Uncommon Fruits
for Every Garden

by Lee Reich

Illustrations by Vicki Herzfeld Arlein

Timber Press
Portland • Cambridge

Grateful acknowledgment is made for permission to reprint portions of the following:

Geoffrey Chaucer, *The Tales of Canterbury*, ed. Robert Pratt. Copyright 1966. Reprinted by permission of Houghton-Mifflin Company.

"Blueberries" from *The Poetry of Robert Frost*, ed. Edward Connery Lathem. Copyright © 1930, 1939, © 1969 by Holt, Rinehart and Winston. Copyright © 1958 by Robert Frost. Copyright © 1967 by Lesley Frost Ballantine. Reprinted by permission of Henry Holt and Company, Inc.

Ovid, *Metamorphoses*, trans. Rolfe Humphries. Copyright 1955. With permission of Indiana University Press.

Plutarch's Lives, trans. Bernadotte Perrin. Copyright 1959. With permission of Harvard University Press.

Lucius Junius Modratus Columella on Agriculture and Trees, trans. E. S. Forster and Edward H. Heffner. Copyright 1968. With permission of Harvard University Press.

"Up and Down Old Brandywine" from *The Complete Poetical Works of James Whitcomb Riley*. Copyright 1932. With permission of The Putnam Publishing Group.

"Paw Paw," a poem in *Heartwood*, copyright © 1983 by Norbert Krapf, reprinted by permission of The Stone House Press.

Mention of trademark, proprietary product, or vendor does not constitute a guarantee or warranty of the product by the publisher or authors and does not imply its approval to the exclusion of other products or vendors.

This revised, expanded work incorporates portions of the book published in 1991 by Addison-Wesley Publishing Company, Inc., as *Uncommon Fruits Worthy of Attention: A Gardener's Guide*.

Published in 2004 by
Timber Press, Inc.
The Haseltine Building
133 S.W. Second Avenue, Suite 450
Portland, Oregon 97204-3527, U.S.A.

Timber Press
2 Station Road
Swavesey
Cambridge CB4 5QJ, U.K.

Printed through Colorcraft Ltd., Hong Kong

Library of Congress Cataloging-in-Publication Data

Reich, Lee.
    Uncommon fruits for every garden / by Lee Reich ; illustrations by Vicki Herzfeld Arlein.—2nd ed.
        p.   cm.
"A previous edition of this work was published in 1991 by Addison-Wesley Publishing Company, Inc., as Uncommon fruits worthy of attention: a gardeners Guide"—T.p. verso.
    ISBN 0-88192-623-X (hardcover)
    1. Fruit. 2. Fruit-culture. I. Reich, Lee. Uncommon fruits worthy of attention. II. Title.
    SB355 .R45 2004
    634—dc22

                                                                                    2003016711

A catalog record for this book is also available from the British Library.

Contents

Contents

Color plates follow page 96

Preface

As I write, the sun is shining brightly, the ground is covered with snow, and the mercury hovers around ten degrees Fahrenheit. But in a few weeks riotous pleasures will unfold, with awakening buds followed by cheery flowers and verdant leaves. And then will come fruits, dangling from stems in a variety of shapes, sizes, and colors, the flesh within luscious blends of sweetness, tang, and distinctive aromas.

My mouth waters at remembrances of those fruiting treasures now quiescent outdoors. I recall, early on summer mornings, refreshing myself with handfuls of pineapple-flavored, white alpine strawberries, the night's chill still within them. I recall, in midsummer, fat 'Achilles' gooseberries bursting open as I bit down upon them, their sweet juices exploding in my mouth. I recall, in autumn, spooning out the custardy flesh of pawpaw, velvet and vanilla on my tongue. Yes, these are uncommon fruits, but each of them is also uncommonly delicious.

I have been enjoying uncommon fruits for over two decades, my enthusiasm for them increasing with the years. Evidently, I am not alone in my enthusiasm. The carefree and attractive plants of this book have proven ideally suited for the trend toward "edible landscaping," where fruit plants are set in backyards and front yards rather than in orchards to be enjoyed for both their beauty and their bounty. Cornelian cherry, Nanking cherry, and juneberry, three fruits of this book, are actually common landscape plants that too often have their tasty bounty overlooked or merely regarded as colorful additions to the spectacle.

In backyards and on farms, "sustainable agriculture" has become a buzz-word for a new kind of agriculture that is kinder to our planet, and, in a related vein, more and more of us want to eat "organically" grown foods. Because they can usually be grown without pesticide sprays, the uncommon fruits of this book, whether farm- or backyard-grown, also have a natural kinship with these trends.

Preface

This book is as much about uncommon fruits for every gardener as it is about uncommon fruits for every garden. Novice gardeners will especially appreciate the ease with which these plants can be grown; once settled in place, beach plum, clove currant, and American persimmon plants require nothing more than the picking and eating of their fruits. (I sometimes hear faint, mocking giggles from my uncommon fruits as I fuss with detailed pruning and pest control on the apples, grapes, and other common fare that I also grow.) Garden mavens will grow these plants to round out their larders with delicacies as yet unavailable in the markets. Savvy orchardists will see the market potential in these wonderful fruits.

Uncommon Fruits for Every Garden builds on my previous book, *Uncommon Fruits Worthy of Attention: A Gardener's Guide*, published in 1991 and now out of print. Information has been thoroughly updated, and more than a decade of research, testing—and tasting!—has prompted me to add new fruits to that original roster. (None have been lost: the original uncommon fruits are all still "worthy of attention" and still not sufficiently well known to have shed the epithet "uncommon.")

As previously, the criteria for entrance to this roster are that a fruit be able to tolerate winter cold, be uncommon, and—most important—be good for fresh eating. Though many of these fruits cook into delectable tarts, jams, and butters, as "those that are skillful in Cookerie can better tell than my selfe" (John Gerard, *The Herball*, 1597), doctoring in the kitchen is not necessary to bring out their best. So join me out in the garden in the months and years ahead, savoring the medley of flavors that these uncommon fruits offer. What you will find in the pages that follow is a guide to growing and enjoying these fruits and fruit plants, arranged not in any sort of alphabetical or botanical order but rather like a fruit salad, to be enjoyed in a like manner.

Lee Reich
New Paltz, New York
February 2003

Acknowledgments

For assistance in accessing the literature, I thank Mary Van Buren of the New York State Agricultural Experiment Station Library, Patricia Carroll and Candice Watson of the MacDonald Dewitt Library (Ulster County Community College), Carol David of the Arnold Arboretum Library, John Hillbrand of the North American Fruit Explorers Library, and the staff at the National Agricultural Library. Alexander Eppler, Ninele Slonin, Johanna Sayre, Tomasz Ziety, and Dariusz Swietlik assisted with translation of works in Russian and German.

The following people have provided helpful commentary on selected chapters of the manuscript draft: John Baird, A. J. Bullard, Ray Cacchiotti, Alexander Eppler, James Gilbert, Ed Hasselkus, Jerry Lehman, Porter Lombard, Paul Lyrene, Steve McKay, Tom Merckel, Elwyn Meader, Roger Meyer, Daniel Milbocker, Paul Miller, R. Neal Peterson, John Smagula, Eldon Stang, Cecil Stushnoff, and John Thieret.

Thanks to Russell Gilmore, Joseph Reich, and Christine Marmo for their careful reading and critique of portions of the manuscript, and also, for this, to Vicki Herzfeld Arlein, in addition to her artful and botanically lucid illustrations. The writing and research for some of this material was helped along by a grant from North American Fruit Explorers (based on a donation by Michael Damroth).

Finally, thanks to all the other gardeners with whom, over the years, I have been able to share my experiences growing these uncommon fruits.

Juneberry

A Cosmopolitan Blue Berry

BOTANICAL NAME
Amelanchier spp.

PLANT TYPE
Deciduous shrub or tree, depending on species and cultivar

POLLINATION
Mostly self-fertile

RIPENING SEASON
June (of course), some in July

I am usually suspicious of any plant that parades under a number of different names. The vine peach, mango melon, and orange melon, for example, all are names for an annual vine producing rather insipid fruits (that admittedly do look like peaches or mangos). This distrust of aliases is unnecessary when applied to the juneberry, which also goes under such monikers as shadbush, serviceberry, or sarvisberry, and, in the case of one species, saskatoon. Besides "juneberry," which refers to the ripening season, these other names refer, respectively, to the trees' blossoming season coinciding with the time when shad spawn, the trees' resemblance to the European service tree (*Sorbus* spp.), and the Indian name for the fruits.

Juneberry fruits are blueberry-sized and usually dark blue or purple. Comparisons with the blueberry seem unavoidable, but such comparisons are valid only as far as the appearance of the fruit. The juneberry, unlike the blueberry, is not even a true berry botanically, but is a pome fruit, kin to the apple and the pear. The best juneberries, while not tasting at all like blueberries, are juicy and sweet, with the richness of sweet cherry along with a hint of almond. Juneberry fruits do not always resemble blueberries even in appearance, for some clones bear fruits that are red or even creamy white.

Juneberries have a wide natural range, with species turning up in Asia, Europe, and North America. We find most species in North America, where they are native to every province of Canada and every state in continental United States. American Indians pounded the berries with the meat and fat of deer, moose, caribou, or buffalo to make pemmican, and juneberries were a staple, frequently the only, fruit of early white settlers on the northern plains. Once again, comparisons with the blueberry seem unavoidable, and for those who garden where blueberries cannot be grown because winters are too cold or soils not sufficiently acid, the cosmopolitan juneberry fills the bill for a blueberry look-alike. There even exists at present a commercial juneberry industry in Alberta and Saskatchewan, Canada. And why not? Indians once harvested and sold to settlers juneberries growing wild along the Yukon River.

Description of the Plant

The almost two dozen species of *Amelanchier* are distinguished with difficulty even by botanists. The genus includes scrubby plants that hug the ground, trees fifty feet tall, and all sizes of trees and shrubs in between. Some species spread slowly by stolons, which are horizontal shoots that grow outward from the base of a plant and take root.

In early spring, about a week before crab apples bloom, juneberry plants burst into clouds of white blossoms. In the greys and browns of the early spring forest, wild juneberries stand out as plants that appear to have caught delicate, white veils dropped from the sky. A juneberry in bloom is a quiet beauty, unlike the more flamboyant crab apples and magnolias of that season.

Summer brings fruit and a raiment of soft, green leaves. Berries, borne in racemes of three to sixteen fruits, follow the blossoms by six to eight weeks. As fall approaches, juneberries continue to earn their keep as their leaves burst into shades of purple, orange, and yellow. The fiery leaves are held late in the season, but once they fall all is not lost, for then the attractive striated, grey bark is revealed. The bark and the neat form of the plants—especially those grown as small trees—pleasantly engage the eye through winter until the plants once again burst into bloom the following spring.

All species of *Amelanchier* have edible fruits, but those of just a few species are of interest to the grower of uncommon fruits. Sweet and juicy fruits are borne by one bushy species from the Pacific northwest and a number of tree and bushy species native to eastern North America.

The saskatoon (*Amelanchier alnifolia*)—its name is a corruption of the Cree Indian name for the fruits, *mis-sask-quah-too-min*—is a native of the northwest prairies up to the southern Yukon and down into Colorado. (The

Juneberry

capital of Saskatchewan is the city of Saskatoon.) As might be surmised from its native range, the saskatoon is very cold-hardy, tolerating cold to at least minus sixty degrees Fahrenheit. The plant, a slowly spreading stoloniferous shrub reaching a height of eight feet, tolerates a wide range of soils, except those that remain sodden. Spikes of a few to twelve or more flowers open after leaves have fully expanded and stay open for a relatively long period of time. Berries that follow blooms are juicy and very sweet, typically bloomy purple and sometimes over half an inch across. Fruit color also comes in blue, creamy white, and red.

In eastern North America, the Allegheny serviceberry (*Amelanchier laevis*), the thicket serviceberry (*A. canadensis*), and the apple serviceberry (*A. ×grandiflora*, a hybrid of the Allegheny and thicket serviceberries) are trees—or at least large shrubs—that produce tasty fruits. The Allegheny serviceberry grows wild in moist upland woods and was a favorite fruit of American Indians of the east. Now it's also a favorite in Europe—as an ornamental. This nonsuckering plant yields a droopy spike of six to twelve white flowers, sometimes pink while in bud, that share the stage with leaves unfolding a coppery red color. The thicket serviceberry grows as a tall, multistemmed, suckering shrub, holding its flowers erect. Native stands of the thicket serviceberry are confined to the eastern seaboard. Allegheny and thicket serviceberries sometimes are confused with the downy serviceberry (*A. arborea*), another eastern native that is inferior in fruit and beauty. The most ornamental of the eastern species is the apple serviceberry, whose large flowers are followed by large and succulent fruits; the latter, unfortunately, are not produced in abundance.

A number of species of low-growing, stoloniferous juneberries (*Amelanchier stolonifera, A. humulis, A. obovalis*, and *A. sanguinea*) have good fruits. Generally, they are native to poor, dry soils. For landscaping, they perhaps find their best calling in naturalized plantings.

The names of many juneberry cultivars with particularly good fruits read like a map of northwest Canada: 'Moon Lake', 'Pembina', 'Forestburg', and 'Sturgeon'. These saskatoon cultivars were selected by enthusiasts in their native territory. In the United States a few cultivars have been selected for their fruits and many for their ornamental qualities.

The few deficiencies of the juneberry as a fruiting plant could be overcome with breeding, especially considering the wide range of species from which to draw specific qualities. To my taste, fruit destined for juice, jelly, or compote could benefit from a slight acid bite to offset the sweetness. The fruit might also be improved if the small yet bony seeds were even smaller and fewer—not too small or few, though, because it is those seeds that impart the delightful almondy flavor. Saskatoons, the juneberries most frequently eaten, have among the largest seeds, but breeding with smaller-seeded species such as *Amelanchier bartramiana* could potentially yield a plant bearing berries that were large, sweet, and juicy, yet small seeded.

Harvesting a fruit as small as a juneberry from a ladder rapidly becomes tedious, so the ideal plant for fruit production would be no higher than six feet. Fruits on short plants are also easier to protect from birds.

Cultivation

There is not much to say about growing juneberries, for they are easy to grow and thrive without special care. The plants are indifferent to extreme cold in winter and are adapted to USDA Hardiness Zones 3 through 8. Juneberries will fruit in sun or partial shade and tolerate a wide variety of soils. Among juneberries, saskatoons are a bit more demanding in their needs, thriving best in exposed sites in full sun and well-drained soils high in humus; think of the periodically burned-over, northern prairies this species calls home. Juneberries begin to bear fruit two to four years after planting.

Set plants a little deeper in the ground than they were in the nursery. Spacing depends on the species or cultivar and the intended use. For instance, to get maximum yields from saskatoons, each plant should stand at least eight feet from its neighbor. But to grow saskatoons as a fruiting hedge, plant them six feet apart in the row so that they eventually grow to stand shoulder to shoulder.

Juneberries have the unfortunate habit (shared by pears) of sometimes sulking for the season following planting. This habit could be related to juneberries naturally shutting down extension growth early in the season, which is an asset for a plant hardy to very cold winter climates. A warm, well-aerated soil and plenty of nutrients can get such plants growing although planting in fall rather than spring frequently bypasses the problem altogether.

For best fruit production on juneberry species grown as bushes, prune every winter. The best fruit is produced on wood that is between one and four years old. Fruit on older wood tends to be small and dryish. Therefore, cut away at their bases any shoots older than four years and thin shoots that grew the previous season from ground level so that only half a dozen of the most vigorous ones remain. Heading cuts can be used to keep plants at a height—six to seven feet—convenient for picking with feet on terra firma.

Juneberries grown as trees do not need annual pruning. But periodically head older branches back to plump buds near the trunk, and thin younger growth to keep plants open.

Especially on backyard juneberries, leaves and stems are generally free of pest problems. That said, in some gardens pests wreak havoc on the berries. (My garden is, unfortunately, in this category, although I know of a stand of juneberry plants only eight miles away that bear consistent, excellent crops.) Among notable insect pests, we find the saskatoon bud moth (*Epinotia bicordana*) causing flower bud drop and the saskatoon sawfly (*Hoplocampa* spp.) causing drop of young fruits or hollow fruits; fruits attacked by the apple curculio (*Anthonomus quadrigibbus*) stay on the plant but are misshapen and often hard and rendered further unappetizing by resident larvae.

Potential disease problems include rust (*Gymnosporangium* spp.), which spreads from junipers and shows up as rust-colored lesions on leaves and fruits; mummyberry (*Monolinia amelancheris*), evidenced by dried-up "mummies" left hanging on plants into winter; and angular leaf spot (*Entomosporium mespili*), leaving foliage spotted with angular brown spots, sometimes with yellow halos. Good air circulation and cleanup of infected plant parts can lessen disease problems, but don't try to remove junipers to control rust because rust spores can travel for miles. Like other members of the rose family, juneberries are also susceptible to fire blight, a disease causing the rapid collapse of new growth. Prune off any blighted limbs twelve inches below the infection, sterilizing the pruning tool in alcohol between cuts. Commercial saskatoon growers in Canada control insects and diseases with two sprays of a combination insecticide-fungicide, the first spray at petal fall and the next spray ten days later. Severity of pest problems may differ in other regions, or with other species.

Birds liken juneberries to blueberries (or is it the other way around?) and are as fond of one fruit as the other. In some cases, they will devour virtually the entire crop. Possibly, birds would avoid white-fruited juneberries. The only sure prevention is netting.

Propagation

It is not difficult to propagate one or two juneberry plants from a neighbor's plant. Propagation on a commercial scale becomes more of a challenge.

If the plant produces suckers, merely dig suckers from an established plant in early spring, taking a good supply of roots with each sucker. Coddle the suckers in a nursery row for a year before planting them out at their permanent locations.

Not all juneberries produce suckers (nor are suckers desirable for a plant grown as a tree), and the easiest way to propagate a nonsuckering plant is from seed. Juneberries are highly self-fertile and plants grown from seeds often closely resemble their parent—about eighty percent of plants will be "true" from seed. (Exceptions are the white-fruited juneberries, which must be cross-pollinated, so do not come true from seed.)

There are two keys to good seed germination: do not allow seeds to dry out; and stratify the seeds for three or four months. If seeds do dry before they are stratified, they might need a long period of warm stratification followed by cold stratification, that is, if you sow dried seeds in spring, they may not emerge until the following spring.

Cuttings are another means of propagating juneberries. Stoloniferous species of juneberry can be propagated by root cuttings. Hardwood stem cuttings are difficult to root, but softwood stem cuttings, if taken at the right stage of growth, root easily. Softwood cuttings taken too early rot; taken too late, they do not root. In Canada and the Northern Tier states, the best time to take cuttings from new growth is between late May and late June. Hormone dips sometimes facilitate rooting, but bottom heat is unnecessary. The etiolated shoot method, described in Appendix 5 ("Propagation"), would be another, more reliable, method of propagating juneberries by cuttings.

Grafting has not been a very satisfactory method of juneberry propagation. Grafts often take on rootstocks of other genera, such as mountain ash, hawthorn, and other members of the rose family, but the grafted plants sometimes stop growing. Stocks generally used have included *Cotoneaster acutifolius, C. bullatus, Sorbus intermedia*, and *S. aucuparia. Amelanchier alnifolia* is apparently the juneberry most compatible with other genera. Plant juneberries grafted onto other genera low enough in the ground to allow the juneberry scion to root. The rootstock, in this case, acts as a temporary nurse root, but may have the unfortunate habit of continually sending up sprouts. *Crataegus arnoldiana* as a juneberry rootstock reputedly shuns this bad habit.

Interestingly, one *Amelanchier* species is not always graft compatible with another. When grafting a juneberry scion onto juneberry roots, choose a nonsuckering clone for roots or you will constantly be finding shoots thrown up from the rootstock.

Harvest and Use

A friend telephoned me one Friday in June to share his just-ripe juneberries. When I finally made it to his house the following Tuesday, birds had stripped the branches clean and what fruits were left had shrivelled or rotted. Harvest juneberries posthaste.

Expect the first real taste from juneberries that you plant within about four years. An average yield is around eight pounds per plant, but individual saskatoon bushes have been known to yield forty pounds of berries!

The berries are topnotch out of hand, as tasty to me as any other fruit you'll find in this book or on market shelves. Besides being used in pemmican, juneberries have also found their way into jelly and juice. Be careful when heating juneberries, because heat can drive away the flavor; even frozen juneberries cannot match those popped fresh into your mouth. For cooking or juice, juneberries do need the addition of something acidic, such as lemon juice. The early settlers spiked cooked juneberries with rhubarb. Out in the garden, the same sprightliness can be had by picking a few fresh currants or gooseberries—which ripen in the same season as juneberries—along with the juneberries.

Cultivars

'Altaglow': *Amelanchier alnifolia* from Alberta selected primarily for its ornamental qualities; the eighteen-foot-high plant makes few suckers; leaves turn shades of gold, red, and deep purple in the fall; the large fruits are white but bland; yields are low; needs cross-pollination; hardy to Zone 1.

'Autumn Brilliance': *Amelanchier ×grandiflora*; multistemmed large shrub growing fifteen to twenty-five feet tall and half that width; the large, pink-tinged flower buds open to snowy white blossoms that become red fruits; leaves turn a spectacular orange, sometimes red or yellow, in autumn.

'Autumn Sunset': *Amelanchier arborea* or *A. ×grandiflora* (possibly *A. lamarckii*) selected in Georgia; a round-topped tree from twenty to twenty-five feet high; its leaves persist late into fall and turn pumpkin orange; heat- and drought-tolerant; cold-hardiness unknown.

'Ballerina': *Amelanchier ×grandiflora* selected in the Netherlands; upright shrub or small tree with spreading branches, fifteen to twenty feet tall and hardy to Zone 4; leaves turn purple-bronze in the fall; flowers are over an inch across, followed by tender, sweet, purplish black fruits up to half an inch in diameter.

'Bluff': *Amelanchier alnifolia* from Alberta; plant reputedly hardy to Zone 1; blue-black fruit is a half-inch across and has few seeds; retains flavor when cooked; ripens evenly.

Juneberry

'Cole's Select': *Amelanchier* ×*grandiflora* with exceptional red-orange fall color.

'Cumulus': *Amelanchier laevis*; upright tree, twenty to thirty feet tall; leaves turn bright orange in fall; hardy to Zone 4.

'Forestburg': *Amelanchier alnifolia* selection from Alberta; somewhat spreading, almost ten feet tall; few suckers; productive and precocious; the fruit is large (five-eighths inch) but somewhat insipid, soft, and watery; hardy to Zone 2.

'Hollandia': *Amelanchier spicata* (possibly *A. sanguinea*) from Winchester, England; grows to seven feet high; a suckering ornamental selection.

'Honeywood': *Amelanchier alnifolia* from Saskatchewan; grows seven feet tall; limbs are spreading, but plant produces few suckers; late-flowering; leaf spot resistant; a precocious and reliable cropper, producing large clusters of flavorful, half-inch fruits relatively later than other saskatoons; hardy to Zone 2.

'Indian': *Amelanchier alnifolia*(?) from Michigan; an ornamental and productive plant bearing large fruits.

'Jennybelle': probably *Amelanchier obovalis*, possibly from North Carolina; heavy bearing and adapted to warmer regions, such as the Mid-Atlantic.

'Martin': *Amelanchier alnifolia* from Saskatchewan; a seedling of 'Thiessen', to which it is similar except for somewhat larger fruit that ripens more evenly; hardy to Zone 2.

'Moon Lake': *Amelanchier alnifolia* originating near Saskatoon; grows six to ten feet high; later-flowering; the fruit is of excellent quality and large (five-eighths inch), but production is sporadic from season to season; hardy to Zone 2.

'Nelson': *Amelanchier alnifolia* from Saskatchewan; a small bush whose relatively late flowers are followed by good yields of half-inch-diameter fruits having few seeds; possibly rust-resistant; fruits are large, flavorful, and somewhat tart.

'Northline': *Amelanchier alnifolia* from Alberta; grows about six feet high and produces many suckers; precocious and productive; fruit is large (five-eighths inch) and purple with excellent flavor; ripens evenly; hardy to Zone 1.

'Paleface': *Amelanchier alnifolia* from Manitoba; grows to become a pyramidal plant seven feet tall; few suckers; prolific producer of large, snowy white, mild fruits; needs cross-pollination.

'Parkhill': a selection, possibly of *Amelanchier sanguinea* or *A. alnifolia*, from Michigan; low yield of half-inch-diameter fruits that ripen fairly evenly; susceptible to powdery mildew; flavor is not as good as saskatoons in Canada.

'Pembina': *Amelanchier alnifolia* selection from Alberta; columnar plant growing ten feet high and producing few suckers; very productive (though less than 'Smoky'); the large, sweet, full-flavored fruits are borne in long clusters; hardy to Zone 1.

'Prince Charles': *Amelanchier laevis* (possibly *A. canadensis*) selection from Wisconsin; billed primarily as an ornamental yet bears large fruits.

'Prince William': probably a hybrid with *Amelanchier canadensis* as one parent; shrub eight feet high and hardy to minus thirty degrees Fahrenheit; leaves turn orange-red in the fall; fruits are half an inch across.

'Princess Diana': *Amelanchier* ×*grandiflora* from Wisconsin; small tree selected for ornamental qualities.

'Regent': an ornamental selection of *Amelanchier alnifolia* from North Dakota; leaf spot resistant; productive; bush is six feet high and produces very sweet fruit with few seeds, though the flavor is reputedly inferior to that of the better *alnifolia* selections from Canada; hardy to Zone 3.

'R. J. Hilton': *Amelanchier laevis* from Nova Scotia; disease-resistant tree with good fall color; flowers are deep pink in bud, then open with pink-flecked white petals; the purple fruit is small but very sweet.

'Robin Hill': *Amelanchier* ×*grandiflora*; grows twenty to thirty feet tall and is hardy to Zone 4; large flowers are pink in bud, unfolding to white; the earliest of all to bloom.

'Rubescens': *Amelanchier* ×*grandiflora*; grows twenty to thirty feet tall and is hardy to Zone 4; flowers are purple-pink in bud, unfolding to light pink; a seedling originating in western New York early in the twentieth century.

'Shannon': *Amelanchier alnifolia*(?) from Michigan; a productive plant with large fruits; good for landscaping and eating.

'Shanty Rapids': *Amelanchier bartramiana* from Michigan; large-petalled ornamental cultivar.

'Smoky': *Amelanchier alnifolia* from Alberta; the six- to eight-foot plant produces many suckers; productive; the reddish-purple, very sweet, yet mild-flavored fruits are large and borne in medium-sized clusters; many large seeds; uneven ripening; note that more than one 'Smoky' may exist; hardy to Zone 1.

'Strata': *Amelanchier* ×*grandiflora*, whose branches tend to grow horizontally; orange-tinged fall color.

'Sturgeon': *Amelanchier alnifolia* selection from Alberta that is upright growing and about nine feet tall; produces large clusters of large, flavorful, meaty fruits.

'Success': The first juneberry cultivar to be named; probably *Amelanchier sanguinea*, but also has been billed as *A. alnifolia*, *A. canadensis*, and *A. oblongifolia* (I did say earlier that juneberry taxonomy leaves even botanists scratching their heads); originated in the 1800s in Illinois from seed that was brought from Pennsylvania; bush is six feet high by four feet wide and produces large racemes off fruit; H. E. Van Deman, who named the bush in 1878, stated that fruits were "attractive and toothsome," while others bill them as "bland"; the fruit clings tenaciously to the stems.

'Thiessen': *Amelanchier alnifolia* selected in 1910 from the shores of the Saskatchewan River; the plant grows fifteen feet high and wide and flowers relatively early; a prolific producer of very large (greater than five-eighths inch), juicy fruits ripening later in the season than do other saskatoons; uneven ripening; one of the best-tasting cultivars; hardy to Zone 2.

Beach Plum

A Tasty Fruit Not Just for the Beach

BOTANICAL NAME
Prunus maritima

PLANT TYPE
Wide spreading bush or small tree

POLLINATION
Generally needs cross-pollination

RIPENING SEASON
Late summer and fall

The first time I put a fresh beach plum into my mouth, I spat it out; the second time, I started plucking more fruit. My experience pretty much describes the spectrum in flavors that one might experience from beach plums.

Fresh or doctored up with sweeteners, beach plums were appreciated by Native Americans and early settlers, who harvested them from wild bushes that snuggle along the Atlantic Coast right in beach sand from Massachusetts to North Carolina. In 1524, in what is now southern New York, Giovanni da Verrazano wrote, "we found *Pomi apii*, damson trees [actually beach plums; damsons are European plums whose leaves resemble those of beach plum], and nut trees." Also in New York, but a bit later, Henry Hudson reported finding "a good harbor, abundance of blue plums, some currants brought by the natives dried and the country full of great and tall oaks." Growing as they do on beach sand, beach plums had to be among the first plants the Pilgrims encountered upon landing in the New World.

Beach plum was assigned its botanical name, *Prunus maritima*, in 1787 by a Hessian mercenary, F. W. J. van Wagenheim. The variability I experienced in tasting the fruit also extends to other characteristics of the plant, with the result that in the hundred years or so following van Wagenheim's naming, numerous explorer botanists assigned each form of beach plum its own botanical name. *Prunus pygmaea, Prunus acuminata, Prunus sphaerica, Prunus pubescens*, and all the others were finally lumped back together as *Prunus maritima*, the beach plum.

Beach plum fruits range from a "pitty" half inch across to an inch or more, although pit size itself can be yet another variable. Fruit color is most commonly deep blue and dusted with a white bloom, but some plants bear fruits clothed in purple, red, even yellow skins. The attractiveness of the fruit can in fact be more than skin deep, as one investigator found that beach plum astringency—that which caused me to eject the first fruit I tasted—is due to tannins, and these are much reduced in clones with yellow fruits. As a general rule, those tannins also are apparently less in clones that mature earlier as well as those whose fruits are softer and larger. Taste, of course, is more than just absence of astringency, and the best beach plums are sweet and juicy, with "plum good" flavor.

Beach plum got its biggest boost around 1940, the hope being to have beach plum follow on the heels of blueberries, another native American fruit that was studied, improved, and then commercially exploited, all in the early part of the twentieth century. J. Milton Batchelor, of the Soil Conservation Service, scouted the Atlantic coast for superior plants, the Arnold Arboretum and the University of Massachusetts teamed up in development of the industry, and the Massachusetts legislature allocated $500 for study of the propagation, cultivation, and pest control of beach plums. James R. Jewett, Emeritus Professor of Arabic at Harvard and—more significantly—longtime summer resident of Cape Cod, donated $5000 to the Arnold Arboretum to further the beach plum cause. The Cape Cod Beach Plum Growers Association was formed. Alas, their Bulletin #10, published in 1958 and including beach plum jelly recipes, a proposal for varietal test plots, and a logo contest, was their last.

So beach plums remain an uncommon fruit, perhaps for no other reason than being eclipsed by their tennis-ball-sized commercial cousins. For the epicure's garden, however, where snowball bloom and tasty, albeit relatively small, plums requiring a minimum of care would be welcome, beach plums are just the ticket.

Description of the Plant

Beach plum is another of those plants that has straddled the fence between being a landscape plant and an edible plant, generating enthusiasm on both

Beach plum

sides, but then never coming into more general cultivation in either guise. Although sometimes growing like a small tree, the plant more commonly grows as a scraggly bush of decumbent stems from which grow upright shoots, frequently rooting where they touch soil. New stems might also arise from creeping roots, the combined effect producing a wide-spreading thicket with old, wild plants.

That above-ground thicket is not mirrored by an abundance of roots below ground. Beach plums have relatively few fine roots, and roots generally are not balanced radially in the soil. Seedlings and cuttings typically develop one or two major roots that keep growing in whatever direction they're initially headed.

Plant height will reflect a plant's genetic makeup as well as growing conditions. Stems on mature plants usually reach a height of about six feet, but ten- or fifteen-foot-tall plants are not unheard of. At the other extreme are plants growing to heights of only a couple of feet or less. Such apparently dwarfed plants growing in beach sand might not, in fact, be dwarfs but merely plants whose older parts have been constantly buried by shifting sand.

One true diminutive type of beach plum does exist, the botanical variety whose full name is *Prunus maritima* var. *gravesii* (sometimes listed as *Prunus gravesii*). This beach plum is found growing in only one place, in Groton, Connecticut, facing the Long Island Sound. With fruits that are small and not notable in flavor, this plant is not worthy of further attention here.

Beach plum's pointy leaves are usually dull green on their upper sides and slightly hairy and lighter-colored below. Although unspectacular in autumn, on most bushes the leaves do retain a clean, healthy appearance right through the season.

Bloom time, following on the heels of apple and juneberry blossoms, is when beach plums unfold in all their ornamental glory. Each branch then is smothered in fleecy white petals from myriad blossoms, the blossoms each three-quarters of an inch across and grouped in clusters of two to five. Blossoming is so profuse that in 1932 two scientists from the Arnold Arboretum were able to plot the distribution of wild stands by observing them from an airplane at bloom time.

Beach plum's second season of attraction is in late summer and early fall. In good years, the ripe fruits dangle all along the branches profusely enough to put on a show of their own.

Cultivation

In the wild, beach plum typically inhabits sites that are drenched in sunlight and whipped with salt-laden wind, and where the soil is low in moisture, poor in nutrients, and relatively high in salts—that is, a beach. This is not to say that beach plum demands or even thrives best under such conditions, just that it survives or tolerates such conditions better than many other plants.

Beyond its need for full sunlight and good soil drainage, little is known of the growing conditions that would make a beach plum most happy, but nothing in the plant's genetics or morphology suggests that it needs conditions different from those enjoyed by most other cultivated plants: to wit, a moderate amount of soil fertility and humus, and soil kept moist with rainfall or irrigation. This statement is borne out by the performance of the beach plums I've grown.

As far as spacing, a common recommendation is to set plants four to five feet apart, in which case they will eventually grow into a hedgerow. Plant spread will reflect soil fertility, a plant's genetic disposition, and the amount of pruning it receives. My plants, even in rich soil, have been easily contained (with pruning and occasional droughty summers) to a spread of six feet or less and a height of four to five feet.

Like wild beach plums, my cultivated ones also bloom profusely and regularly. Much may occur 'twixt blossom and fruit, however, and beach plums are notable for their lack of consistent production—in my garden as well as in the wild. A number of reasons have been suggested. The problem might reside in the nature of the flowers themselves. They are generally considered to be not only self-sterile, but in some clones at least, the female part of the flower matures and protrudes through the flower before it fully opens. Also, some clones can be all male, while others have both male and female parts. Any of these factors might account for consistent poor production of wild stands, where large expanses overrun by few clones might prevent better pollination.

In a garden, with relatively few branches of a few clones, poor production may also reflect the effects of weather on blossoming. As with other fruiting plants, unfavorable wind, rain, or cold can prevent the happy marriage of male and female flower parts, resulting in little or no fruit. Despite its rugged constitution for survival and growth, beach plum's fruiting seems more subject to the vagaries of the weather than that of other fruits. Perhaps a plant so capable of asexual increase—single plants have been known to spread into colonies over a hundred feet across!—has less need for sexual reproduction.

Pests are another possibility in the beach plum's feast-and-famine cycle of fruit production. Insects and diseases are known to interfere with fruit production of cultivated plums, so why not beach plums? Beach plum has reportedly been attacked by the same insects and diseases that attack many of its cultivated kin. That said, beach plum crops do more often seem to be all-or-nothing affairs, and the plants, when they do crop, seem to have few pest problems. With the exception of a fruit insect, probably plum curculio or plum gouger, I have not observed any of these other pests on my own beach plums, nor have I ever resorted to spraying anything on my plants.

Your site and garden style will influence how much you prune your beach plums. With time, plants do spread; contain them if desired by lopping back decumbent branches before they root. Also look the plants over while they are dormant, and cut away any dead or diseased branches, as well as any weak or inward-growing ones causing congestion in the center of the bush. Fruit is borne on one-, two-, and, to a lesser extent, three-year-old wood, so shortening some stems and cutting some of the oldest ones to the ground or to vigorous suckers will maintain and stimulate enough new growth for good, annual blooms—and, in good years, fruits to follow.

Propagation

In 1714, John Lawson wrote, in *History of Carolina*, that beach plums "grow anywhere if planted from the Stone or Slip: bear a white blossom, and are a good fruit." And that's still how beach plums are generally grown.

Where plants are wanted in quantity rather than quality, seeds will do. Two to three months' stratification is needed for best germination. Resultant seedlings will show a range in fruit and plant characteristics.

Cuttings are one way to make exact replicas of an existing plant, that is, to clone it. The best reported results—eighty percent rooting—were with softwood cuttings of entire, but short, new shoots two to four inches long. Shoots were collected when fruits had swelled to about one-eighth inch in diameter (which was in early June at the study site). Lower leaves were stripped off, then shoots were dipped in Hormodin No. 1 rooting powder and plunged into sand in a shaded greenhouse. Hardwood cuttings should also be successful for beach plums.

The simplest and easiest way to clone new beach plum plants, provided they are growing on their own roots (that is, not grafted), is by root cuttings. Cut pencil-thick portions of healthy roots into lengths of three to four inches, then lay them horizontally in the soil two to three inches deep. Alternatively, the cuttings could be set vertically, with the ends that were closest to the mother plant upwards and just below the soil surface. If such cuttings are set outdoors, where conditions are less ideal than in a pot, set the vertical cuttings deeper, beneath an inch of soil. Chances for success with root cuttings is high enough so that they could even be set in the ground where mature plants are to stand—but do put a few cuttings at each location and mulch them in winter to keep frost from heaving them out of the ground.

Grafting is a way to get quick growth on a cloned plant. Beach plum naturally grows a sparse root system, which makes bare-root transplanting more chancy. Various rootstocks have been used with success. *Prunus tomentosa* has been used as a rootstock to make transplanting less difficult, although these days, potted plants also could overcome such problems. Grafts of beach plum on *Prunus americana* exhibited early bearing and strong growth, while those on *Prunus domestica* grew into excessively large plants. A suitable rootstock, with the graft union sufficiently high above ground level, might be utilized to keep a beach plum in place rather than spreading. Where the rootstock is being used only for propagation, bury the graft union to let the beach plum eventually take root itself, although rootstock suckering could then be a problem with certain rootstocks. A wire twisted around the graft union solves this problem, eventually strangling the rootstock as the stems age and thicken but after the scion portion has formed its own roots.

Harvest and Use

For best fresh flavor, beach plums must not be picked before they are dead ripe. Like other stone fruits, beach plums will not ripen after harvest; they will soften and some complex carbohydrates may turn to sugar, but they will not develop the aroma and sweetness of bush-ripened fruits.

If your beach plums yield more than you, your family, and friends can vonsume fresh, you'll have to make some jelly. Although beach plum jelly is a signature Cape Cod comestible, in fact the fruits have just barely enough acidity (pH 3.3) and pectin (0.9%) to make a good jelly. In 1942, two scientists at the University of Delaware set out to quantify just what makes a beach plum jelly that has good structure, color, and flavor; here, verbatim, are their instructions:

To one pound of washed [ripe] fruit add one pint of water and boil moderately in a covered vessel for 15 minutes. Strain through one thickness of cheesecloth without pressing. Return the pulp to the kettle, add another pint of water, and extract again for 10 minutes. In straining this time express all the juice. Mix the two extractions, concentrate to one pint, and clarify by straining through four thicknesses of cheesecloth. To the clarified extract add 12 ounces of sugar in which has been mixed 2.7 grams (one level teaspoon) of 100 grade dried citrus pectin, or two ounces (one fourth of a bottle) of Certo. After adding the sugar, concentrate rapidly to a jelly test of 65 to 68 percent soluble solids. The temperature at the finish point is 9–10 degrees F. above the boiling point of water. A yield of 18 ounces of jelly per pound of fruit is obtained by this procedure.

(S. G. Davis and A. C. Levine, "Composition and Utilization of the Beach Plum," *The Fruit Products Journal*, August 1942)

If your bushes don't yield enough all at once for a batch of jelly, fruits can be picked as they ripen, then stored in a freezer at zero degrees Fahrenheit or lower.

I'd eat a fresh beach plum rather than beach plum jelly any day, but for those years when beach plums don't crop or on a winter day, the jelly will have to do.

Cultivars

For a fruit still so little removed from the wild, beach plum has spawned a number of cultivars, most of them culled from the wild. The first named variety was 'Bassett's American', introduced in 1872 by William Bassett of Hammonton, New Jersey. After being sold by nurseries for a few years, this variety disappeared—thankfully, considering that its fruit were dull red, a ho-hum three-quarters of an inch in diameter, and poorly flavored.

No less a breeder than Luther Burbank recognized the qualities of beach plums, and hoped to infuse larger Japanese and American plums with the beach plum's hardiness, late bloom, productivity (when it bears!), and general ruggedness. Burbank actually introduced three varieties—'Burbank's Giant Maritima', 'East', and 'Pride'—all of which had large size but allegedly disappeared for lack of commercial qualities such as firmness and texture to withstand shipping.

In one recorded case, beach plum took it upon itself to hybridize with another species without human intervention: the mate was *Prunus americana*, both plants growing near to each other in Highland Park in Rochester, New York. A Mr. John Dunbar collected the seed in 1899 and grew it into a plant that bore purple fruits larger than those of beach plum, which was one bit of evidence of its hybrid origin. As an ornamental, it surpassed both its parents when in bloom.

Few, if any, of the cultivars in the following list are available, perhaps even in existence, today. But who knows when a lost fruit might be dredged out of obscurity? As far as new cultivars, my enthusiasm for beach plums was spurred by fruits I tasted on some test plants at Rutger's Cream Ridge experiment station; they are not available (yet, at least) and at present have the nonluscious designations NJBP1-13, NJBP1-64, NJBP3-13, and NJBP3-55. Ripening times of the clones listed here are those where the clone originated.

'Alpha': selected in 1899 by E. M. Winsor; purple fruit.

'Arrowhead': blue fruit with oval shape.

'Beta': selected about 1899 by E. M. Winsor; yellow fruit.

'Cotuit': originated in Cotuit, Massachusetts; spreading bush two to three feet high; leaves bright apple green; prolific production of fruits three-quarters of an inch to one inch in diameter, with small seed and sweet, fine flavor; early-ripening, often in late July.

'Eastham' ('HC-1248'): selected in Eastham, Massachusetts, by J. M. Batchelor in the 1940s; three to four feet high, very spreading but with strongly upright stems; leaves light green; heavy production of deep purple crimson fruits one to one and three-eighths inches in diameter with tart to mildly acidic flavor; ripens in early September.

'Hancock' ('HC-1244'): selected in Fort Hancock, New Jersey, by J. M. Batchelor in the 1940s; three-foot-high bush elongating only a half a foot per year; fruit has a blue skin and a juicy, golden flesh with a small pit; the fruits, seven-eighths of an inch to one inch in diameter, have a sweet flavor that makes for excellent fresh eating; begins ripening in the middle of August.

'Jersey': vigorous plant is treelike, to thirteen feet high; reddish fruits have good flavor and ripen from late summer to early fall.

'Premier' ('HC-1358'): originated in Plum Island, Massachusetts; four-foot-high bush; very susceptible to brown rot; moderate production of blue, inch-wide fruits.

'Raribank' ('NJ#1'): selected in Old Bridge, New Jersey, in 1932; large, treelike plant (similar to peach); notably resistant to brown rot and Japanese beetle; purplish-red fruits are good for canning and jelly and ripen in early September.

'Safford' ('HC-1252'): originated in Plum Island, Massachusetts; prostrate bush up to four feet high; heavy yielder of deep blue, inch-wide fruits with good, sweet flavor; begins ripening in the middle of August.

'Snow': annual production of round fruits with excellent flavor.

'Wheeler Selection No. 6': originated in Truro, Massachusetts; upright bush as high as three to five feet, with deep green leaves; heavy yields of light blue fruits an inch and an eighth in diameter, "real beach plum flavor ripening to very sweet and good flavored, quality fruit" (George Graves, *Arnoldia*, 1949).

Alpine and Musk Strawberries

Diminutive Delectables

BOTANICAL NAME
Fragaria vesca and *Fragaria moschata*

PLANT TYPE
Herbaceous perennial

POLLINATION
Alpine strawberries are self-pollinating; musk strawberry cultivars
are somewhat self-pollinating though the species is dioecious

RIPENING SEASON
Spring through fall for alpine strawberries; spring for musk
strawberries

It is said that if you order strawberries in a deluxe Parisian restaurant, those strawberries will be very small and very expensive (but of course!), but also very delicious. Such fruits are not scaled-down or poorly grown versions of common, cultivated strawberries, but different species of near-wild strawberries: the alpine strawberry or the musk strawberry.

Alpine and musk strawberry fruits are expensive not because they are hard to grow, but because the plants are not very productive. This should not preclude growing them in the backyard garden, where flavor is as important as productivity. Fruits of the alpine strawberry have an intense, wild strawberry flavor. The flavor of the musk strawberry tastes like a mixture of strawberry, raspberry, and pineapple. Delicious!

For centuries, Europeans planted both species in gardens and harvested them from the wild. Cultivation of alpine and musk strawberries abated two and a half centuries ago with the development of the "modern" strawberry, which is a large-fruited and prolific hybrid of two American species.

Today's strawberry breeders do not pay much attention to alpine or musk strawberries. Incorporating genes of these two species into the modern hybrid strawberry is no easy task because of chromosome differences between the alpine strawberry (a diploid), the musk strawberry (a hexaploid), and the modern hybrid strawberry (an octoploid). Undiluted with the genes of other species, the alpine and musk strawberry are unacceptable for commercial production. Aside from low yields, the fruits are too perishable and too small.

"I am sure that the very practical . . . strawberry growers will never fool with either of the two European species. One look at these wild strawberries from Europe will convince them that there is nothing there for them," wrote Henry A. Wallace, who was United States Secretary of Agriculture in the 1930s. Yet Mr. Wallace was so taken by the flavor of alpine and musk strawberries that he chose to count himself among the "unpractical." His retirement years were spent growing alpine and musk strawberries and attempting to incorporate their unique flavor components into modern hybrid strawberries in his garden in South Salem, New York. The exotic flavors of these two strawberries have similarly stirred the enthusiasm of other gardeners to become amateur strawberry breeders.

Description of the Plants

ALPINE STRAWBERRY (*Fragaria vesca*)   The alpine strawberry is one botanical form of wood strawberry (often referred to by the French name, *fraise de bois*). Wood strawberries are dainty plants that grow wild along the edges of woods in Europe, North and South America, and northern Asia and Africa. The wood strawberry is the wild strawberry of antiquity, mentioned in the writings of Virgil, Ovid, and Pliny, the strawberry that garlanded medieval religious paintings and was later depicted in grand proportions in Bosch's *Garden of Delights* (c. 1500). Although occasionally cultivated in gardens as far back as the fifteenth century, the fruits were mostly gathered from the wild. Cultivation did not improve the fruit sufficiently to justify growing it, and more than a tad of fruits (and vegetables) in the diet was long deemed to be unhealthy.

The alpine form of wood strawberry was discovered about three hundred years ago east of Grenoble in the low Alps and it soon surpassed other wood strawberries in popularity. Fruit of the alpine strawberry is generally larger than that of the wood strawberry. And whereas most wood strawberries bear fruits only in spring, alpine forms fruit continuously throughout the growing season. Especially in older texts, the alpine strawberry is sometimes referred to as the "perpetual strawberry" or *fraise de quatre saisons*.

Alpine strawberry

Most strains of alpine strawberries do not send out runners, the horizontal stems that cause strawberries to strew (hence "strewberry," which became strawberry) all over the ground. The first runnerless alpine, selected in 1811, was called 'Bush Alpine', or 'Gaillon'. Others include 'Érige du Poiton', 'Monstreuse Caennaise', and a strain once widely cultivated in England and France, 'Fressant'. I have grown the strains offered by American nurseries—'Baron Solemacher', 'Alexandria', 'Ruegen', 'Mignonette', and 'Charles V'—and find no dramatic differences among them in flavor or yield. With good soil and adequate water, all bear delectable, though small, berries continuously from June to October.

Some strains of alpine strawberry produce fruits colored creamy white, though they are often advertised as being yellow-fruited. Such fruits were described as long ago as 1536. These whitish cultivars include 'Bush White', 'Pineapple Crush', 'Alpine Yellow', and 'Alpine White' (the profuse runnering habit of the last-named cultivar distinguishes it from 'Alpine Yellow'). 'Pineapple Crush' fruits have a hint of pineapple flavor melded with the alpine strawberry flavor—though I do admit to the power of suggestion from the name and color of the fruits. Come to think of it, 'Alpine Yellow' also seems to have that hint of pineapple. Whether or not there are differences among the various white strains, I prefer growing them to growing the red strains because the white fruits are larger and are ignored by birds—and I like that hint of pineapple.

Novel types of alpine strawberries are worth mentioning. They are not readily available today, but may still exist in the backyard garden of some strawberry dilettante. The petals of one such variety, described in Berlin in 1904, are persistent and red (!) on the ripe fruit. With another novel variety, noted by John Tradescant (the father in the father-son team of British plantsmen) in Plymouth in 1620, the flowers' styles (stalks protruding from the top of a flower's ovaries) are persistent and green on the ripe fruit; not very appealing, but interesting. Other varieties described in nineteenth-century literature include plants with flowers having double rows of petals, flowers without petals, and plants with gold-striped leaves.

MUSK STRAWBERRY (*Fragaria moschata*)   The musk strawberry is larger than the alpine strawberry both in plant and fruit. Musk strawberries grow wild to a limited extent in dappled shade in the forests of central Europe, north into Scandinavia, and east into Russia. This fruit is the *Moschuserdbeere* or *Zimmerterdbeere* of the Germans, the *hautbois* strawberry of the French. In English the species has been referred to as the musk, the musky, or in anglicized French, the hautboy strawberry.

Musk strawberry

Alpine and Musk Strawberries

The musk strawberry is not commonly seen in garden catalogues or gardens in America, though it has been cultivated on a small scale in Europe. Nonetheless, it was the first strawberry of any sort with a cultivar name, which was 'Le Chapiron' (1576). By 1591, the cultivar was called 'Chapiton', then later 'Capiton'. This is probably the 'Capron' mentioned by Louis XIV's gardener, Quintinye, in 1672. Maintaining the thread, 'Capron' was the name tag on the musk strawberry plants I imported from Italy back in 1980.

Wild forms of musk strawberry are dioecious, which is one reason the musk strawberry was never widely cultivated in the past. Before the principles of sex in plants were elucidated, nonfruiting, male musk strawberry plants were rogued from gardens, leaving no pollinators for, and hence no fruit from, the remaining female plants.

Cultivated forms of musk strawberry have perfect flowers and are somewhat self-pollinating. Many of these cultivated varieties have exotic names to match their flavors: 'Framboise', 'Abricot', 'Précoce Musquée', 'Verlander Erdbeere', and 'Profumata di Tortona', to name a few. The last-named cultivar was cultivated commercially as recently as the middle part of the twentieth century outside Tortona, Italy. In my garden, this cultivar is more vigorous, more productive, and larger fruited than the aforementioned 'Capron'. Other cultivars, flavorful in fruit though not in name, have included 'Black', 'Peabody's New Hautbois' (new in the nineteenth century, that is), 'Monstrous Hautbois', 'Globe', 'Prolific', and 'Royal'.

The flowers, whether male or hermaphroditic, are ornamental in their own right. They are held aloft, well above the foliage, in trusses atop thin stalks that (hopefully) eventually topple from their weight of fruit.

THE FUTURE OF "WILD STRAWBERRIES"? Although these wildings, in their pure form, will always be grown by those of us who relish their unique flavors, these strawberries could also find themselves—or rather, their genes—in many more gardens and even commercial strawberry fields. Some of the barriers to hybridization have been overcome. So from Germany comes, for example, 'Florika', a hybrid of *Fragaria vesca* with the modern garden strawberry. Hybrid vigor is expressed in its profuse runnering, leading this strawberry to be billed as a "*vescana* strawberry meadow," yielding quantities of disease-resistant and tasty berries. Breeders in Canada have succeeded in combining the genes of musk and alpine strawberries, along with those of garden strawberries and other species. Time will tell what flavors emerge from these melting pots.

Cultivation

Alpine and musk strawberries are remarkably easy to grow. The alpine strawberry can be grown from USDA Hardiness Zones 3 through 10. My experience with musk strawberries is that they are hardy to at least the colder parts of Zone 5—not surprising, considering their native range into Scandinavia. Both come through winters unscathed even without the winter mulch needed by regular cultivated strawberries.

Plants of both species fruit with as little as four hours of sun per day, but they are more finicky when it comes to soil. The soil needs to be well aerated, moisture retentive, and rich in organic matter. Assuming a site above the water table, the best means to ensure fertility, aeration, and water retention in a soil is to add organic matter. Ideally, two or three inches of peat moss or compost should be dug into the top six inches of soil before planting. Soil nitrogen can be augmented with an annual sprinkling of two cups of any fertilizer having about ten percent nitrogen over every hundred square feet, applied at any time between late winter and midsummer. I use soybean meal, which releases nitrogen slowly throughout the growing season.

The main body of the strawberry plant consists of a crown, which is actually a shortened, woody stem producing successive leaves at close intervals. New leaves and flowers grow atop the crown, and, below ground, new roots form above the old roots. The roots are short-lived and ninety percent of them are in the top six inches of soil. Plant with the soil surface just below the top of the crown, so that the roots are covered but the crown is not smothered.

Always keep in mind the plant's shallow root system, susceptible to the effects of searing summer sun, careless hoes and tillers, dry soil, and competition from hungry weeds. A mulch around the plants suppresses weeds and obviates hoeing. Mulch also keeps the upper layers of the soil cool and moist. Organic mulches continually enrich the soil as they decompose; consequently, they need annual replenishment. Suitable organic mulches include sawdust, compost, pine needles, leaves, and the traditional mulch, straw (use of the latter mulch, according to some etymologists, is another possible derivation for the word strawberry).

Alpine strawberries planted six inches apart will make a solid miniature hedge. At a distance of twelve inches, the plants remain separate mounds of green.

Musk strawberries need a half foot to one foot between plants, the latter distance for vigorous clones such as 'Profumata di Tortona'. The plants need some regimentation if they are to bear reasonable crops. Plants set in the ground at their minimum spacing need to have all their runners removed through the summer to avoid overcrowding. Pinch the runners off while they are still young and succulent.

An alternative planting plan, which economizes on the number of plants needed, is to set plants wide apart and allow runners to grow and fill in the spaces. Space the mother plants at twice the recommended distance and allow each plant to develop only one or two runners, or set the plants three feet apart each way and let them run wild!

My preference is to keep the plants under strict control by setting mother plants in a double row, with a foot between the rows and between the plants, then ruthlessly removing all runners. This is admittedly strict treatment for a near-wild plant, but I feel it is necessary, considering the low yields of musk strawberries under even the best of conditions.

All strawberry beds need periodic renovation for best fruit production. As plants age, the roots are increasingly exposed to cold and desiccation. An inch of compost spread over the bed each spring keeps the soil level rising along with the crowns. Eventually, old plants become woody and less productive, at which time they should be dug out and replaced with young plants (see the following section on propagation).

No matter how diligent I am in removing runners from musk strawberries, they seem to sneak ahead of me so eventually the bed becomes overcrowded. Renovation is the time to catch up, thinning plants back to the original spacing and removing the oldest plants.

Strawberries bloom early and are especially susceptible to late spring frosts because the plants are low to the ground, where cold air settles. In the case of the alpine strawberries, the loss of a few blossoms is tolerable; the everbearing plants will put forth new blossoms. Not so for musk strawberries, and the blossoms most apt to be nipped by frost are the first ones to open, which are the ones that produce the largest fruits.

Protecting strawberry blossoms from frost entails nothing more than throwing an old blanket or sheet over the plants when frost is predicted. Mulch also could be piled over the plants. Ideally, the berries should not have been planted in low-lying areas, into which dense, cold air has a habit of settling on frosty spring nights.

Though alpine strawberries bear continuously the whole season, their main crop comes during spring, with a lesser crop during fall, and only a few berries in midsummer. The crop each season depends to a large extent on the prevailing temperature. The hotter it gets, the sparser the fruits. The plants can be coerced to change their seasonal bearing. A century ago, the French horticulturalist Vilmorin-Andrieux suggested removing at least some of the flowers in spring and summer, so that the plants would channel more energy into a fall crop.

With a sunny window or a greenhouse, the harvest season can be extended even further into fall (alpine strawberries only) or advanced in the spring (for both alpine and musk strawberries). A six-inch pot is adequate in size, though I have fruited plants in pots as small as two inches in diameter. Any porous potting mix is suitable. Fertilization and watering should be commensurate with plant growth. By late winter plants need weekly doses of fertilizer and, often, daily applications of water. In clay pots, which are attractive and allow air to pass through to the roots, twice-daily watering may be called for by late winter. To insure pollination indoors, touch each fully opened flower with a small paintbrush.

I have reaped more musk strawberries per plant from pots in sunny windows in late winter than from plants in the garden during the growing season. Strawberries generally make fruit buds when days are short, and runners when days are long, so the fecundity of my indoor plants could be due to the opportunity they have to grow while the days are still short. By the time plants outdoors in the garden begin to grow, the days are already long enough to stimulate runners more than flowers. Plants sitting at a cool, bright window probably can also develop flower buds through the winter. In southern areas, outdoor plants might fruit more prolifically than they do in my Zone 5.

I have also found that although musk strawberry cultivars are billed as self-pollinating, they evidently are only partially so. A bona fide male clone (which could be raised by planting musk strawberry seeds) won't itself fruit, but seems to greatly increase the number and size of fruits on any nearby female or perfect-flowered (hermaphroditic) plants.

Musk and alpine strawberries are subject to many of the same pests as are common garden strawberries. But, as with garden strawberries, these pests do not present a problem with good cultural conditions: a site with good air circulation and a well-drained soil, sufficient water, and the prompt removal of diseased plants or plant parts. Keep an eye out for whiteflies and aphids on indoor plants.

Propagation

Alpine strawberry plants are usually propagated by crown division or seed (the plants come quite true from seed); musk strawberry plants (and runnered alpines) are usually propagated by runners. A problem, if any, in growing either species is their tendency to propagate too readily. Alpine strawberries self-sow prolifically and musk strawberries runner prolifically. In either case, a planting soon becomes overcrowded, necessitating the annual thinning out of plants to maintain productivity.

Grow alpine strawberries from seed just as you do tomatoes: sow seeds indoors in late winter, then transplant seedlings to the garden when warm weather settles in the spring. Sprinkle the tiny strawberry seeds evenly over a flat filled with a well-drained potting mix, just barely cover the seed with sphagnum moss, then water from below by setting the flat in a pan of water. The seeds will not all germinate at once, and the seedlings should not be disturbed for a while. The frailty of indoor-sown seedlings in their early stages belies the almost weedy nature of seedlings that self-sow around mother plants outdoors. After about a month of growth, the seedlings begin to show vigor and are ready to be pricked out and spaced two inches apart in a larger flat.

Set plants in the ground outdoors as soon as the last frost date is passed. Plants grown from seeds ripen their first berries during the summer of the year they are planted, and in years to follow fruits can be picked beginning in spring.

Crown division is a way to multiply established plants and, as with any herbaceous perennial, is a necessity every few years to rejuvenate old plants. The crowns branch with age, and plants can be dug in early spring and cut into pieces, each with a crown branch and some attached roots. Replant young growth from the outside of the clump rather than old, woody growth near the center.

Although the musk strawberry can be propagated by crown division, runners are the most convenient way to make new plants. Pegging runners in place in a flowerpot or in the ground with a hairpin ensures quick rooting. Sever daughter plants from the mother plant a few weeks after pegging. These runners are clones, all genetically identical to one another and to the mother plant. The plants will bear fruit the following season, and the sooner the runners are rooted, the greater the harvest.

Musk strawberry seeds grow into plants different from their parents, which is fine if you want to try your hand at developing new cultivars, but not if you want to propagate a desirable cultivar. To raise seedlings, first mash the fruits in water to extract the seeds, then sow them immediately or dry them for storage. Remember that most seedlings, in contrast to cultivated varieties, will have either male or female flower parts, but not both. Save some male plants to pollinate the female plants.

Harvest and Use

I would not suggest replanting a regular strawberry bed solely to alpine and musk strawberries, for the bed would never produce enough fruit to stock a freezer. True, the French king Charles V had twelve hundred wood strawberries planted in the Louvre garden in 1368, but he had no choice, for the modern strawberry had not yet been created.

Alpine and musk strawberries, nonetheless, do have a place in today's gardens. Aside from bearing delicious fruits, the plants are ornamental—green mounds, with white blossoms staring out above the foliage from atop thin flower stalks. The neat, compact habit of nonrunnering alpine strawberries makes them ideal for edgings. The profuse runnering habit of musk strawberry plants can be put to use as a groundcover (at some expense to fruiting). Both species also make attractive specimen plants in pots.

Both alpine and musk strawberry fruits are flavorless until they are dead ripe. And even when ripe, musk strawberry fruits do not turn completely red. Rather, each fruit ripens unevenly to some drab shade between pale red and dark purple. When ready to harvest, alpine and especially musk strawberry fruits become so aromatic that a single ripe berry perfumes the air around a plant. At this stage the fruits are so soft that they almost crush when picked— yet another reason why alpine and musk strawberries are unsuitable for large-scale commercial cultivation, but good for backyards, where the ripe fruits need travel no further than arm's length.

Pawpaw
Banana of the North

BOTANICAL NAME
Asimina triloba

PLANT TYPE
Small, pyramidal, deciduous tree

POLLINATION
Except for a few cultivars, all need cross-pollination

RIPENING SEASON
Late summer and early fall

I have three banana trees planted in the ground in my front yard, even though winter temperatures here reliably plummet well below zero. Okay, they are not bona fide bananas, but pawpaws, the fruits of which have been known as poor man's banana, Hoosier banana, Michigan banana, or "whatever-state-the-pawpaw-happens-to-grow-in" banana. The reason for these monikers is that pawpaw fruits taste and look very much like bananas. Within the pawpaw's greenish yellow skin, which becomes speckled and streaked with brown at ripeness, is a creamy white, custardy flesh. The flavor is much like that of bananas, but with additional hints of vanilla custard, pineapple, and mango.

> And sich pop-paws!—Lumps o' raw
> Gold and green,—jes' oozy th'ough
> With ripe yaller—like you've saw
> Custard-pie with no crust to . . .
> (James Whitcomb Riley, "Up and Down Old Brandywine")

Aside from tropical flavor, the pawpaw also has tropical roots—botanical roots, that is. Pawpaw is a cold-hardy representative of the custard apple family (Annonaceae), which includes such tropical and subtropical delicacies as the soursop, the sweetsop, the cherimoya, and, of course, the custard apple. Even the name, "pawpaw," is a nickname for yet another tropical fruit, the papaya, perhaps because of the slight physical resemblance between the two fruits. But the pawpaw and the papaya are as distantly related as are the apple and the orange.

Pawpaw trees are native throughout the eastern United States, south of New England and north of Florida, and as far west as Nebraska. For centuries, American Indians collected and cultivated the fruits. Four hundred years ago a traveling companion of the explorer Hernando de Soto wrote that "the fruit is like unto peares riall: it hath verie good smell, and an excellent taste." An entry dated 18 September 1806 in the journal of Lewis and Clark offers respite from the usual grueling pictures of exploration: "our party entirely out of provisions subsisting on poppawas . . . the party appear perfectly contented and tell us that they can live very well on poppaws." (They also had a few biscuits left.) Over the decades, America's rural folk came to know and enjoy the fruit; Charles Sprague Sargent (the first director of Harvard's Arnold Arboretum), writing at the turn of the twentieth century, tells us that the fruit was "sold in large quantities in cities and towns in those parts of the country where the tree grows naturally." Count Daniel Boone and Mark Twain among pawpaw's fans. And four states—Illinois, Kentucky, Michigan, and West Virginia—even have towns named Paw Paw. Pawpaw—the fruit—is our largest native edible fruit.

Description of the Plant

The pawpaw is a small, pyramidal tree with long, drooping leaves, the latter (once again) more reminiscent of tropical climes than of those with frigid winters. The tree signals the coming of winter with its leaves changing color to a beautiful clear yellow.

Pawpaws grow wild in forests in the shade of larger trees. Although usually reaching between ten and twenty-five feet in height, individual specimens have been known to soar to almost fifty feet. Branches are brittle, something to keep in mind when eyeing a luscious cluster high out of reach. Sprouts commonly shoot up from horizontal roots at some distance from the trunk, so a single tree eventually spreads to form a thicket. A family of sprouts with a single root system might cover a quarter of an acre. Sprouts from backyard trees are easily kept in check with a lawnmower.

Pawpaw

Recently pawpaw shoots have been eyed as more than just hangers for delectable fruit. Most parts of the plant—including the unripe fruits and the seeds as well as the bark—have been found to contain powerful pesticides and antitumor agents. On a commercial scale, there is talk of extracting active ingredients from prunings of trees that were annually pollarded (pollarded trees would not bear fruit, though). While scientists are quantifying and characterizing these compounds, clever gardeners could perhaps concoct a crude, homegrown pesticide by macerating, then soaking in alcohol, twigs collected during summer months, when bioactive compounds are most concentrated.

Getting back to the living tree, it has some details worth a closer look. In winter, the dormant buds are rusty brown and fuzzy. Those that are vegetative—these will give rise to shoots the forthcoming season—are long and pointed. Flower buds look like small, plush buttons.

Come spring, those small, plush buttons swell and unfold petals that initially are green, then change to pink. When the flower finally opens to its full breadth, between an inch and a half to two inches across, the petals deepen in color to lurid purple. You have to get up close and below the blossoms to appreciate them fully because they hang downwards.

The flowers open late enough so that they rarely get frosted. In only one year out of my almost two decades of growing this fruit has frost struck these blossoms, in this case a heavy frost, and it struck twice that spring, even burning the leaves. But pawpaws have a long blossoming period, and new blossoms continued to open for four weeks even after that devastating frost. Depending on the cultivar and the length of the season, fruits that develop from late blossoms may or may not have time to ripen.

Pawpaw flowers are born singly, each flower containing several separate ovaries, typically three to seven, but up to nine, so potentially a flower could give rise to a cluster of fruits of that number. Large clusters occur under only the best of conditions. Rarely is fruit set abundantly in the wild, because the flowers are not readily pollinated. One reason is that the female parts of the flower are no longer ready to receive pollen by the time the male parts get around to shedding it. And even when both female and male flower parts are ready, the flowers need cross-pollination to set fruit, yet few insects perform this job with efficiency or enthusiasm. It is not uncommon for less than one percent of the flowers on wild plants to set fruits, mostly thanks to a few beetles and flies. Bees, the usual pollinators of fruit trees and bushes, show no interest in the pawpaws' dark, fetid flowers.

Fruits from a single flower hang together, pointing outward or upward—once again reminiscent of bananas, which hang from the banana plant much the same way in "hands." Fruits range from three to six inches long by one to three inches wide.

According to folklore, there are two distinct types of pawpaws: a large, yellow-fleshed, highly flavored, early-ripening type; and a white-fleshed, mild-flavored, late ripening type. However, botanists do not distinguish these as separate types, and the two probably represent extremes of a continuum in flesh color, with a tendency for the yellower-fleshed clones to taste better.

The fruits part company with bananas in that there are two rows of brown seeds the size of lima beans embedded in the pawpaw's creamy flesh. The fruit separates easily from the seeds, though—fortunately, because of the toxins they contain.

> I stood in thickets,
> turned your flat
> seeds with my tongue,
> and sucked the juices
> off those magic stones.
>
> (Norbert Krapf, "Paw Paw")

Over the past hundred years, there have been periodic flurries of interest in selecting and/or breeding superior pawpaws. In 1916 the American Genetic Association offered a prize of one hundred dollars as "stimulus to the search for superior specimens"—fifty dollars for the largest tree, and fifty dollars for the best fruit. In the early part of the twentieth century a handful of enthusiasts put together collections of the best pawpaws available. Many of those collections have since been threatened by or lost to neglect or development. (For example, the Beltway circling Washington, D.C. went right through the collection of David Fairchild, who headed the USDA's first Office of Foreign Seed and Plant Introduction.) There are efforts to save what is left of those collections and to develop or find even better pawpaws.

Since 1905, various pawpaw clones have been notable enough to receive names and, often, be propagated. Aside from those on the list at the end of this chapter, a few other cultivars are worth mentioning. 'Gable', 'Jumbo', 'Osborne', 'Shannondale', and 'Tiedke' were late ripening. 'Hope's August' was an old cultivar distinguished for its early ripening, and 'Glaser' was notable for its large fruits. Other old varieties that should be mentioned for completeness include: 'Rees', 'Cheely', 'Hann', 'Early Best', 'Arkansas Beauty', 'Scott', 'Endicott', and 'Hope's September'.

THE FUTURE OF THE PAWPAW?   Among wild pawpaws, it is not difficult to find ones that produce good fruits. But there is room for improvement. The ideal pawpaw would produce abundant fruits ripening before frost, be large, and have few and/or small seeds. This fruit would have a firm texture, and the flavor would be sweet, delicate, and rich but not cloying. If the fruit were ever to be grown commercially, it would need a thicker skin to tolerate shipping and handling. The tree itself, while quite good right at the go-get, could stand some improvement, mostly in terms of peduncle borer resistance and consistent, good yields.

Compared with the fruits you find on today's market shelves, relatively little work has been done in improving the pawpaw. Most named varieties were superior wild plants found in a relatively narrow geographic area (in contrast to the pawpaw's extensive native range). It could be that at this very moment the ideal or almost-ideal pawpaw is lurking somewhere in an American forest. In 1981, pawpaw improvement and promotion got a boost when Neal Petersen founded the PawPaw Foundation, "dedicated to the research and development of Asimina triloba as a new fruit for American farmers and consumers."

Some of the pawpaw's deficiencies could be overcome by hybridization with other members of the genus *Asimina*, to wit some of the Southern species, with which pawpaw readily crosses and which excel in complementary qualities. For example, *A. parviflora* is an upright shrub or small tree that is cold-hardy to the coastal plain of Virginia, is self-fruitful, and ripens its (barely) edible fruits weeks before the pawpaw. To make the flowers more attractive to insects, one might introduce some blood of the fragrant-flowered *A. reticulata*. Pawpaws might even be grown for their flowers as well as their fruits if they had the lovely, four-inch-diameter flowers of *A. obovata*.

Delicious hybrids also might result from cross-breeding the pawpaw with some of its tropical and subtropical relatives, such as the cherimoya (*Annona cherimola*) and sugar apple (*Annona squamosa*). Thus far, such hybrids are elusive.

Cultivation

The pawpaw is an easy plant to grow. As might be expected of a plant with a wide natural range, the pawpaw is not particularly finicky as to soil or climate. Any well-drained soil with a pH level ranging from 5.0 to 7.0 is suitable.

A thick surface mulch of leaves or straw will reproduce the cool, moist soil conditions found in pawpaw's native habitat. Though pawpaw trees are hardy to below minus twenty degrees Fahrenheit, the fruit needs enough summer warmth and about 160 days to ripen, or about 2600 growing degree days calculated between fifty and eighty-six degrees Fahrenheit (USDA Hardiness Zones 4 through 8). Winter cold is needed to awaken the pawpaw each year, with four hundred or more total hours of cool temperatures signaling that wake-up call. Therefore, pawpaws can be grown everywhere in temperate climates except extreme northern regions and areas with cool maritime summers.

Pruning is rarely necessary except perhaps to remove wayward branches here and there, more to please the gardener than the tree. Periodic pruning might be used to stimulate some new growth each year on old trees, for it is new wood that produces fruit the following season.

The pawpaw does have three foibles that require attention. First of all, care is needed in transplanting. Pawpaw has a long taproot that reaches deep into the ground, even on small plants, and the roots are brittle. One way around this shortcoming is to avoid transplanting: sow seeds at trees' permanent locations. Another way is to plant a tree that has spent its youth in a pot, so the roots are not disturbed during transplanting. Bare-root transplanting is possible, though. Wait until pawpaw buds begin to grow in the spring, then move the plant with as much of the root system as possible. Some nurseries dig and sell sprouts from pawpaw thickets; such plants, with their sparse root systems, rarely survive. Best survival comes with large trees transplanted from commensurately large (mostly deep) containers.

The second foible of the pawpaw concerns shade. Not only does the pawpaw feel at home in the shade, but young seedlings demand it. Plants that are grafted or otherwise start out in life "mature" do not require shade. And although pawpaws are naturally found growing in shade and will grow well there, they actually fruit best in full sun, so make that shade for young trees only temporary.

The third bugaboo in growing pawpaws, one not always requiring attention, is getting the plants to produce fruits in abundance. The plants usually flower extravagantly and late enough to avoid spring frost, but it is pollination that limits yield. Most cultivars need cross-pollination, which is ensured by a pawpaw's female floral parts being receptive to pollen before the flower's male parts are ready to offer it. Various flies and beetles seem to be the primary pollinators of pawpaw, but their efforts are often not sufficiently enthusiastic to result in a good crop.

If plants flower but bear little fruit, try hand-pollination. The pollen is ripe when the anther ball within the flower is brownish and loose, and the pollen grains come off readily onto your finger. Pick off a few such flowers and remove their petals. Then gently rub that flower onto the tips of the central stigmas of another plant's flowers (the stigmas indicate their readiness for the pollen when they look fresh and shiny). The central style is very delicate, and care must be taken not to break it. Alternatively, shake the pollen from a number of flowers into a small container, then transfer it to receptive flowers with an artist's brush. With hand-pollination, only the strength of the branches limits the quantity of fruit that a plant can produce.

Few insects or diseases seem to find either the leaves or the fruits toothsome enough to warrant any spraying. Probably the worst pest is the pawpaw peduncle borer (*Talponia plummeriana*), a quarter-inch-long larva that bores into the fleshy tissue of the flower, causing the flower to drop; in most years, in my experience, the pest causes no trouble. In some years devastation can be quite extensive. Look within the flower stalk—the peduncle—of a wilted blossom for the caterpillar, or, at least, its tunnel if it has departed. Another caterpillar sometimes chews on a few pawpaw leaves, but this one is happily tolerated because it is the larva of the beautiful zebra swallowtail butterfly. An as yet unidentified disease attacks, sometimes killing, a small percentage of trees, causing branches to wilt, beginning at their tips, right after leaves have emerged and staining wood beneath the bark blue or black. On the West Coast pawpaw leaves are sometimes feasted upon by slugs and snails, and when they finish in early summer, other insects have been reported to eat the foliage and leave just a rattail midvein of each leaf. Elsewhere, possums, raccoons, and foxes are the only competitors for the fruit.

Propagation

The easiest way to get pawpaw trees started is to plant seeds, which should not be allowed to freeze or dry out once extracted from the fruits. In contrast to older pawpaws, seedling pawpaws require shade, about fifty percent, for their first year or two, whether in a greenhouse or outdoors. Before germination can occur, the seeds need cold stratification for between sixty and a hundred days.

Once seed has been stratified and planted an inch deep, patience is needed, not so much in waiting for the plants to fruit, but in watching for any sign of life to appear above the soil. Roots are well established before a shoot pokes through the soil surface, which occurs forty-five to ninety days after sowing. Warming the soil to about ninety degrees Fahrenheit can hasten the seedling up out of the soil by ten days.

Under natural conditions, or even those of the average garden, seedling growth is very slow, measured in inches the first two, even three, years. But then the pace picks up and the plant begins to bear at between five and seven years of age, at which time the tree is five or more feet tall.

Sow the seeds either outdoors in hills at their permanent locations (and thin the seedlings to the one or two most vigorous plants per hill after a couple of years), or in containers. The containers need not be wide, but must be deep enough to accommodate the taproot: special "deep root" containers are available commercially, or make your own with twelve-inch lengths of PVC pipe with screens at their bottoms. Seedlings planted outdoors usually do not emerge until about July, sometimes not until the following spring.

If seeds are sown early in the season in a greenhouse, it is possible for plants to make the equivalent of two seasons of growth by the end of their first summer. The seeds must not be sown too early, however, for they are responsive to daylength, and seedlings that poke through the ground while days are still short act as if fall is approaching and stop growing. On the other hand, if you sow the seeds early and provide artificial light to bring daylength to sixteen hours, air temperatures to around seventy-five degrees Fahrenheit, and root temperatures to about ninety degrees Fahrenheit, you could coax five feet of growth in a single season! Feed biweekly with waterings and repot as needed to keep plants actively growing rather than setting terminal buds.

Pawpaw cultivars are easily propagated by most types of grafting except for T-budding. Keep scionwood dormant in a refrigerator and graft sometime between when the leaf buds on the rootstock begin to show green in the spring and when the leaves have fully expanded.

Other methods for propagating pawpaws include transplanting suckers and taking root cuttings. Pawpaws will grow from transplanted suckers as long as the suckers are severed from the mother plant with a shovel, but left in place, a year before transplanting. Success in growing plants from root cuttings is variable, dependent on the particular clone. The advantage of clones grown from root cuttings and suckers is that they are on their own roots. If a plant dies back or sends up root suckers, all new growth still will be of the desired clone. Thus far, tissue culture has not been very successful, especially of mature plant material.

Harvest and Use

A good-yielding pawpaw tree produces between twenty-five and fifty pounds of fruit, or about a bushel. Some people harvest pawpaws when they are dead ripe on the tree, at which time the greenish yellow skin turns brown or almost black. Other people pick fruits when they just begin to soften, to finish ripening indoors (acting like a banana again, isn't it?). Perhaps the fully ripe flavor is too strong for some people.

Large fruits fall when almost ripe, which is another good reason for a thick, soft mulch beneath the trees.

Fully ripe fruit does not store very well, perhaps three days at room temperature, a week in the refrigerator. Eat dropped fruit quickly. If picked almost ripe, the fruit will keep for three weeks or more in a refrigerator, and can be removed to finish ripening at room temperature after about a week. Keep the storage temperature no lower than forty degrees Fahrenheit, though, or pawpaw will develop off flavors. (Doesn't a banana do this also?) Harvested fruit will finish ripening faster than fruits left hanging on the branches.

Pawpaw pulp freezes well once it has been divested of its skin and seeds, a little lemon juice or citric acid mixed in for added pizazz. Pawpaw pulp also can be dried for storage. Extracted or dried pulp has been used in all sorts of delectable drinks and foods, including ice cream (a favorite in taste tests) and cookies. For something cooling and refreshing, substitute pawpaw for all or some of the pineapple in a piña colada.

I would be remiss not to point out that there are people who experience an adverse reaction to pawpaw, even though these sensitive people might actually like the flavor. Reactions may include a rash, nausea, or diarrhea. Usually it is the pawpaw's skin or leaves that are responsible, and adverse reactions are probably no more severe or extensive than what some people experience from strawberries.

The way to eat a fresh pawpaw is by halving it and using a spoon, or by removing the skin à la banana, though the latter method is not quite that easy. Pawpaws do not take kindly to cooking, as their flavor is fugitive and easily driven away by any more than a little heat. Within this constraint, the pawpaw still can be used to make a tasty pudding, marmalade, beer, brandy, and, of course, custard pie.

Cultivars

Many of the cultivars mentioned here may not be available or even exist anymore; then again, one or more of them may turn up sometime. This list is far from inclusive of every pawpaw that someone decided tasted good and then gave a name, and with current interest in the fruit, new cultivars are on the horizon. Actual ripening dates depend on time of bloom and summer heat accumulation, so, for instance, expect fruits to ripen a few weeks earlier in Indiana than in New York.

'Buckman': fruit is late-ripening, white-fleshed, and has a mild flavor.

'Davis': not very vigorous tree, with variable production; fruit is midseason to late-ripening (first week in October in Michigan), large, with a green skin when ripe; up to four ounces and five inches long; selected from the wild in 1959, but has been superseded by better cultivars, such as 'Overleese'.

'Dr. Potter': a cultivar mentioned in 1917; originated in Indiana; small, yellow fruit with mild flavor; late-ripening; ships fairly well.

'Fairchild': productive tree with early-ripening fruit; considered to be the best cultivar by Dr. G. A. Zimmerman (a pawpaw enthusiast whose collection spanned the years between 1917 and 1941); a seedling of 'Ketter'.

'Ford Amend': origin in Oregon in 1950; slightly smaller and earlier than 'Sunflower'; greenish yellow skin and orange flesh; ripens late September in Oregon.

'Ketter': origin in Ohio; tough skin keeps its good yellow color; large; flesh yellow, mild but not insipid; the winner of the American Genetic Society's pawpaw contest in 1916 for the best fruit; early-ripening, considered the second-best pawpaw by Dr. Zimmerman.

'Martin': origin in Ohio; late-ripening and cold-resistant, but the fruit is small and has poor flavor (also has been reported as being large and good quality!); yellow flesh.

'Mary Foos Johnson': origin in Kansas; fruits up to eight ounces with yellow skin and flesh; few seeds; ripens first week in October in Michigan.

'Mitchell': origin in Illinois; ripens midseason; average production; medium-to-large, oval-to-round fruits with excellent flavor, comparable to or better than 'Overleese'; yellow skin and golden flesh.

'NC-1': very vigorous hybrid of 'Davis' and 'Overleese' selected in Ontario in 1976; ripens mid-September in Ontario; ten to twenty ounces with few seeds; yellow skin and buttery yellow flesh with very good flavor.

'Overleese': origin in Indiana about 1950; a late-ripening cultivar similar to 'Davis'; the oval-to-round fruits have few but large seeds, excellent flavor, and are borne in clusters of three to six; size is variable; flesh is yellow to orange and skin is green, not darkening.

'PA-Golden': includes four cultivars differentiated as #1, #2, #3, and #4; origin in

New York in 1972; all have yellow skin and golden flesh with excellent flavor; ripen in mid-September in New York.

'Prolific': vigorous tree with medium to high productivity; medium-sized fruit with light green skin and yellow flesh of very good quality; long ripening season and keeps moderately well.

'Rappahannock': uniformly medium-sized fruits (average seven ounces) have flesh with firm texture and relatively low percentage of seed; skin is pale yellow-green and flesh is yellow; large blossoms; the foliage is less drooping, which eases picking; ripens midseason, in the first half of September in Maryland; sets in clusters of three or less; prune off excessive vertical growth that this cultivar tends to develop.

'Rebecca's Gold': origin in California in 1970; kidney-shaped three-to-six-ounce fruit with yellow flesh.

'SAA-Overleese': origin in New York in 1982; ten-ounce fruit has green skin, yellow flesh, and few seeds; ripens mid-October in New York.

'SAA-Zimmerman': origin in New York in 1982; six-to-eight-ounce fruit has yellow skin and flesh, and few seeds; ripens in late September in New York.

'Shenandoah': the large fruits, averaging nine ounces, have a luscious, firm yet custardy flesh of which a relatively small percentage is seed; pale green skin and creamy yellow flesh; mild flavor appeals to many people; ripens in clusters of one to three fruits mid- to late season, around the middle of September in Maryland.

'Sunflower': origin in Kansas about 1970; reportedly self-fertile pawpaw with moderate vigor and reliable production; fruit ripens late (first week in October in Michigan), has few seeds, and weighs about half a pound to almost a pound; the flavor is reported by some as excellent and by others as mediocre; I find them "excellent."

'Susquehanna': among the largest (average eleven ounces) and sweetest of pawpaws; also among those with the lowest percentage of seeds; rich flavor, too rich for some people; clusters of one to five fruits usually; skin is yellowish green and flesh is firm and smooth; leaves have a naturally slight pucker; ripens mid to late season, just after the middle of September in Maryland.

'Sweet Alice': large fruits of good flavor.

'Taylor' ('Taylor 1'): origin in 1967 in Michigan; similar to 'Davis' in ripening, color, and size, but has better flavor and is reportedly self-fertile; borne in clusters of as many as seven fruits; green skin with yellow flesh; ripens first week in October in Michigan.

'Taylor 2' ('TayTwo' or 'Taytoo'): origin in 1967 in Michigan; moderate vigor; late-ripening; medium-sized; excellent flavor; light green with yellow flesh; has been reported by some as a shy and by others as a prolific bearer; fruit keeps well.

'Uncle Tom': origin in Indiana; the first-named cultivar of pawpaw, from the turn of the twentieth century; fruits borne singly or in pairs.

'Wells': origin in Indiana in 1960; fruit up to fourteen ounces, with green skin and yellow flesh; winner of the 1990 contest sponsored by Kentucky State University.

Raisin Tree

Candied Fruit for the Picking

BOTANICAL NAME
Hovenia dulcis

PLANT TYPE
Deciduous tree

POLLINATION
Self-fertile

RIPENING SEASON
Fall

When you eat from the raisin tree, you bypass the dark, dry, pea-sized fruit itself to nibble instead on the peduncle, or fruit stalk. Unlike other fruits, whose peduncles remain gracefully svelte, each of the raisin tree's peduncles swells into a gnarled, meaty mass. The peduncles are small but multitudinous, a profusion of them terminating nearly every twig on a mature tree. If truth be known, the peduncles do not look very appetizing, and it must have been a hungry human that sampled the first raisin-tree "fruit."

The peduncles live up to the tree's common name in appearance and taste. Late in the season, these peduncles darken to a reddish brown color and shrivel slightly. Their taste is sweet, with just a hint of astringency, to me more reminiscent of a combination of candied walnut and Asian pear than of raisin. The Japanese name for the "fruit" is *kenpo nashi*, *nashi* being the Japanese word for pear; one Chinese name is *chi-chao li*, which translates as "chicken-claw pear."

The "fruits" have been sold and harvested in China since pre-Confucian times. The plant was introduced to the West in about 1820, but has remained rare as an ornamental and virtually unknown for its savory peduncles.

Raisin tree

Raisin Tree

Description of the Plant

The raisin tree is native to shady, moist glens and mountains of China, but cultivation spread long ago to Japan, Korea, and India. In leaf, form, and texture, the plant resembles the American basswood (*Tilia americana*) and, like the basswood, possesses a beauty that is quiet rather than striking. The raisin tree can grow to a height of seventy feet or more, but cultivated specimens usually grow about thirty feet high, with a breadth equal to about two-thirds of the height. The leaves are large, ovate, and glossy green, beautiful in their season but, unfortunately, lacking in fall color. With age, the smooth bark separates into vertical strips to reveal a reddish interior that makes a pleasant contrast with the greyish brown outer bark.

The flowers bloom quite late, waiting until late June or early July, and are self-fruitful. They are cream colored and compensate for their small size by being clustered together in great masses. Where summers are cool, such as in England, bloom might be delayed even until the end of summer with the result that fruit does not form or ripen.

Cultivation

The raisin tree tolerates a wide range of soil conditions, except for sogginess, and has no pests to speak of. Though the tree is native to partially shaded sites, fruiting would probably be more prolific, and flowering and ripening hastened, in full sun. Growth rate is moderate, perhaps a foot or two a year, more when young and less when old.

Because the tree is so little grown, its northern limits for winter survival and fruit ripening can only be approximated. The plant seems cold-hardy to about minus ten degrees Fahrenheit (Zones 6 through 10), and fruits ripen in eastern North America at least as far north as southern New York (and farther north along Lake Ontario). Within seedling populations, there may turn up plants that survive and ripen in colder regions.

Propagation

No superior clones of the raisin tree are available, so the usual method of propagation is from seed. Plants grown from seed usually bear fruit within seven to ten years though bearing within three years is possible under good conditions: adequate moisture and fertility, and a long growing season.

The seeds have an impermeable seed coat that severely inhibits germination. Scarify the seed coat either by nicking it with a file or by soaking the seeds in concentrated sulfuric acid for two hours. Wash the seeds thoroughly with water following the acid soak. (Be careful of the exothermic reaction of sulfuric acid with water!) After scarification, germination usually occurs within a week to a couple of months.

The plant also has been propagated by softwood cuttings taken in late summer, and by root cuttings.

Harvest and Use

Raisin tree peduncles do not become tasty until very late in the season. Do not rush the harvest because until they are ripe their flavor is no better than the stalk of an apple or of any other fruit.

The peduncles are small and tedious to pick. Even the Chinese—not ones to shy away from hand labor—have traditionally relegated the task of picking off the peduncles to small children. The fruits form terminally on the branches, so one can imagine the difficulty and danger of harvesting peduncles high up in a tree. The usual procedure is to lop off large branches so that stalks can be picked off with the safety and comfort of terra firma against one's feet.

Besides eating the peduncles out of hand, the Chinese use them and other parts of the tree to prepare a sweet extract called "tree honey." The Chinese also credit the peduncles—and the real fruits—with counteracting the effects of large quantities of alcohol.

Lingonberry

Dainty Looks, Sturdy Disposition, and Tasty Berries

BOTANICAL NAME

Vaccinium vitis-idaea var. *vitis-idaea*, *V. vitis-idaea* var. *minus*

PLANT TYPE

Low-growing, evergreen, semi-woody subshrub

POLLINATION

Self-fertile, but benefits from cross-pollination

RIPENING SEASON

Midsummer, and then again in fall

Merely utter the word "lingonberry" to someone Scandinavian and watch for a smile on their lips and a dreamy look in their eyes. Each year, thousands and thousands of tons of lingonberries are harvested from the wild throughout Scandinavia, destined for sauce, juice, jam, wine, and baked goods. A fair number of these berries are, of course, just popped posthaste into appreciative mouths.

This relative of our Thanksgiving cranberry has long been a favorite of not only Scandinavians but of other northern peoples throughout the world. Despite having tiny, evergreen leaves and slender stems, lingonberry is a plant of rigorous climates. In such places, any palatable fruit is appreciated, making truly delectable lingonberries all the more dear. So important was the fruit in thirteenth-century Iceland that law books limited berry picking on other people's lands to what could be eaten on the spot.

This fruit is the *Preiselbeere* of the Germans, the *kokemomo* of the Japanese, the *puolukka* of the Finns, the *wisakimin* of the Cree, the *airelle rouge* of the French, the *keepmingyuk* of the Inuit—and the *lingon* of the Swedes. In English, the plant parades under a number of monikers, including partridgeberry (Newfoundland), cowberry (Britain), foxberry (Nova Scotia), mountain cranberry, and rock cranberry.

Not to be unpatriotic, but the cosmopolitan lingonberry outshines its close relative, our native American Thanksgiving cranberry, in a number of respects. Yes, both fruits are used in the kitchen in similar ways, and neither fruit is sweet. But a lingonberry fruit couples just enough sweetness with a rich, unique aroma so that the fruits—if picked dead ripe—are delicious plucked right off the plants into your mouth or mixed with, say, your morning cereal. As far as I'm concerned, a cranberry is never palatable until doctored up with plenty of sugar and heat.

While you're picking lingonberries, take a look at how pretty the plant is. It grows only a few inches high but spreads sideways to blanket the ground with thick, yet dainty, evergreen leaves having the same green gloss as those of holly. Again outshining the Thanksgiving cranberry, whose leaves turn a muddy purple with the onset of cold weather in late fall, lingonberry leaves retain their lush, green color right through winter. Along the front of my home, a rock retaining wall anchors a bed of lingonberries whose glossy greenness is livened in autumn by the red leaves, then, in winter, the red stems, of interplanted lowbush blueberries. Good eating and good-looking!

Description of the Plant

Lingonberry is a plant that can be enjoyed year round with your eyes, and almost year round with your mouth. Let's start in spring, when the cutest little urn-shaped blossoms dangle singly or in clusters near the ends of the thin, semi-woody stems. These urns hang upside down (upside down for an urn, that is) and are white, blushed with pink. They're not going to stop traffic from the street, but are best appreciated when plants are grown where they can be looked at frequently and up close—such as in that bed at the front of my house.

If you miss the spring floral show, you get another chance because lingonberries blossom twice each season. This second show, appearing in mid- to late summer on young stems, is absent at far northern latitudes.

The flower shows are, of course, followed by fruits, pea-sized and somewhat of a show in themselves. The bright red—or, rarely, white—berries hang on the plants for a long time, well into winter, making a perfect Christmas decoration in situ. Fruit yields are greater from the second flowering than from the first, and although cold and time will eventually darken and shrivel

Lingonberry

the berries, I find them tasty whenever I find them on the plants. Vitamin C concentration of the fruits, at 25 milligrams per 100 grams, is moderately high.

Hybridization of lingonberry with cranberry has been tried with the goal of imbuing the tasty but small lingonberry fruits with the large size of cranberry fruits. Thus far, success has been achieved only when cranberry was the pollen parent, and the resulting plants showed intermediate characteristics between the two parents except that none produced underground runners. Unfortunately, like a mule, the hybrids have all been sterile and so bear no fruit.

Although "lingonberries" have been discussed thus far as if they were but a single kind of plant, there are actually two botanical varieties, which differ a bit from each other in morphology and range. The larger of the two, botanically *Vaccinium vitis-idaea* var. *vitis-idaea*, grows about two feet high and has inch-long, pointed leaves. The more diminutive lingonberry, *Vaccinium vitis-idaea* var. *minus*, stays under eight inches and has commensurately smaller leaves, one-third by one-sixth of an inch, oval, and rounded at their tips. The larger lingonberry, hardy to Zone 4, is native to lowlands of Europe and northern Asia. Variety *minus* frequents mountains in Scandinavia and extends westward to Iceland, Greenland, and northern portions of North America; it is hardy to Zone 2. Natural hybrids of these two lingonberries occur in Scandinavia.

Both botanical varieties of lingonberry can grow into Zone 7 provided summers are not too hot for too long, but are admittedly at their best in cooler areas. In fact, in cold climates lingonberry stands in well for low-growing boxwood—in parterres, for example, a use first suggested in 1651 by André Mollet, the French gardener to Queen Christina of Sweden.

Grubbing beneath lingonberry plants of either variety, we find a dense mat of fine roots. These roots grow off stems that run underground just beneath the surface and are responsible for the spread of the plants. Plants that are raised from seed, in contrast to those propagated from rooted cuttings or runners, also have taproots.

Above-ground shoots originate from buds near the ends of the underground stems. How those above-ground shoots look and what they do reflects growing conditions, with increasing light resulting in more profuse flowering and branching.

Cultivation

If site conditions are suitable, lingonberry is an easy plant to grow. The plant is found growing naturally on raised bogs, rocky barrens, lichen woodlands of boreal taiga, dry heaths, tundra, mountaintops, and other cold, sometimes exposed habitats—that is, among the harshest conditions in the world, especially for an evergreen. What the lingonberry has going for it is that it hugs the ground, where it's sheltered from wind, nearer the earth's warmth, and often further protected by snow cover. All the soils that lingonberry inhabits are extremely rich in humus (decomposed organic material), so provide good drainage and at the same time hold moisture—these are the conditions that suit it best.

These conditions are similar to those enjoyed by blueberry, cranberry, mountain laurel, rhododendron, and other lingonberry relatives, and must be met for lingonberry to thrive. In addition to good drainage and abundant organic matter, lingonberries enjoy the same very acidic conditions—with a pH ideally between 4.5 and 5.5—required by their kin.

Adapting site conditions to suit lingonberry is not at all difficult on a garden scale (or a small farm scale as long as natural conditions are not too far off the mark). After ridding an area of weeds, against which lingonberries are poor competitors, mix a bucketful of acidic peat moss into each planting hole to provide the needed humus and its associated benefits as well as to acidify the soil. Peat moss is a humus source that is poor in nutrients so is especially suitable for lingonberries, which do not like rich soils. Such soils can burn lingonberries' delicate roots and encourage ranker growing weeds. Backfill soil used behind my rock wall, where I planted my lingonberries, was nothing more than a great quantity of old potting soil, most of which was fifty percent peat moss.

If you do not have sufficient natural acidity—which means that the soil has a sufficiently *low* pH, lower, say, than about 6.5—also dig elemental sulfur into the top six inches of ground before planting. Use three-quarters of a pound per hundred square feet in sandy soils, or two pounds per hundred square feet in loams, for each pH unit that the soil is initially above a pH of 4.5. Where soils are naturally very alkaline (pH higher than 8), such as in many parts of the western United States, either excavate soil at the planting site and replace it with a fifty-fifty mix of peat moss and sand or use this mix in containers plunged into the ground up to their rims. If the soil at the planting site tends to stay wet, build up mounds of soil and peat, and plant the lingonberries on the mounds, where their shallow roots can stay above the water level.

Lingonberries thrive in full sun but can tolerate some shade. Being a plant of northern climes, lingonberry will appreciate the coolness of some shade or—like the lingonberries on the east side of my house—a site shielded from hot afternoon sun. Be careful of shading plants too much, though, because the plants will appear lusty, with even more stem growth than they would make in the sun, but yield will suffer.

Lingonberry looks and feels at home in a rock garden and makes an attractive, edible groundcover. When growing it as a groundcover, plant lingonberry to eventually fill in a bed with a uniform mat of stems. Under farm conditions, lingonberries are planted in rows four to five feet apart, then kept to solid ribbons—like strawberries—of plants thirty inches wide. *Vaccinium vitis-idaea* var. *vitis-idaea*, being more vigorous, can fill in the row in a reasonable amount of time with an initial eighteen-inch spacing along the row; *Vaccinium vitis-idaea* var. *minus* plants need to be set about ten inches apart in the row. Utilize these in-row spacings in all directions to get a lingonberry groundcover established.

For best fruit production, plant at least two varieties. The plants are somewhat self-fertile, but yield and berry size are larger with cross-pollination. Best pollination occurs at about sixty degrees Fahrenheit. Little pollination takes place at temperatures below fifty degrees, which are common during the early bloom period in spring; fortunately, the plants bloom again when conditions are more conducive to good pollination.

Right after planting and then each year sometime between fall and spring, mulch the plants. The ideal is a two-inch depth of some finely divided, organic material that is not too rich in nutrients: sawdust, woodchips, chopped straw, or shredded leaves, for example. Such mulches sift down through the leaves and stems, keeping the ground cool and moist, preventing frost from heaving plants in winter, and decomposing to maintain high humus levels in the soil, provide some nutrients, and buffer soil acidity—all of which translates to larger berries and more of them. New roots, which form mostly in spring and autumn, will also eventually form along covered portions of stems. Sand has also been used as an annual mulch, as it is for cranberries, but has the drawbacks, especially in a backyard garden, of being heavy to move and providing no nutrition or buffering of acidity.

Plants need care their first season if they are to thrive, perhaps even survive. That care can be summed up mostly in one word: water. One-half gallon per week per square foot of planted area, which is the equivalent of an inch depth of water, keeps plants happy whether it comes from the sky, a sprinkler, or drip irrigation. High levels of soil humus from initial additions of peat moss and maintenance applications of organic mulches, as well as the plants' natural drought tolerance, will pretty much eliminate the need for further watering once plants are established.

Just because lingonberries thrive in lean soils does not mean they never get hungry. Those additions of organic materials will probably make nitrogen the only foodstuff, if any, needed by the plants. An ideal source of nitrogen for these plants (for all plants, in fact) is soybean meal, available at feed stores. Soybean meal is inexpensive and doles out its nutriment slowly and in synch with growing conditions (because these are the same conditions—heat and moisture—that stimulate soil microbes to work on the soybean meal). As a general recommendation, spread a pound of soybean meal per hundred square feet each year sometime between late fall and spring. Plants tell you they're hungry for nitrogen by yellowing of their oldest leaves. Be careful, though, not to over fertilize, because too much fertilizer might burn lingonberries' delicate roots as well as encourage growth of weeds, against which lingonberries are poor competitors.

Soils that are not sufficiently acidic require periodic adjustments to keep acidity in lingonberry's preferred range. Every few years I spread elemental sulfur over the ground. Yellowing of the youngest leaves, with their veins staying green, is a sign of iron deficiency, which is the result of, among other things, insufficient acidity.

Lingonberry bears flowers and fruits on its youngest shoots, and pruning can be used, as it is with lowbush blueberries, to stimulate growth of young, fecund stems. Plants are slow to establish, so there's no need for pruning until the planting is five or six years old. Then, while the plants are dormant, mow or cut a portion of the planting down to within an inch of the ground. Current recommendations for the timing of this drastic pruning run from as frequently as every three or four years for the slower-growing *minus* varieties, or every two to three years for the more vigorous *idaea* varieties, to as long as every fifteen years for any lingonberry. Being evergreens, lingonberries will not bounce back from a drastic pruning with as much enthusiasm as do their deciduous relative, lowbush blueberries.

Beyond annual mulching, occasional pruning, perhaps additions of fertilizer and sulfur, lingonberry is a carefree plant. Insect or disease pests are rarely significant, so your main "job" will be picking and enjoying the berries.

Propagation

A number of techniques can be used to propagate lingonberries, each with its advantages and disadvantages.

Sowing seed is the most basic method and can produce oodles of plants, but the seeds do have their quirks. If you can get your hands on lingonberry fruits, all the better, because fresh seeds germinate the best, although even then germination is somewhat erratic, averaging about eighty percent. To extract seeds in quantity from the fruits, crush them in water and let the mix ferment for a few days. Then wash away the pulp and skins. Sound seeds sink.

A one-to-one mixture of sand and peat moss, equal parts sand, peat, and soil, and straight, milled sphagnum moss are all good sowing mediums. Barely cover the seeds because they need light to germinate. A cool, moist stratification period of about three months seems to improve germination although fresh seeds may sprout without such treatment. Seeds sprout within a few weeks, then seedlings grow slowly and begin fruiting, on average, within three years. It is probably because of that three-year juvenile period, when all a plant's energy is directed to growth rather than growth and fruiting, that seed-propagated plants spread faster than plants grown by other methods.

The advantage of cuttings is that they are easy to root, bear a year after rooting, and are genetic replicas of the plants from which they originate. Expect best success with cuttings of succulent, new shoots or of ripened, mature shoots (the younger the better). Two-inch lengths treated with rooting hormone and kept in a humid atmosphere, preferably with bottom heat, root in about two months. Rhizomes tend to develop slowly on rooted stem cuttings.

Pieces of rhizomes two to four inches long also can be made to grow into new plants. Best times to propagate from rhizomes are spring and fall, probably because these are peak periods for new root growth.

To create just a few new plants, older plants can be dug up in spring or late summer and divided just as you would any perennial. Take clumps having roots and shoots for replanting. The same technique can be used to move plants or parts of plants from the wild, success being in large part a function of the kind of soil in which the plants are growing. Take care to minimize damage to the thin, fragile roots when moving or dividing plants, which can most easily be accomplished with plants that are growing in a soil rich in humus.

Micropropagation, which is the creation of new plants under sterile conditions from just a few cells of a mother plant, has been used successfully with lingonberry. Rare would be the gardener or farmer set up to practice this technique, but this method of cloning does result in the maximum number of plants in the least amount of time.

Small plants, whether seedlings, cuttings, or micropropagated plants, grow best if coddled for a year or two in a nursery bed enriched with abundant humus. Mulch that is spread over the plants in the dead of winter and, perhaps, additional protection with coverings of glass or plastic help as yet poorly rooted plants keep their roots in the ground as it freezes and thaws.

Harvest and Use

A wait of three to six years after planting is needed before a reasonable crop can be expected, but even then yields vary considerably depending on growing conditions. Under suboptimal growing conditions, including fertilized forest stands, yields might be five to ten pounds per hundred square feet (one to two tons per acre). With skillful cultivation and planting of better varieties, you can expect yields of twenty-five pounds or more per hundred square feet (five tons per acre).

Patient souls or those wanting only a nibble can pluck off individual berries by hand. A berry comb like that used for harvesting lowbush blueberries speeds picking, although the resultant harvest will need some cleaning to rid it of leaves and unripe fruits. (Sources for berry combs include Hartmann's Plant Company, Inc., 310 60th Street, Grand Junction, MI 49056, 616-253-4281; The Hubbard Rake Company, RR1 Box 3115, Mason's Bay Road, Jonesport, ME 04649, 207-497-5949; and Raintree Nursery, 391 Butts Road, Morton, WA 98356, 360-496-6400.) A "berry hungry" Scandinavian can rake about five pounds of fruit in an hour.

No need to rush eating or picking lingonberries. They keep well on or off the bush, in part because they contain benzoic acid, a natural preservative. Refrigerated, you can enjoy the harvested berries for at least eight weeks, longer for the variety *idaea* than for the variety *minus*. In nineteenth-century Sweden, lingonberries were kept from one year to the next as "water lingon," made by merely filling a jar with the berries, then pouring water over them.

There is seemingly no end to the uses for lingonberries. In Finland, for example, the berries are the traditional accompaniment to blood sausage or blood pancakes. Lingonberries also find their way into meat stews, sauces, juice, and wine. They make excellent jam alone, and especially so combined with rosehips. The juice is delightfully refreshing mixed with that of other berries.

A refreshing, albeit potent, drink can be made from lingonberries and vodka. One recipe calls for soaking a quart of berries in a quart of vodka for two months, then pouring off the liquid into a bottle and adding half a quart of sugar to the berries. Let the berries and sugar sit about a week while the sugar draws out more liquid, then pour it in with the first decantate. Let that mix age for a month before tippling.

Lingonberries also find their way into the dispensary. Arbutin in a tea made from the leaves is reputedly good for intestinal and bladder disorders, and the fruits reputedly combat bladder and kidney infections, lower cholesterol, and treat rheumatic diseases.

I don't admit to ever having used lingonberries for curative purposes, nor have I tasted them in all their culinary incarnations. One guise in which I do have great affection for the berries is plucked right from the plants—dead ripe—into my eagerly waiting mouth.

Cultivars

'Ammerland': a selection of the botanical variety *vitis-idaea* introduced from Germany; very similar to the popular 'Koralle' in growth and yield, with slightly larger berries.

'Erntedank': a selection of the botanical variety *vitis-idaea* from Germany, introduced by Zillmer in 1975; the plant has relatively pale leaves and poor growth; produces very heavy yields of small- to medium-sized berries.

'Erntekrone': a selection of the botanical variety *vitis-idaea* from Germany, introduced by Zillmer in 1978; these vigorous, stiffly upright plants have roundish, dark green leaves and are high-yielding; fruits are dark red and large.

'Erntesegen': a selection of the botanical variety *vitis-idaea* from Germany, introduced by Zillmer in 1978; a prominent variety that won a Gold Medal in the German Garden Show in 1981; a very vigorous plant with large leaves, growing sixteen inches tall; productive, with profuse second bloom; berries are late-ripening, bright red, and very large.

'Ida': a Swedish selection introduced in 1977; this vigorous, compact plant grows about eight inches high; precocious; profuse second bloom; fruits ripen early and are large; an outstanding ornamental for its beautiful leaves and abundant and repeated bloom.

'Koralle': represents a seedling population of thirty-five plants from the botanical variety *vitis-idaea*, introduced from Holland in 1969 by H. van der Smit, so some variation depending on the clone from which a plant was propagated; 'Koralle' is the most popular lingonberry in Europe and winner of the prestigious Award of Merit, 1976; the plants spread at only a moderate rate and are productive if given suitable soil; stems are upright and bushy, reaching twelve inches high; berries are bright red and small to medium sized, ripening midseason.

'Masovia': a selection, from 1985, of the botanical variety *vitis-idaea* from Poland; vigorous with heavy yields.

'Red Pearl': a selection of the botanical variety *vitis-idaea* introduced from Holland in 1981; although not the most productive cultivar, 'Red Pearl' spreads rapidly and gives consistent yields. Stems are upright, reaching sixteen inches high; the dark red fruits are medium sized and have excellent flavor.

'Regal': selected in Wisconsin in 1990 from Finnish seeds; plants spread moderately fast with stems growing eight inches high; precocious; low yield; small red fruits.

'Sanna': introduced from Sweden in 1988; plants spread moderately fast, with erect stems that grow eight to twelve inches high; productivity is excellent, perhaps the highest of any variety to date; bears attractive crops of bright red berries in both the summer and the fall.

'Scarlet': a selection of the botanical variety *vitis-idaea* from Norway; grows twelve to eighteen inches high.

'Splendor': selected in Wisconsin in 1990 from Finnish seeds; plants spread moderately fast with stems growing six to eight inches high; precocious; low yield; the carmine berries are medium sized.

'Sussi': introduced from Sweden in 1985; this low-growing variety, whose stems are only four to eight inches high, spreads rapidly; production of the dark red, medium- to large-sized berries is moderate.

Actinidia

Emeralds in the Rough

BOTANICAL NAMES
Actinidia chinensis, Actinidia deliciosa, Actinidia arguta,
and *Actinidia kolomikta*

PLANT TYPE
Deciduous, twining woody vines

POLLINATION
Except for a few cultivars, all need cross-pollination from
a separate, nonfruiting male vine

RIPENING SEASON
Late summer and early fall

J ust look at these plants and it is easy to see why actinidias—the grocery store kiwifruit and other lesser-known but equally delectable and more cold-hardy related species—have not been longer and more widely known for their fruits. Who would suspect a sparkling, emerald green interior to lie beneath the skin of the hairy, brown kiwifruit? The more cold-hardy kiwifruits generally have green skins when they are ripe and often go unnoticed beneath the foliage. One taste would have rescued any of these fruits from obscurity sooner. The flavor is a savory commingling of acidity and sweetness that is akin to a dead-ripe pineapple, but, in fact, each actinidia has its own unique essence.

Within or along the margins of humid mountain forests in eastern Asia, where actinidias are native, these fruits have been eaten for centuries. Then as now in those regions, the bulk of the fruit is harvested from the wild. (One hundred thirty thousand tons were picked from wild vines in China in 1983.) Actinidias were first botanically described outside China in the middle of the eighteenth century. Plant explorer Robert Fortune collected vine specimens of *A. deliciosa*, but no mention was made of the fruit. Carl Maximowicz of the

Botanic Garden in St. Petersburg (once Leningrad) described *A. kolomikta* in 1856.

The first seed lots of *Actinidia deliciosa* to leave Asia were shipped by the well-known plant explorer E. H. ("Chinese") Wilson to England, France, and the United States around 1900. James Veitch & Sons, a British seed company that received some seeds from Wilson, listed kiwifruit in its 1904 catalogue, describing the plant's "edible fruits the size of walnuts and the flavor of ripe gooseberries" and stating, "Apart from its flowering and fruiting qualities it is a remarkably handsome plant, and will be of great value as a pillar or pergola plant in the open garden."

How true of so many of the *Actinidia* species! Actinidias are twining woody vines, clambering up trees or sprawling over the ground in their native habitats. The foliage varies among species but is extremely handsome in all cases. Cup-shaped flowers, opening white then turning to muddy gold, usually remain hidden and unappreciated beneath the foliage. How many visitors pass beneath the many handsome, hardy-kiwifruit vines planted early in the twentieth century on public estates, unaware of the savory fruits also hidden beneath the foliage?

Most actinidia introductions outside Asia emphasized ornamental qualities of the vines; not so in New Zealand. From a single seed lot of *A. deliciosa* planted in New Zealand early in the twentieth century and fruiting in 1910, superior fruiting sorts were selected. In the 1930s a farmer near the Bay of Plenty decided to put in a commercial planting on a half-acre parcel of land. Other farmers followed suit, the first fruits were exported in the 1950s, and the rest is marketing history. New Zealand was exporting over a half a million tons of the hairy brown fruits by the 1980s and commercial plantings were soon established in the United States, mostly in California.

An important part of the marketing success involved changing the fruit's name from Chinese gooseberry to kiwifruit. The earlier reference to flavor kinship with the gooseberry was meant as a compliment, but too few buyers appreciated gooseberries. How many avocados would leave grocery shelves today if marketed under their old name of alligator pear?

Description of the Plants

Actinidias are vining plants, the vigor of the vine varying among species. Wild plants, left to their own devices in their native haunts, can form impenetrable thickets, often shrublike if given full sun with nothing on which to climb.

Actinidia

Gender expression of actinidias can be described with the botanical mouthful "polygamodioecious," which means that flowers of individual plants usually are male or female, though some plants have two types of flowers, those that are perfect (male and female parts on the same flower) and those that are either male or female. To further complicate the matter, all this can change with growing conditions from year to year.

KIWIFRUIT (*Actinidia deliciosa*)   Primarily because of its large fruits that store well, *A. deliciosa* has become the actinidia of commerce, the kiwifruit of the grocery store. In China, the fruit has been called *hou tao* (monkey peach, after votaries of the fruit, not its appearance), *orr mei* (goose fruit, indicating the size), and *van zhou* (soft date, for the flavor). The vine itself is strong growing, with thick, maple-sized leaves.

Kiwifruits can be grown in temperate climates experiencing some, but not excessive, winter cold (USDA Hardiness Zones 7 through 9). At least thirty days of cool weather—between about thirty and forty-five degrees Fahrenheit —are needed before vines can resume normal growth in late winter or early spring, though some cultivars will resume growth with a shorter cold period. The latter are referred to as low-chill cultivars. Kiwifruits need a long growing season—200 to 225 days—to ripen their fruits

Ripe fruits are hairy, brown, and about the size of hens' eggs, with vitamin C concentration twice that of oranges. The emerald green interior is speckled near the core with tiny black seeds, and fruit sliced crosswise exhibit the lighter-colored rays that are the source of the generic name (*actin* means ray in Latin).

HARDY KIWIFRUIT (*Actinidia arguta*)   Here is a fruit that, along with the species that follows, has so rapidly become popular in America that it has yet to receive a common English name of its own. As an ornamental vine, the plant has been sold as "bower vine," so perhaps bowerberry is an appropriate name. How about transliterating its name from other parts of the world, such as *kishmish* (a Russian moniker) or *tara* (meaning wild fig in Korean)? "Kuwi" has been suggested, a name made by combining the common and scientific names: hardy kiwifruit and *Actinidia arguta*. "Peewee kiwi" is yet another possibility. I vote for "Piwifruit."

Hardy kiwifruit is a rampant grower with wild vines sometimes climbing one hundred feet high into trees in the forests of Japan, Korea, north China, and Siberia. Cultivation can suppress and redirect some of this energy. Vigor aside, this plant has a more delicate appearance than the kiwifruit plant. The leaves of hardy kiwi are only the size of apple leaves and attached to the stems on red petioles. The contrast between red and green is pleasant, not harsh, because of the pale intensity of both colors.

As implied by the name and the native habitat, this plant can tolerate cold. Plants generally are hardy to about minus twenty-five degrees Fahrenheit (adapted to USDA Hardiness Zones 4 through 9), and require about 150 frost-free days to ripen their fruits.

The fruit itself looks quite different from that of kiwifruit. Hardy kiwifruits are smaller, an inch or so long. Fruits are borne in clusters and have smooth, edible skins so they can be eaten just like grapes. The hardy kiwifruit has the same emerald green interior as the kiwifruit and a similar, though much sweeter and more aromatic, flavor.

The Russians were breeding hardy kiwifruits through many decades of the twentieth century and some of their cultivars now are available outside Russia. Other available cultivars are the result of limited, recent breeding efforts in North America or are clonally propagated plants from mature vines growing on old estates and public grounds. The latter category includes plants such as 'Geneva' (from a plant at the New York State Agricultural Experiment Station at Geneva, New York), 'Michigan State' (from a plant at Michigan State University campus), and 'Dumbarton Oaks' (from a plant in this old public garden in the District of Columbia).

SUPER-HARDY KIWIFRUIT (*Actinidia kolomikta*) Here is another species producing smooth-skinned, small fruits on a cold-hardy—extremely cold-hardy—vine. The plant tolerates winter lows below minus forty degrees Fahrenheit (adapted to USDA Hardiness Zones 3 through 7) and needs only about 130 frost-free days to ripen its fruit. For want of a better name, this plant has been referred to as hardy kiwifruit, super-hardy kiwifruit, Arctic beauty kiwifruit, or, more descriptively, grape kiwi.

There are a few differences between this species and *Actinidia arguta*. *A. kolomikta* vines bear smaller fruits and often have the nasty habit of dropping their ripe fruits to the ground. The fruit is brimming with vitamin C (an average of a thousand milligrams per one hundred grams of fruit has been reported, as compared with sixty for oranges). The plant itself is less rampant than those of the previous two species and prefers some shade, especially when young. Leaves of male vines and, to a lesser extent, females, have a decorative silvery white and pink variegation, the markings so distinctive that they sometimes look as if they were brushed on by an artist. The variegation is absent on young plants or those grown in too much shade.

THE FUTURE OF ACTINIDIAS? Except for the ornamental leaves of the male *A. kolomikta*, it seems a waste to have to grow nonfruiting male vines. In the early part of the twentieth century, the common garden strawberry also produced separate male and female plants. Breeding undoubtedly could produce perfect-flowered actinidia vines just as it did with the strawberry.

For a purely cosmetic change, how about red actinidias? Another edible species, *Actinidia mellanandra*, produces reddish fruits, and *A. arguta* var. *purpurea* ripens with a smooth, bright crimson skin. By hybridizing these plants with other actinidias, tasty fruit with varying degrees of red flesh could be produced.

A previously overlooked species with great potential is *Actinidia chinensis*. Overlooked outside of China, that is, because this is the preferred actinidia there. Among this species's pragmatic qualities are a more compact vine whose stems do less of that bothersome twisting. The fruit is relatively large (though usually not as large as *A. deliciosa*) with skin covered by only a peach-like fuzz. The flesh color ranges from green to yellow, on some plants even red, in the center. The flavor is very sweet and aromatic, smooth and somewhat tropical, reminiscent of muskmelon, tangerine, or strawberry. The plant has its defects: coming from warmer regions and lower elevations, it is more susceptible to spring frosts and winter cold than many other actinidias (but, on the positive side, is well adapted to warm winter climates); with its thinner, less hairy skin, it also does not keep as well as *A. deliciosa*.

If one could stir together the genes of *Actinidia deliciosa*, *A. arguta*, and *A. kolomikta* into a cauldron along with a bit of some other species, then take out the best from each, an incredible fruit would result. This plant would be productive, laugh off almost any amount of winter cold, and have variegated leaves. The large, edible-skinned fruits could be stored all winter and would be rich in vitamin C. There might even be a bit of red in them for Christmas eating!

Cultivation

The cultivation of all the actinidias for their fruits will be treated together. This is possible because the plants are very similar in their requirements. That said, it must be admitted that cultivation of the more cold-hardy kiwifruits for their fruits has been little studied.

SITE AND SOIL Site selection is among the most important factors leading to success in growing all actinidias. In addition to being cold-hardy, *A. arguta* requires less winter chilling than *A. deliciosa* before it can resume growth in spring, which makes *A. arguta* perhaps the better species to grow in areas with mild as well as severe winters. All actinidias, even the cold-hardy ones, are susceptible to having their early-awakening foliage nipped back by spring frosts of only a few degrees below freezing. Short of moving near the ocean with its moderating effects on temperature, north-facing slopes or sites shielded from low winter and early spring sun by buildings or trees are preferred.

Some regions might provide sufficient winter chilling without excessive winter cold, yet still be unsuitable for growing actinidias because the summer is either too short or too cool. Such is the case with attempts to fruit *A. deliciosa* at latitudes north of Washington, D.C. (though I have seen fruit ripen at the Brooklyn Botanical Garden in New York in warm seasons). Other gardens are unsuitable because temperatures in winter fluctuate too much, with sporadic warm spells causing the vines to lose their cold-hardiness in midwinter and then be shocked as the mercury plummets. The latter conditions, common to many areas of the southeastern United States, are tough on all actinidia vines.

Abundant sunlight—the more the better—generally ensures the best annual production of abundant and large fruits, except in climates, such as those in the southwestern U.S., that experience very intense sun. And the variegated foliage of *Actinidia kolomikta*, especially males, scorches in full sunlight. Offer just a bit of shade in these cases.

Soil for growing actinidias must be well drained. Vines planted where water sits on the surface after rain are likely to develop crown rot. Where less than perfect soil drainage is suspected, plant atop a broad, raised mound of earth.

Other soil requirements of actinidias are not notable. Perfect drainage does not imply that the plants will get along in a dry soil. Like other succulent fruits, actinidias need adequate water for vine growth and to swell out the berries. As is common with other plants native to shaded forests but cultivated in sunny areas, supplemental irrigation might be necessary.

Soil acidity should be between 5.0 and 6.5. A general fertilizer recommendation is to sprinkle the ground beneath each young plant with about a pound of complete fertilizer, progressing to ten pounds when a plant is mature. The plants are sensitive to fertilizer burn, so applications of synthetic (chemical) fertilizers should be split into two or three smaller doses applied from early spring until early summer. Even better: use a bulky, organic fertilizer, which is less likely to cause fertilizer burn (except manure from feedlots, in drier regions of the western U.S.).

PLANTING   Actinidias are rampant growers and their trunks never become sturdy enough to hold the plants well up off the ground of their own accord. Under cultivation, plants must be trained to some sort of support that is both sturdy and allows vines adequate room to ramble. Figure on two hundred square feet per plant, less so for *A. kolomikta*, 'Issai', and any other less vigorous sorts.

A trellis used by commercial kiwifruit growers and suitable for all actinidias consists of wires stretched between six-foot-high T-bar supports spaced between fifteen and twenty feet apart. The supports are made from four-by-four- or six-by-six-inch rot-proof posts set deeply in the ground. Cross-arms between four and six feet wide are bolted to the uprights, and the T-bars are linked together with three, four, or five parallel wires: one down the middle and the others along the cross-arms. (See Figure A.)

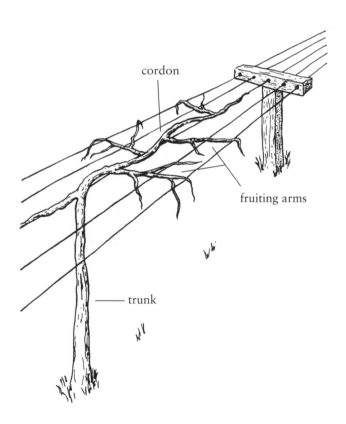

Figure A. Actinidia vine trained on a trellis.

The wires must be stretched tightly in order to support the weight of the vines and the fruit, and the T-bars at each end of a row have to be held firmly upright. High-tensile wire (12 gauge) or nylon monofilament is best to avoid sag. The T-bars at each end are kept upright with either a dead-man or a box-end support. (See Figure B.)

At some sacrifice to fruit production, but with perhaps a gain in beauty, actinidia vines can be coaxed up a variety of other structures such as gazebos and pergolas, or even along split-rail fences.

Actinidia plants are especially touchy about less than perfect site and soil conditions in their youth; some gardeners report better survival from planting larger plants. Winter cold bites hard at plants of all species their first two or three years in the ground, especially in conjunction with intense sunlight. A wrapping of corn stalks, burlap, pipe insulation, or tree wrap material shades the developing trunks and abates the fierceness of the cold. Where very low or fluctuating temperatures make winters brutal, even mature plants should perhaps be wrapped. Remember, the trunks of wild actinidias in those Asian forests are rarely exposed to full sunlight. Some growers coddle their plants in containers for one or even two years. Growth can be phenomenal in carefully watered and fertilized containers, and the plants can be protected during their first couple of winters in an unheated basement or a slightly heated garage.

Pollination is extremely important because almost all of the female flowers should set fruit for full production. The burden of pollination rests mostly with honeybees, though wind and other insects also play a role. With few exceptions, a separate, nonfruiting male plant is needed to fertilize female plants. The male should be no further than thirty-five feet from females. Do not be surprised if it appears that female flowers have stamens, the male flower parts. The stamens are there, but the pollen they shed is sterile. Similarly, male flowers have small, nonfunctional ovaries. One male plant can sire a harem of eight or so females, and male and female plants need not be the same species of *Actinidia* in order to cross-pollinate. Bloom times of male and female flowers must coincide, though. Bloom times of *Actinidia deliciosa* and *A. arguta* generally overlap; not so for *A. kolomikta*.

Hand-pollination is practical if you grow only a few plants. Merely pluck off a male blossom and lightly rub it on half a dozen female flowers. Then go pluck another male, repeat the rubbing, and so forth.

TRAINING AND PRUNING The goals in training and pruning are to make a potentially tangled mass of rampant shoots manageable and easy to harvest,

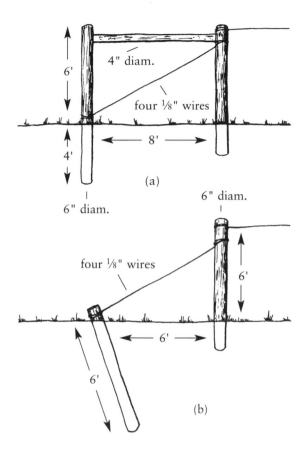

4" diam.

6'

four ⅛" wires

8'

4'

(a)

6" diam.

6" diam.

four ⅛" wires

6'

6'

(b)

Figure B. Supports for posts at end of trellis: (a) box-end support;
(b) dead-man support.

and to keep a vine fruitful by allowing adequate light to fall within the plant canopy. Pruning also stimulates an annual flush of new wood, important because flowers and, hence, fruits, are borne only toward the bases of shoots of the current season that grow from the previous year's canes. Don't let bleeding of the vine following pruning worry you for it does the plant no harm.

Not all the new shoots that grow from the previous year's canes bear flowers and fruits. Lack of flowering could be the result of too much shade or too large a crop the year before (when flower buds are initiated), or the vine may be too young. Those canes that are fruitful will produce fruiting shoots at the six or so bottom-most buds; the buds further out are capable of producing shoots that fruit the next year. Flowers and fruits are just as likely on either of the two kinds of shoots that actinidias produce: terminating shoots, which grow just a few inches, then stop for the season; and nonterminating shoots, which keep growing and growing until they are several feet long.

An established actinidia vine consists of a trunk, permanent cordons, and fruiting arms (or canes). (See Figure A.) Training and pruning are effected by tying shoots to supports and by pruning the plants while they are growing during the summer and again while they are dormant. Late winter, before the buds swell, is the best time for dormant pruning.

First develop the trunk by training a vigorous shoot against a one- to two-inch pole, tying the vine at intervals. If the plant has been grafted, it is important that the developing trunk originate above the graft.

When the trunk reaches just above the center wire of the trellis—either during the growing season or the dormant season—it is time to develop two permanent cordons. Cut the trunk to just below the height of the middle wire and train the two shoots that grow from the topmost buds on the severed trunk along the middle wire in opposite directions. Alternatively, forgo cutting and instead bend the trunk at ninety degrees to run along the wire, then train a shoot that develops from a bud near the bend along the wire in the opposite direction.

Sometimes a developing trunk will grow too weakly its first season, not even reaching the height of the wire. In this case, cut the trunk back by half while the plant is dormant. This will stimulate vigorous growth the following season.

The first dormant season after the cordons have been formed, cut off all excess growth along the trunk and shorten the cordons to about two feet. Shorten the cordons each dormant season, leaving two feet of the previous season's growth, until they reach their allotted length of about seven feet in each direction along the wires. After that, cut back the cordons each dormant season to a length of seven feet.

Fruiting arms will grow out perpendicular to, and be draped over, the wires. The arms should be spaced a foot apart on opposite sides of the cordon; prune away any excess canes during the dormant season. Tie the fruiting arms to the side wires to keep them from blowing around, unless the arms are too stiff to be brought to the wire. The first crop will form on shoots directly from these arms; future crops will form on shoots from laterals growing off these arms.

Throughout the training period, you may notice an occasional shoot starting to get thinner and twisty, whether that shoot is the developing trunk, the cordon, or a fruiting arm. Nip back such growth to encourage new, stronger growth from a bud. Do not let any shoots twist around poles or wires, or self-strangulation can occur.

Training is now complete, and annual pruning will consist, first, in shortening the ends of the cordons each winter, as described previously, and then in maintaining a supply of fruiting arms. The fruiting arms give rise to laterals that fruit at their bases; during each dormant season, cut these laterals to a few buds beyond the point at which they fruited—eighteen inches long is about right for each lateral (or, if you want to be more precise, four buds for *Actinidia deliciosa* and eight for the small fruited species). These buds will grow into shoots that fruit at their bases in the following summer. In the winter after they have fruited, these shoots correspondingly should be pruned to a few buds beyond where they fruited and thinned to remove any that are crossing or spindly. (See Figure C.) Usually only one strong fruiting cane, whether it is the original arm or one of its laterals or sublaterals, is retained in winter pruning. When a fruiting arm with its lateral, sublateral, and subsublateral shoots is two or three years old, cut it away to make room for a new fruiting arm.

Summer pruning of actinidias is aimed at keeping the lusty vines in bounds, maintaining order, and letting the shoots bask in light. Repeat summer pruning, as needed, through the growing season, paying special attention to the vine during the critical, early part of the growing season. The trunks must be kept clear of shoots, so cut away any that form there as soon as noticed. Also, cut back to short stubs excessively rampant shoots growing off the cordons, thus leaving buds for future replacement arms. Any tangled shoots should be cut away before the vine starts to strangle itself and laterals not needed as replacements can also be removed. As always, nip back any shoots that become twisty. One other bit of summer pruning: shorten fruiting arms and their laterals if they get too long. When a vine is getting enough sun, the ground beneath should be in dappled shade.

Because male plants are needed only for their flowers, they can be pruned sharply right after they bloom, removing about seventy percent of the previous year's growth. Cut back any flowering shoot to a new shoot, which will flower the following year. Male vines do not need to put any energy into fruit production, so are generally more vigorous than female vines.

For a punctilious approach to vines on pergolas, allow the plants to grow a few, rather than just two, permanent cordons. Shorten fruiting arms to just a few buds. This drastic pruning of each arm limits the number of fruits per

79

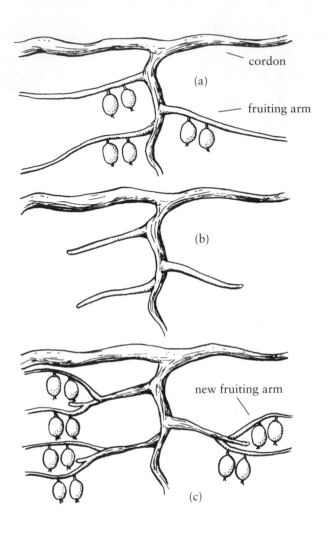

Figure C. Fruiting and pruning of fruiting arms: (a) growing season;
(b) the following dormant season, after pruning; (c) the following growing season.
(Note: for clarity, leaves are not shown.)

arm, but the reduction is compensated for by the increased number of arms on each plant because of the increased number of cordons.

All actinidias need annual pruning for maximum fruit production. That said, let it be known that the vines do fruit with no more pruning than a yearly, undisciplined whacking away aimed at keeping them in bounds. Such was the objective in pruning those hardy kiwifruits planted as ornamentals on old estates. These vines happily and haphazardly clothe pergolas with their small, green fruits hanging—not always easily accessible nor in prodigious quantity—beneath the leaves.

GIRDLING   Girdling is a technique that induces fruiting and hastens maturity and awakening of buds in spring (uh-oh!) by disrupting the flow of nutrients and hormones in the stems. In late summer, make two parallel cuts, one-sixteenth of an inch apart, around the trunk and remove the strip of bark from between the cuts. Do not girdle any vine that is in a weakened condition, or cut too deeply. Remove just the outer bark.

PESTS   Pest problems are minimal or nonexistent for actinidias, though some commercial kiwifruit growers spray pesticides because market fruit must be blemish-free, yields must be high, and large monocultures are a great draw for any pests that happen by.

As mentioned previously, actinidias are particularly susceptible to crown rot (*Phytophthora* spp.) wherever the soil stays overly wet. Symptoms of crown rot are stunted growth and yellowing, small leaves. Snails and slugs can demolish young plants, but established ones grow too fast to be bothered by these pests.

Japanese beetles, unfortunately, are as fond of actinidia leaves as they are of the leaves of grapes, roses, and a host of other plants. Maybe the actinidia foliage reminds the beetles of their Asian "roots." If the beetles become overly voracious, knock them off by hand into a can of soapy water or spray with an insecticide. Milky spore disease (sold as "Japademic," "Doom," etc.), which may provide a long-term and benign remedy in some regions, infects the larval stage of the beetle and is not toxic to anything else.

Actinidias sometimes suffer the attentions of one unique pest: cats. The effect on the animals is similar to that of catnip, and young vines cannot tolerate the chewing and clawing that sometimes ensues. My cats have always been oblivious to my actinidia vines, but when cats do take an interest in young plants, fend off the felines with a cylinder of chicken wire. Mature plants do not need protection from cats.

AN ASIDE   Too many gardeners have become justifiably frustrated from having to wait too long—even eight years, or more—to taste their first home-grown actinidias. One reason for delayed bearing is winter die back of young plants, avoidable by planting larger plants, wrapping plants for protection in winter, and avoiding late summer pruning or fertilization, which would stimulate late, cold-tender growth. The effect of winter die back is similar to hard pruning: vigorous vegetative, rather than fruitful, regrowth ensues. A second reason for delayed bearing could be just that: repeated hard pruning, perhaps induced by fright of the vines' vigor. Do prune your young actinidias, but not haphazardly nor any more than necessary. A third cause for delayed bearing is plants mislabelled as to sex. In this case, you see flowers but don't taste fruits. Look closely at the flowers to determine if you have the requisite male and female plants. And finally, plants do have to reach a certain age before they can bear fruit—but not eight years. One of my 'Ananasnaja' vines bore well in its third year!

Propagation

Actinidias are easily propagated by seed, by cuttings, and by grafting. Keep in mind that propagation by seed, but not by the latter two methods, produces plants that differ from the parent plant. The progeny may be better, may be worse, or may be almost the same as their parents, but different nonetheless. Also, some of the seedlings—usually more than half of them—will be non-fruiting males. Unfortunately, there is no way to determine whether a plant is male or female until it flowers. Vines from seed begin to bear in three or four years, grafts and cuttings in about two years.

Actinidia seeds germinate best when they are fresh, and the best source for fresh seeds is a soft, ripe fruit. Extract the seeds by dropping fruits into a blender with water and blending (not too long or too fast, or the seeds will be damaged), or by mashing the fruits in water by hand. The seeds can be sown pulp and all. After sowing, the seeds need stratification before they will germinate: about two months of cool, moist conditions for *A. arguta* and *A. kolomikta*; two weeks for *A. deliciosa*. Be on guard for damping-off disease, which readily attacks the feeble seedlings until they pick up steam.

Actinidias will grow from root cuttings, hardwood cuttings, and softwood cuttings. A problem with hardwood cuttings is that they often callous so heavily as to inhibit the development of roots. Leaves will begin to grow but, without root support, will flag.

Softwood cuttings are the easiest means of making new plants, often rooting in two to four weeks. Clip off new growth after it has become firm in early summer, discarding the succulent tips. Reduce the number of leaves, and/or reduce their size so the cuttings do not dry out before the roots form. Expect good results from six-inch stem pieces one-eighth to one-quarter of an inch in diameter whose bottoms have been slightly wounded and dipped in rooting hormone, and whose tops have been reduced to two leaves, with those cut in half. Until they are rooted, maintain high humidity with an automatic misting system or at least partial shade under a "tent" of clear plastic or glass.

The time for grafting actinidias is either in midwinter, indoors, with a dormant rootstock and scion, or outdoors, with a dormant scion just after the rootstock has begun to send out shoots in spring. Use either a cleft or whip-and-tongue graft. Grafts made while buds are just swelling in the spring are not as successful because the cut scions bleed. The advantage of grafting over cuttings is that grafted plants grow faster initially.

Harvest and Use

A mature kiwifruit vine can produce over two hundred pounds of fruit. A yield of one hundred or more pounds is possible from a single cold-hardy kiwifruit plant. Even in frigid, northern areas of Russia, vines will produce twenty or more pounds of fruit.

Harvested fruit will ripen off the vine, but only after achieving a certain level of maturity. If fruit is picked before this point, flavor and texture will suffer. Sweetness and firmness are two indicators of when a fruit is ripe for picking. Not all fruits on a plant, even in a single bunch, ripen together so it's best to sample a few fruits for maturity. The most quantitative method would be to use a small, hand-held (but somewhat expensive) device called a refractometer to determine "soluble solids," which are, essentially, sugars. Squeeze a drop or two of juice from test fruits onto the refractometer and look for a reading of eight to ten percent soluble solids before bulk harvest. At this level, or higher, fruit will taste good and store well. The first fruits will also be softening on the vine.

Harvest kiwifruits by snapping them off their stalks when the skins turn brown and samples of cut fruit show black seeds. The fruit will be hard, but will soften and sweeten in a week at room temperature. In a cool room, it will keep for two months. If the fruit is refrigerated to near freezing, and humidity maintained at ninety-five percent (with a plastic bag having just a few small holes, for example), the fruit keeps for nine months! Let firm-ripe fruit soften before eating. This can be hastened by putting the fruit in a bag with an apple.

Hardy and super-hardy kiwifruits drop or come off easily from the vines when they are ripe. Picked soft with their stems attached, hardy kiwifruits store a couple of weeks; firm, they'll keep six weeks or more. Water loss through the thin skin limits long-term storage. Expect super-hardy kiwifruit, with their thicker skins, to store longer than hardy kiwifruit.

A ripe actinidia is a delectable and beautiful (at least on the inside) fruit for eating fresh. Unfortunately, heat, acidity, dehydration, or freezing associated with cooking or processing can easily cause the fruit to lose flavor, become more tart, and turn a muddy green color. Still, the fruits have been canned, dried, or made into wines.

Uses of actinidias do not end with the fruit, though. What to do with all those summer prunings? The leaves reputedly are good food for pigs. What to do with all those winter prunings? The stalks are rich in a glue that leaches out when they are soaked in water. The stem fibers that remain have been made into paper. Even the roots have been processed into an insecticide toxic to aphids and caterpillars.

Perhaps the most novel use of actinidias capitalizes on their effect on cats. An infusion of the leaves is used in Chinese zoos to sedate "large cats."

Cultivars

KIWIFRUIT (*Actinidia deliciosa*, *Actinidia chinensis*)

Unless specified, all kiwifruit listed here are *Actinidia deliciosa*.

'Abbott' (indistinguishable from a cultivar called 'Allison'): female plant with medium-low chill requirement; productive; early-flowering; fruit elongated and medium-sized; more cold-hardy than Hayward.

'Blake': female plant; precocious and productive; once thought to be self-fertile; fruit small, pointed, a month or so earlier than 'Hayward', and with stiff hairs.

'Bruno': female plant with medium-high chill requirement; early-flowering; fruit is large and elongated, with dark, bristly hairs; a bit more cold-hardy than Hayward.

'Chico Male' ('California Male'): male with midseason bloom.

'Dexter': female plant; cultivar for warmer winter regions; prolific; small fruit.

'Elmwood': female plant; for warmer winter regions; very large fruit.

'Gracie': female plant; pear-shaped fruit; early-flowering.

'Hayward' (same as 'California Chico'): female plant, not very vigorous and with a high chill requirement; not as productive as many other cultivars; flowers later in the season than do most other cultivars; fruit has good size, flavor, appearance, and keeps well; late-ripening; this is the one you see on grocers' shelves.

'Jintao': *Actinidia chinensis* female blossoming about a week earlier than 'Hayward' and ripening about three weeks earlier; fruit is large and long with an almost hairless brown skin and greenish yellow flesh that ripens to yellow and orange; excellent flavor, surpassing 'Hayward' in sweetness and vitamin C, and storing just as well.

'Koryoku': female plant; similar to Bruno; high sugar; early-ripening; popular variety in Japan.

'Matua': vigorous male with early and long bloom season; cold-tender.

'Monty': female plant with low chill requirement; precocious; productive (tends to overcrop, and size suffers); late-flowering and -ripening; stiff hairs; more cold-hardy than Hayward.

'Tewi': female plant with low chill requirement.

'Tomuri': late-flowering male.

'Vincent': female plant with low chill requirement; prolific; medium-sized fruit.

Hardy kiwifruit (*Actinidia arguta*)

All of the following cultivars are females.

'74-75': large fruit, moderately good yield; good flavor; ripens early, about three weeks before 'Ananasnaja'.

'Ananasnaja Michurina' ('Michurin's Pineapple', also 'Ananasnaya'): from the Russian plant breeder I. V. Michurin; fruit is large (one by one and one-half inches) and firm; ripens late (mid- to late September in Russia, late September in New York); heavy yielder; excellent flavor; possibly *Actinidia kolomikta* hybrid. 'Ananasnaja' plants presently being sold in America appear to be different from the plant described by Michurin.

'Dumbarton Oaks': relatively large fruit, moderately good yield, very good flavor and appearance; ripens early, about three weeks before 'Ananasnaja'.

'Geneva': relatively large fruit, good yield, excellent flavor, mixed reviews on appearance; ripens early, about three weeks before 'Ananasnaja'.

'Issai': excellent flavor and appearance; good yields; sets some fruit without pollination, but yields larger crops with pollination; precocious, often bearing its first fruit after one year; fruit small; vine is less vigorous than are most actinidias; less cold-hardy than most other *Actinidia arguta* plants; late-ripening, about with 'Ananasnaja'; possibly a hybrid of *A. arguta* and *A. polygama*; reputedly cannot be pollinated by or pollinate either of its parent species.

'Ken's Red' ('Red Princess'): very vigorous plant bearing smooth-skinned fruits that turn red as they ripen; hybrid of *Actinidia arguta* female and *A. mellanandra* male.

'Meader': from the well-known American plant breeder Professor Elwyn Meader; productive; medium-sized fruit. (Professor Meader also developed a 'Meader Male' cultivar of *Actinidia arguta*.)

'Michigan State': very large, elongated fruit; very good flavor.

'National Arboretum': good flavor and size; lower-yielding; ripens early, about three weeks before 'Ananasnaja'.

'Rannaya' ('Early'): another of Michurin's cultivars, this one a wild selection that Michurin described as having a "pleasant" flavor; prolific; ripe in mid-August in Russia; less vigorous than most others.

SUPER-HARDY KIWIFRUIT (*Actinidia kolomikta*)

'Aromatnaya': medium-sized fruit, productive, medium vitamin C content.

'Clara Zetkin': probably a hybrid with *A. arguta*; large fruit; very sweet; less drop; ripe by the end of August in Russia; reputedly ripens more evenly than other cultivars.

'Krupnopladnaya' ("Large Fruit"): large fruited, high in vitamin C.

'Leningradskaya Pozdnjaja': male pollinator.

'Matovaya': small to medium fruit; very high in vitamin C; earliest ripening.

'Nahodka': medium-large fruit; medium vitamin C content; ripe in mid-August.

'Orozainaya' ('Prolific'): medium-sized fruit, high in vitamin C; regular bearer; prolific; precocious, ripe in mid-August in Russia; from Michurin, who described it as "lusciously sweet."

'Pautske': vigorous plant; the name is that of the breeder, V. Pautske, who made this selection in Lithuania.

'Pavlovskaya': large fruit, productive, medium vitamin C content.

'Podznaya' ('Late'): wild selection, ripe in mid-September in Russia, prolific; "pleasant flavor," according to Michurin.

'Sentyabraskaya': medium-large fruit, productive, medium vitamin C content, ripe in mid-August.

Mulberry

A Summer Fruit-of-Many-Colors

BOTANICAL NAMES
Morus alba, Morus rubra, and *Morus nigra*

PLANT TYPE
Large, deciduous tree

POLLINATION
Cross-pollination not needed

RIPENING SEASON
Midsummer

C hildren of the nursery rhyme dancing "round the mulberry bush, all on a frosty morning" no doubt also frequented that bush earlier in the season when the fruits were ripening. All children love mulberries, though the plants do have deficiencies that some grownups find unacceptable. Mulberries are shaped like blackberries, but are even more fragile and can be colored creamy white, lavender, dark red, or black. The dark colors stain readily (and were used for dye in medieval times), but children do not mind fruit-stained fingers and mouths. Nor do children mind repeatedly climbing into the trees for the few handfuls of berries that ripen every day during the extended ripening period.

Children mostly love mulberries because the fruits are sweet—on some trees, too sweet for most adults. But this is where we adults step in and select superior clones with fruits that have a bit of tartness to add character to the flavor. In defense of the mulberry, Henry Ward Beecher wrote in 1846, "I regard it as an indispensable addition to every fruit garden; and I speak what I think when I say that I had rather have one tree of Downing's Everbearing Mulberries than a bed of strawberries."

There is no dearth of mulberry seedlings in America, for not only is there a native species, but mulberry trees native to China were introduced into

America early on in an attempt to begin a silkworm industry. Silkworm eggs were shipped to Virginia in 1621, and settlers were mandated to care for mulberry trees, whose leaves were used to feed the silkworms. Virginia silk made the coronation robes of Charles II. Enthusiasm for silkworm culture reached a peak in the decade of the 1830s when a new, supposedly superior (from the perspective of the silkworm) type of mulberry was introduced. Nurserymen gave up all other business merely to propagate this plant, and there were visions of farmsteads from New England to the Gulf Coast producing their own silk.

The American silkworm bubble burst by 1839, the result of disease, winter cold, and cheap labor in foreign lands. The legacy of American silkworm culture was more mulberry trees to mingle with, and in some cases replace, the native species. From the exotic mulberry species introduced in the 1830s, there was even one cultivar, 'Downing', selected for its fruit. (Yet another legacy was the gypsy moth, which had been imported for silkworm breeding, then accidentally escaped out a window in Medford, Massachusetts, in 1869.)

Description of the Plant

The "mulberry bush" of Mother Goose represents just one form of the plant; some mulberries grow to become large trees. Mulberry leaves are variously lobed, even on the same plant, just like those on fig (a relative of mulberry) and sassafras trees. Some leaves are unlobed, some are mitten-shaped, and some are the shape of a crude glove.

Mulberry trees are either dioecious or monoecious, and sometimes a tree even will change from one sex to another. High temperatures, strong light, and long days favor maleness in mulberries, with their opposites, as well as high humidity, bringing out female flowers. (What can we anthropomorphize from this?) Flowers appear in axillary positions on current season's shoots and on spurs on older wood. Pollination is not usually a problem, because mulberries are wind-pollinated, and some plants—the cultivars 'Illinois Everbearing' and 'Hicks', for example—will set fruit without any pollination whatsoever.

Three species of mulberries are grown for their fruits: the white mulberry, the red mulberry, and the black mulberry. There also are wild and deliberate hybrids of the white and the red mulberry. (Red and white mulberries have the same number of chromosomes; the black mulberry has a different number.) In spite of the common names, white, red, and black, do not look at the fruits

Mulberry

to identify a mulberry by species. White mulberries, for example, might produce white, lavender, or even black fruits.

Many mulberry cultivars were named during the nineteenth and twentieth centuries; some of these exist today, but a large share of them have disappeared from cultivation. To this day, mulberry enthusiasts are naming and propagating superior trees. The most notable cultivars are mentioned under each species in the text that follows.

White mulberry (*Morus alba*) is a variable species. The fruits are generally very sweet but often lack tartness that gives flavor *éclat*. Fruit size is also variable, with the largest-fruited cultivars—'Pakistan', for example—bearing berries over three inches long. The white mulberry can be characterized more by its thin, glossy, light green leaves than by the color of its fruit. White mulberry is the most cold-hardy of the three mulberry species, though cold-hardiness varies from clone to clone. At the extremes, there are those clones damaged at twenty-five degrees Fahrenheit above zero and those unfazed by twenty-five degrees Fahrenheit below zero. White mulberry is the plant that was introduced into America for silkworm fodder but then went on to naturalize and hybridize with the native red mulberry.

Many clones of white mulberry were selected for their fruit and, because of their cold-hardiness, were grown primarily in the northeastern part of the United States. (Some of these cultivars might also have been infused with a bit of red mulberry "blood.") The most widely planted, and probably the best, cultivar was 'New American', found in Connecticut about 1854. The tree produced large, tasty, glossy black fruits all summer long. 'Wellington' is a cultivar offered today whose origin is unknown, but which is very similar to, though slightly less cold-hardy than, 'New American'. Other white mulberry cultivars include 'Trowbridge', 'Thorburn', 'White English', 'Stubbs', and 'Westbrook', all of which bear prolific amounts of good-quality fruits, but none of which is worthy of planting in lieu of 'New American'.

The silkworm craze of the 1830s was fueled in part by the introduction into America of a botanical variety of white mulberry, *Morus alba* var. *multicaulis*, that was supposed to be especially good silkworm fodder. After the "multicaulis craze" subsided, these strong-growing trees remained and spread their progeny. Their leaves are large and dull green; their fruit, black and sweet.

A few *multicaulis* plants were selected for their fruits, the best of which was 'Downing', originating in New York about 1846. 'Downing' trees produced tasty, black fruits but, like other *multicaulis* plants, proved to be insufficiently cold-hardy in the northeast. 'New American' was often sold under the name 'Downing'.

Mulberry

The Russian mulberry (*Morus alba* 'Tatarica') is yet another type of white mulberry, an especially cold-hardy type that was introduced into the American West by Mennonites in about 1875. Russian mulberries are diminutive in size of tree, leaf, and fruit. The fruits are black and sweet, but vary from plant to plant. A number of cultivars, such as 'Ramsey's White', 'White Russian', 'Barnes', and 'Victoria', were propagated as fruit trees, though the quality of the fruits was considered poor. One notable Russian mulberry was found in the nursery row of John C. Teas in Missouri in 1883. The original plant just crept along the ground, so when a scion of this plant was grafted high on a straight stem of an upright Russian mulberry, the resultant plant was an attractive weeping mulberry—'Teas' Weeping Mulberry', as the cultivar came to be known. Nonetheless, the main value of the Russian mulberry was as a hedge plant for the rugged climate of the Midwest.

Red mulberry (*Morus rubra*) is the largest of the three mulberry species grown for fruit and is native to the eastern United States from New York west to Nebraska, and down to the Gulf coast. The tree has large, sometimes lobed, leaves with blunt teeth. These leaves are rough on their upper surfaces and pubescent underneath. The fruits are usually deep red, almost black, and have a flavor that, in the best clones, almost equals that of the delectable black mulberry.

Red mulberries were cultivated primarily in the American South. 'Johnson', the first mulberry selected for its fruit in America, was a red mulberry, and numerous others followed. 'Johnson' fruits were large and black, and had a "rich vinous" flavor. Other good-tasting red mulberry cultivars include 'Travis' (from Texas in 1900), 'Wiseman', and 'Cooke'.

Some of the natural hybrids of red and white mulberries produce notable fruit. 'Hicks', a prolific bearer of cloyingly sweet fruits, was widely planted in the South to feed hogs and poultry. 'Illinois Everbearing' was found in 1958 and is noted for bearing flavorful, large, nearly seedless fruits throughout the summer. My tree tends to cling to its fruits even when they are ripe, which makes for clean ground underfoot but harder picking, especially from near the ends of branches. Other tasty cultivars are 'Muddy River' and 'Collier'.

The third mulberry species, the black mulberry (*Morus nigra*), is a native of western Asia and is the species most cultivated worldwide for its fruit. Long ago, this species found its way to ancient Greece and Rome, and thence to other parts of Europe. As if foreshadowing the discrepancies between common names and fruit colors, the Roman author Ovid, in the first century A.D., recounts in his story of Pyramus and Thisbe that the black mulberry was originally white fruited. The fruit turned dark red as commemoration of the blood of these two lovers, forbidden by their families to marry, whose rendezvous beneath a mulberry tree turned to tragedy. Pyramus, mistaking blood on a fallen veil to be that of Thisbe, plunged his sword into his heart, and then Thisbe, arriving later and realizing what had happened, took the sword and followed him into death.

> The whiteness of the mulberry soon fled
> And ripening, sadden'd in a dusky red.

Let's look to the leaves and twigs, rather than the fruits, for identification: black mulberry leaves are rough and often unlobed, like those of red mulberry, but the black mulberry has sturdier twigs with fatter buds. This tree does not grow as large as the other two species, perhaps to thirty feet, and is often a bush unless deliberately trained as a tree. Fruits of *M. nigra* are large and juicy, with a congenial blend of sweetness and tartness that makes it the best-flavored species of mulberry, in my opinion among the best-flavored of all fruits!

The black mulberry has been grown for its fruits in Europe for centuries, and Europeans turn up their noses at the fruit of the other species. This nose-turning is not entirely justified—'Illinois Everbearing', for example, approaches a black mulberry in quality. There is little difference among most black mulberry cultivars (they all are excellent), and 'Black Persian' and 'Noir of Spain' are the ones most commonly grown. In Greece, the cultivar 'Mavro-mournia' is reputedly delectable and has sufficient firmness to give it market potential. Black mulberries have been planted only to a limited degree in America, mostly on the Pacific Coast. Some were planted in the South early in the twentieth century, but did not fare well in the humid summers and colder winters.

Black mulberry is the least cold-hardy of the fruiting mulberries, but just how much cold the plant can tolerate is open to question. Some claim that this species is as hardy as a peach and will grow in protected sites as far north as New England; others claim it to be only as hardy as a fig and unadapted in regions colder than USDA Hardiness Zone 7. The discrepancy is probably the result of differences between clones and how well a plant hardens off in the fall in preparation for winter cold.

Mulberries are among the last trees to begin growth in spring—a signal for many gardeners that frost is past. (Mulberry's generic name, *Morus*, comes from the Latin word *mora*, meaning delay.) This sluggish start in the spring often saves mulberry flowers from being nipped by late spring frosts, which makes mulberries very reliable croppers and, as described in *Fruit and Its Cultivation* by Thomas William Sanders, "the wisest of trees." Those wise trees, or the most wise of mulberries, are *M. nigra* trees, which leafs out almost two months after the other two species. In contrast to the other two species, which ripen in spring, on the heels of strawberries, *M. nigra* fruits ripen latest, from midsummer into autumn.

Cultivation

The white mulberry is the second most common weed tree in New York City, which should be testimonial enough to mulberry's tolerance to abuse in the form of drought, pollution, and poor soil. In cold regions, siting to avoid spring frosts is not as critical as it is for most other fruit plants because of mulberries' relatively late start in spring. Even if the buds are nipped by late frost, mulberries can set a partial crop from secondary buds that push out.

Mulberries do need full sun and adequate space: fifteen feet of elbow room all around for most cultivars. Also, do not plant a mulberry near a walkway, or stains from fallen fruit will find their way indoors on the bottoms of shoes.

Once a mulberry tree's branches have been trained to a sturdy framework, no special pruning techniques are required. Just remove dead, exhausted, and overcrowded wood. If desired, mulberry trees can be kept to a tidy form by developing a set of main branches, then pruning laterals to six leaves in July in order to develop spurs near the main branches.

"Popcorn disease" is occasionally a problem with mulberries. Infected fruits swell to resemble popped corn. The disease carries on from one season to the next in these "popcorns," so collecting and burning infected fruits is one means of control. Mulberries are subject to a number of other pest problems—cankers, scale, dieback—that rarely require attention. But keep an eye out for them, especially on young plants.

Birds are very fond of mulberries. Unlike juneberry and blueberry bushes, which birds often strip clean of fruit, mulberry trees usually produce enough fruit to satisfy fruit-loving humans as well as birds.

Propagation

Growing mulberries from seed is a long-term proposition, for the plants sometimes take a decade or more until their first crop. If you want to give it a try, sow seeds as soon as you extract them from the fruits, or, in the case of the white mulberry, stratify the seeds for one to three months for better germination. Give seedlings a bit of shade during the first few weeks after they emerge from the ground. Even after plants start to flower and bear fruit, exercise restraint in discarding apparently poor plants or lauding apparently good ones. Plants grown from seed are sexually unstable while they are young, bearing perhaps only male flowers one year, female flowers another year, and both types of flowers yet another year.

In the early part of the twentieth century, S. D. Willard of Geneva, New York, used a method called "sprig budding" that became widely adopted for grafting mulberries. (See Figure D.) When the bark slips (peels easily from the wood) in the spring, make a T-cut in the rootstock just as you would when T-budding. On the lower end of a scion two or three buds long, make a smooth, sloping cut. Then insert the scion into the T, and wrap and seal the graft. Other types of grafts are usually successful also. Be aware of a possible incompatibility between the white and the black mulberry, though the Russian mulberry seems to be a good rootstock for all types of mulberries.

Hardwood, softwood, and root cuttings also are suitable methods for propagating mulberries. Suggestions for enhancing the rooting of hardwood cuttings include splitting the lower ends of cuttings, or taking each cutting with a small "heel" of two-year-old wood. Softwood cuttings have been known to root without fail when taken in midsummer and treated with a rooting hormone (8,000 ppm IBA). Red mulberries are reputedly difficult to root.

A novel method for propagating mulberries was suggested in *The French Gardinier*, published in 1669. The instructions were to rub ripe mulberry fruits on an old rope, then bury the rope in the ground. Voilà! (Mulberries are easy to propagate, but not that easy.)

Harvest and Use

Ripe mulberries fall readily from the trees (some even before they are ripe). To harvest large quantities of fruit, spread a clean cloth or plastic sheet on the ground, then shake the limbs. Separate ripe fruits from the leaves, twigs, insects, and unripe fruits that also fall by dumping the whole mess into a pail of water. Everything except the ripe berries will float and can be decanted. A mature tree bearing a good crop produces about ten bushels of fruit over its extended ripening season.

94

Mulberry

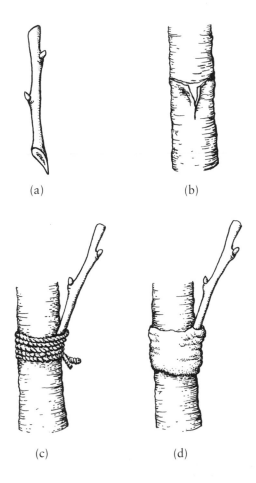

Figure D. S. D. Willard's method of grafting mulberries: (a) scion; (b) rootstock ready to receive scion; (c) scion inserted and graft tied; (d) the graft waxed.

The ripe fruit is delicious eaten out of hand but also can be made into wine. In medieval England, mulberries were made into murrey, a blue-black purée added to spiced meats or used as a pudding. Harvest mulberries slightly underripe for cooking into pies and tarts.

Dried mulberries are a winter staple for some of the peoples living in the rigorous climate of the high foothills of the Himalayas. J. Russell Smith, in his classic book *Tree Crops: A Permanent Agriculture* (1950), related that "for eight months the people live entirely on these mulberries. They grind them and make a flour and mix it with dried almonds." (I guess he meant "almost entirely.")

Red mulberry trees rarely live more than seventy-five years, but black mulberries have been known to bear fruit for three hundred years. A tree in England planted when Drapers Hall was built in 1634 lived until 1969. At any rate, once a tree outlives its usefulness in providing fruit and shade, the wood becomes useful for decay-resistant posts—a kiwifruit arbor, anyone?

Cultivars

Of the many mulberry cultivars, the following are among the most prominent.

'Black Persian': *Morus nigra*; the fruit is large, over an inch long and almost an inch wide; juicy with a rich, subacid flavor; the tree is fairly drought-tolerant once established.

'Collier': A hybrid of *Morus alba* and *M. rubra*; tree is productive and hardy; fruit is medium-sized and almost black; very good flavor, sweet with a trace of tartness, about like 'Illinois Everbearing'.

'Downing': The original 'Downing' was a *multicaulis* plant grown from seed sown about 1846; the fruit was black with excellent flavor and ripened from June to September; the tree was not hardy in the north; other varieties have subsequently been sold under the name 'Downing'.

'Geraldi Dwarf': *Morus macroura*; compact tree suitable for Zones 5 through 8; good flavor.

'Illinois Everbearing': Slender black fruits with excellent flavor; the main crop ripens with raspberries, and fruiting continues into July and August; the tree is hardy to thirty degrees Fahrenheit below zero, so is a good choice for northern gardens; the tree was discovered growing wild in 1958 and probably is a hybrid of red and white mulberry.

'Pakistan': *Morus alba* originating in Pakistan; tree not very winter-hardy; heart-shaped leaves; fruit very large, sometimes over three inches long, with a firm flesh and excellent flavor.

'Shangri La': *Morus alba* seedling originating in Naples, Florida, but hardy to Zone 7; fruits are watery and insipid.

'Weeping': possibly the same as 'Teas' Weeping Mulberry'; at any rate, weeping form and very tasty, very dark fruits.

'Wellington': Fruits are slightly smaller than 'Illinois Everbearing', but tree also yields well over long period; the fruits are reddish black and medium-sized, with good flavor; may be the old variety 'New American' that was also sold under the name 'Downing'.

PLATE 1. The white blossoms of a bushy juneberry light up the spring woods in the Shawangunk Mountains that rise up behind my house.

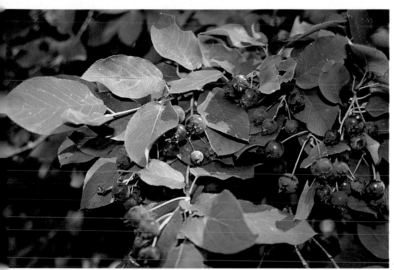

PLATE 2. These juneberry fruits, dusted with a natural powdery bloom, taste best traveling no farther than arm's length.

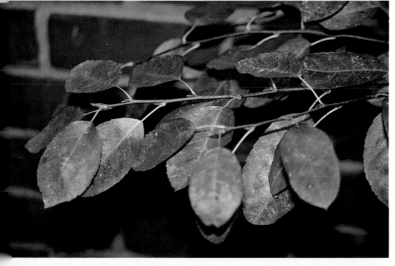

PLATE 3. The juneberry cultivar 'Autumn Brilliance' shows off its brilliant orange-red leaves against the wall of my house in autumn.

PLATE 4. The white blossoms of a tree species of juneberry stand out against the muted color of the spring woodland.

PLATE 5. Good genes make these particular beach plum fruits delectably meaty and sweet right off the bush.

PLATE 6. Musk strawberry fruits are not much to look at, but their flavor is a superb blend of the best that a strawberry plant can offer, with a hint of raspberry and pineapple mixed in.

PLATE 7. Ripe alpine strawberries, red ones and white ones, held in front of the bush bearing the white ones.

PLATE 8. Pawpaw's blossoms hang downward so their lurid purpleness is fully experienced only if you are positioned below a branch looking upward.

PLATE 9. A row of dark brown, inedible seeds lined up within the custardy, rich flesh of a pawpaw fruit.

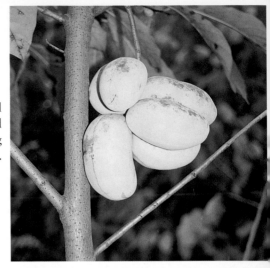

PLATE 10. Pawpaw's kinship with tropical fruits goes beyond just flavor, as evidenced by this bunch of pawpaw fruits hanging together like a "hand" of bananas.

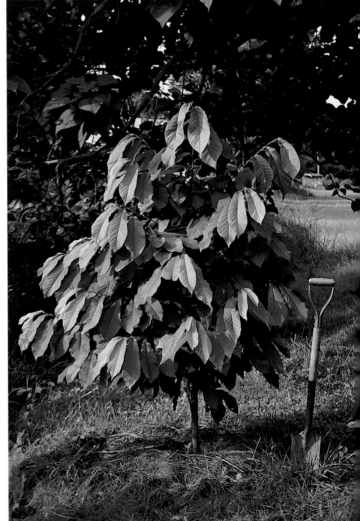

PLATE 11. Pawpaw's long, lush, lance-shaped leaves make the tree seem as if it would be more at home in a tropical jungle than in its native woodlands in the eastern United States.

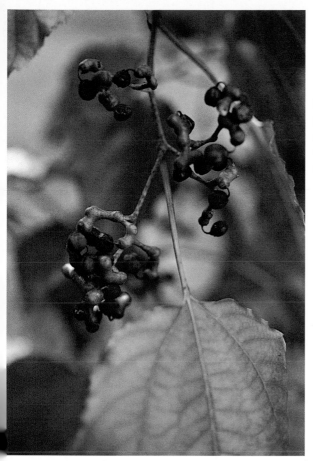

PLATE 12. The edible "fruits" of the raisin tree are actually the gnarled, swollen fruit stalks (peduncles), which look and taste like candied walnut to me.

PLATE 13. Lingonberry plants spread to blanket the ground with small, glossy green leaves accented by their bright red berries.

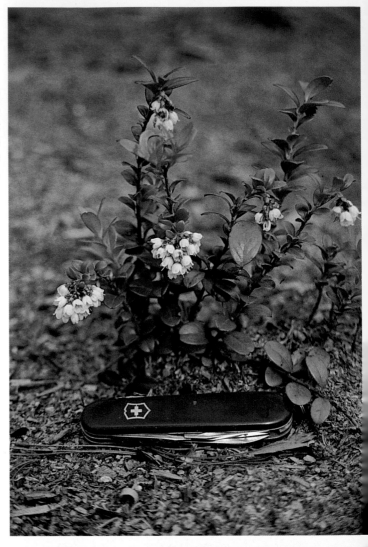

PLATE 14. Lingonberry in flower—and it does so twice a year—is a sight to behold, but get up close to appreciate the tiny blossoms.

PLATE 15. In ornamental plantings, the fruits of hardy kiwifruit vines often go unnoticed because they are camouflaged within the leafy canopy.

PLATE 16. Hardy kiwifruits and market kiwifruits look similar within, but the skin of the hardy kiwifruit is edible and the two fruits differ in flavor and size.

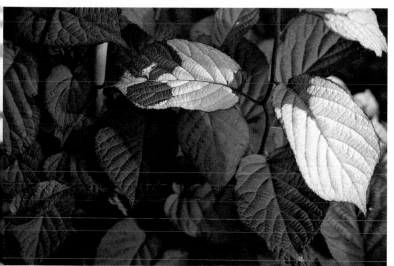

PLATE 17. Looking as if painted by an artist's brush, *Actinidia kolomikta* leaves—mostly the males—show regular and irregular patches of silvery white and pink variegation.

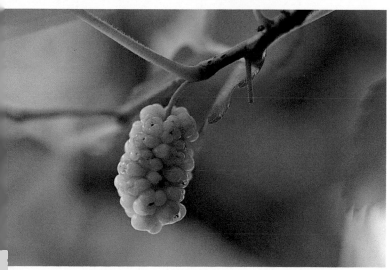

PLATE 18. A supersweet fruit hangs on one of the many white mulberries naturalized over much of the United States.

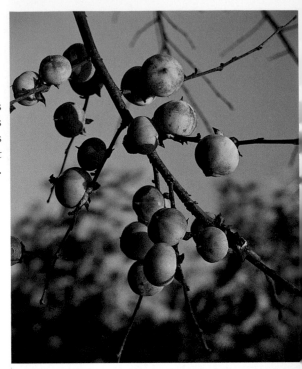

PLATE 19. 'Szukis' persimmon fruits hang on and decorate the branches well after the leaves fall, the fruits retaining their spicy, honey-sweet flavor for weeks.

PLATE 20. An interesting bark pattern and languid, blue-tinged leaves make my American persimmon trees admirable in summer even before their fruits ripen.

PLATE 21. Autumn lights up my American persimmon tree's leaves in a show of amber yellow.

PLATE 22. A myriad of small, golden fruits on this 'Charlie's Golden' autumn olive bush cast a golden haze over the leafless branches in autumn.

PLATE 23. Bright red fruits of 'King Red' Russian olive stand out against the tree's silvery leaves.

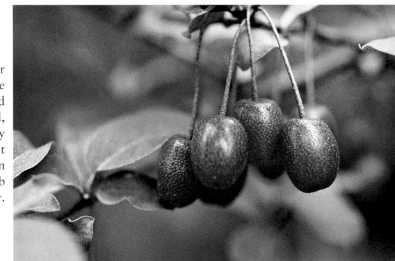

PLATE 24. A silver flecking adds sparkle to both the fruits and leaves of gumi, and, along with sprightly flavor, gives this fruit another common name, rhubarb silverberry.

PLATE 25. The spectrum in size and color of gooseberry cultivars is evident here; you have to taste them to appreciate the range in flavors also.

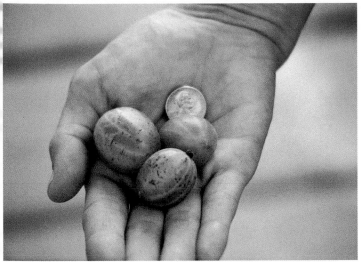

PLATE 26. 'Jumbo' gooseberry, here living up to its name, is a sweet variety with a "cracking" texture, so each berry explodes with juice when you bite into it.

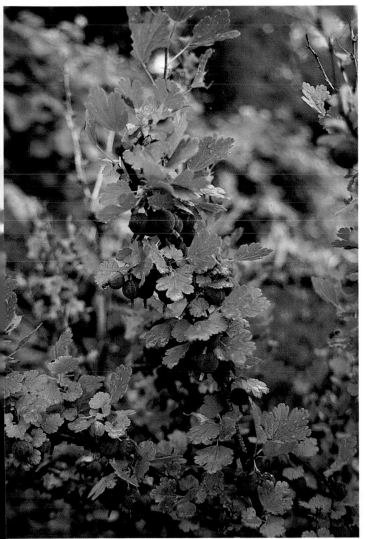

PLATE 27. The wine-red berries of 'Lepaa Red' gooseberry look decorative hanging on the bush.

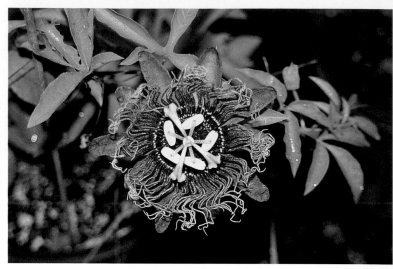

PLATE 28. It is hard to believe that a blossom as breathtaking as that of 'Incense' maypop could offer even more than beauty, going on to become a tasty fruit.

PLATE 29. Combine the appearance, flavor, and texture of mulberry and fig fruits and you get something that looks, feels, and tastes like these che fruits.

PLATE 30. The yellow trumpets of these clove currant flowers perfume the spring garden with their spicy, sweet aroma.

PLATE 31. Clove currants are rugged plants that yield these aromatic, sweet-tart berries over a period of weeks in summer.

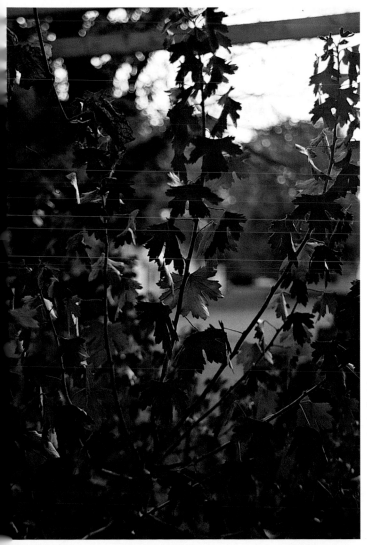

PLATE 32. Come autumn, clove currant bushes make their exit with leaves that turn a muted, purplish red.

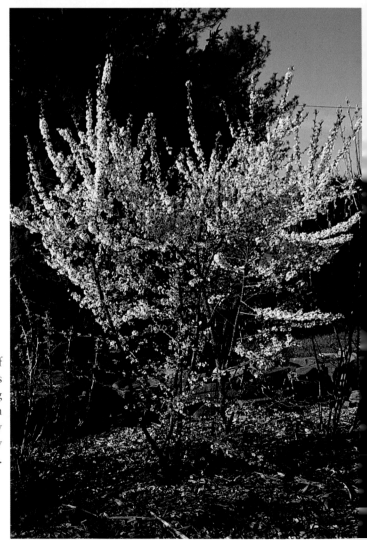

PLATE 33. These 'Consort' black currant fruits have a robust flavor and are rich in vitamin C.

PLATE 34. A profusion of blossoms practically hides the branches of Nanking cherry bushes, which cheerfully and reliably put on their show early each spring.

PLATE 35. Nanking cherry's profusion of blossoms is followed in early summer by an equal profusion of cherries.

PLATE 36. Cornelian cherry's individual blossoms are small, but they are produced in great masses and are among the first flowers of the season.

PLATE 37. Cornelian cherry trees produce a reliable crop of cherrylike fruits that ripen over a long period from midsummer on.

PLATE 38. 'Albatross' and 'Pink Champagne' are as pretty as jewels and are among the best flavored red/white currants.

PLATE 39. The only problem with my red currant espalier is that I have trouble bringing myself to ruining its appearance by plucking off any berries.

PLATE 40. With five or more flowers per bud, and flower buds clustering together on short spurs, it's no wonder that Asian pears produce such a good show in spring.

PLATE 41. This display shows some of the variation in size, color, and shape among a few of the thousands of Asian pear cultivars.

PLATE 42. Jostaberry fruits and leaves show the influence of both their black currant and gooseberry parents.

PLATE 43. This young lowbush blueberry plant will never grow much taller than shown, but will spread via underground stems to fill its bed.

PLATE 44. Nodding, bell-like flowers help make lowbush blueberry plants as valued for their beauty as for their tasty fruits.

PLATE 45. Lingonberry and lowbush blueberry plants keep the bed in front of my house pretty year round. (Shown here in autumn, the blueberries' fiery foliage contrasts against the lingonberries'glossy, green evergreen leaves and scarlet fruits.)

PLATE 46. These jujube fruits, just ripened, hang like buffed mahogany orbs among the tree's glossy, green leaves.

PLATE 47. As jujube fruits ripen, either on or off the tree, the flavor and texture start out reminiscent of a crisp, sweet apple (on right) and end up reminiscent of date (on left).

PLATE 48. The delicate flavor of these shipova fruits matches their delicate beauty.

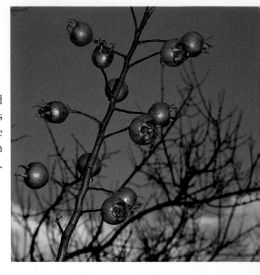

PLATE 49. Once these medlars are harvested and brought indoors to blet, their insides will soften and their flavor will become something like rich applesauce livened with cinnamon and wine.

PLATE 50. Medlar's autumn color is a warm mixture of reds and yellows.

PLATE 51. Each medlar flower opens cradled in a whorl of leaves, then reliably goes on to become a fruit.

Kaki and American Persimmons

Fruits of the Gods

BOTANICAL NAME
Diospyros kaki and *Diospyros virginiana*

PLANT TYPE
Deciduous trees

POLLINATION
Most kakis do not need pollinators; most American persimmons
do need pollinators

RIPENING SEASON
Midsummer to late fall

Millions upon millions of people have enjoyed eating persimmons, so why include this fruit in a book about uncommon fruits? Because most of those people are in Asia. The kaki, or Oriental persimmon, was the most widely grown fruit in the Far East until the twentieth century, when apples became popular. Few people outside Asia are familiar with—let alone grow—the kaki. Few people anywhere in the world know or grow the American persimmon.

Persimmons are neither widely known nor grown because they are somewhat hard to transplant (but not hard to grow), because many cultivars are too soft for commercial shipping (not a problem when you stand under the tree and eat the fruits, or bring them in a bowl into the kitchen), and because the unripe fruits of some cultivars are astringent (but how good is an unripe peach?). With respect to the last complaint, Captain John Smith of the Jamestown colony wrote: "The fruit is like a medlar, it is first green, then yellow and red when it is ripe. If it is not ripe it will draw a man's mouth awrie with much torment."

But the captain did go on to say of the persimmon that "when it is ripe, it is as delicious as an apricot." Farther south, Thomas Hariot of the Roanoke colony wrote that persimmons "are as red as cheries and very sweet: but whereas the cherie is sharpe sweet, they are lushious sweet."

Eating a thoroughly ripened persimmon is as pleasurable a gustatory experience as eating an unripe one is horrible. The best fruits of either species have a soft, smooth, jellylike texture, a honeylike sweetness, and a richness that is akin to apricot. In some cultivars, ripe fruits are so soft as to be almost liquid inside the skin. The fruits are very much the size and shape of tomatoes—small tomatoes (an inch or so across) in the case of the American persimmon—in colors ranging from pale yellow through orange, to crimson and deep red. The American persimmon is softer and drier than the kaki, with a richer flavor, something like a wet, dried apricot that has been drizzled with honey and given a dash of spice. Persimmon fruits might contain as many as half a dozen or more large, brown seeds, though some cultivars of both species set seedless fruits. The generic epithet, *Diospyros*, translates, with good reason, as "food of the gods" (or, more poetically, "Jove's grain").

Description of the Plant

Drooping leaves and branches—the branches made more so by their weight of fruit—give the persimmon a relaxed, languid appearance. Later in the season, this languid appearance is livened by the brightly colored fruits ripening amongst the dark leaves. Autumn color can be spectacular on both the American persimmon and the kaki, with leaves anywhere on the spectrum from clear yellow to crimson. In colder areas, however, the green leaves are sometimes frosted off the plant before they have a chance to put on their show. Even after the leaves have dropped to the ground, the fruits commonly hang on the limbs, festooning the leafless trees like Christmas ornaments.

Persimmon trees are usually either male or female, but some trees have both male and female flowers. Especially on male trees, occasional bisexual flowers occur. To further complicate matters, a tree's sexual expression can vary from year to year. Most kaki cultivars will fruit without pollination. Most, but not all, American persimmons do need pollination. If plants of either species that do not need pollination are pollinated, the resulting fruits have seeds and may be larger, ripen earlier, and have a different flavor and texture than do their unpollinated, seedless counterparts.

Persimmons flower on one-year-old wood. The flowers do not appear

American persimmon

directly from buds on this wood, but in the leaf axils of new shoots that grow from the buds, especially those near the tips of the branch. Blossoming is relatively late in the season, occurring after growth of new shoots is well under way. For the American persimmon, this may be as late as mid-June in the north, or the end of April in the south. The flowers are pale green, inconspicuous, and insect- or possibly wind-pollinated.

KAKI (*Diospyros kaki*)   The kaki is native to China, where it has been cultivated for centuries and more than two thousand cultivars exist. Marco Polo saw kakis for sale in the city of Kinsai (now thought to be Shanghai) in the thirteenth century. Long ago, kaki culture wended its way through Korea into Japan, where the fruit achieved great popularity and improvement.

Kaki trees can be long-lived. A six-hundred-year-old, grafted 'Saijo' tree is still growing in Japan, as is the original, now three-hundred-year-old, tree of the cultivar 'Hiratanenashi'.

Most available kaki cultivars are cold-hardy to about zero degrees Fahrenheit (suitable for growing in USDA Hardiness Zones 7 through 10). Cold-hardiness for any given cultivar is enhanced if growth is not overly lush and the soil is well drained. Trees can be killed or injured even in warm-winter areas when hard freezes occur after growth has begun in spring. Kaki does not require winter chilling and will grow in subtropical as well as temperate climates.

If completely dormant, kaki may even be as cold-hardy as is the American persimmon. In China, kaki have been grown on the edge of the Gobi desert, where temperatures drop below minus fifteen degrees Fahrenheit, and trees tolerate similar cold in Korea. The dryness of these regions may contribute to plants' cold-hardiness. Cultivars planted outside the Orient have originated mostly in Japan, where tolerance to extreme cold is not needed.

Among the most cold-hardy cultivars is 'Eureka', a seedling that originated in America. This cultivar has survived winter cold below minus twenty degrees Fahrenheit, though damage can occur from cold snaps in fall or spring. 'Saijo' and 'Giombo' are two cultivars that survive winters in Zones 5 and 6. Other cold-hardy kaki cultivars include 'Great Wall', 'Peiping', 'Kyungsun Ban-Si', 'Niu Nai', and 'Sheng'.

Kaki cultivars can be classified into two general categories: those that bear astringent fruits (astringent until they are ripe, that is) and those that bear non-astringent fruits. Within each of these categories, there are cultivars whose fruits are influenced by pollination ("pollination variant") and cultivars whose fruits are unaffected by pollination ("pollination constant"). (Actually, it is the seeds that influence the fruit, not pollination *per se*.)

An astringent cultivar must be soft—as soft as an overripe tomato—before it is fit to eat, and such cultivars are best adapted to the cooler regions where kakis can be grown. (With some types of artificial ripening procedures, these cultivars will become edible while firm.) The flesh color of pollination-constant astringent (PCA) cultivars is not influenced by pollination. Pollination-variant astringent (PVA) cultivars have dark flesh around the seeds when pollinated.

A non-astringent kaki can be eaten when it is as crisp as an apple. These cultivars need hot summers, and the fruit might retain some astringency when grown in cooler regions. Pollination-constant non-astringent (PCNA) kakis are always edible when still firm; pollination-variant non-astringent (PVNA) kakis are edible when firm only if they have been pollinated.

Kaki fruits can be large, often weighing more than a pound. They vary from those that are shaped like a tomato ('Fuyu'), to those that are shaped like an acorn ('Giombo', 'Tamopan'), to those that are lobed ('Saijo').

AMERICAN PERSIMMON (*Diospyros virginiana*)   The American persimmon has rarely been cultivated, but humans and animals have been eating the wild fruits since time immemorial. Eastern America, from Connecticut to Florida and west to Kansas, is the native home of this plant. The trees are fast-growing when young, then settle down to a moderate growth rate as they begin to bear fruit. In their native forest habitat, occasional trees grow over seventy-five feet high, but fifty feet is the more usual maximum height. On mature trees the checked pattern on the bark makes the trunk appear to be wrapped in alligator skin (attractive, not frightening).

Though its fruit is smaller than that of the kaki, the American persimmon survives and ripens fruit farther north than do the kaki cultivars that are now available. American persimmon trees are cold-hardy to Zone 4, but at the northern limit of cultivation, the problem is finding a cultivar that can ripen its fruit rather than one that can survive the winter.

There exist two races of American persimmon, a ninety-chromosome, "northern" race and a sixty-chromosome, "southern" race. The "northern" race is native to the upper Midwest of the U.S. and is the earlier ripening and more cold-hardy of the two races. Also, the pubescent leaves and larger fruit (which occasionally are bluish) of the "northern" race contrast with the smooth leaves and smaller fruit of the "southern" race.

Compared with the kaki, already benefiting from centuries of improvement through breeding, the American persimmon is a pomological upstart. About 1880, an early-ripening, flavorful, small-seeded American persimmon was discovered on a farm in Alton, Illinois. This wilding was deemed worthy of being named and propagated—the first American persimmon cultivar. 'Early Golden', as this cultivar was called, began a lineage of high-quality persimmon cultivars that includes 'Garretson', 'Killen', 'John Rick', 'Meader', and others. Other seedlings, many unrelated to 'Early Golden', were also selected and named, beginning in the early part of the twentieth century. In 1915 a publication from the United States Department of Agriculture listed twelve cultivars besides 'Early Golden'.

High-quality cultivars for the lower Midwest include 'John Rick', 'Garretson', 'Killen', 'Early Golden', 'Craggs', 'Beavers', 'Wabash', and 'Florence'. The foliage of 'Wabash', incidentally, turns red in early fall, rather than the characteristic yellow of other American persimmons. Moving northward, where growing seasons are shorter and winters are colder, the cultivars 'Hicks', 'Meader', 'Szukis', 'Mohler', 'Dooley', and 'Pieper' are recommended.

A male pollinator is needed to ensure fruiting except for those cultivars that can set seedless fruits. Pollinators can be male seedlings, male cultivars such as 'Mike', 'George', and 'William', or female cultivars, such as 'Szukis' and 'Killen', that bear some male flowers. The male must have the same chromosome number as the female fruiting tree, and kakis cannot usually pollinate American persimmons, or vice versa.

THE FUTURE OF PERSIMMONS?   Though the American persimmon has been eaten for hundreds of years, its full potential as a fine dessert or culinary fruit has yet to be realized. Besides pushing the limit of American persimmon cultivation farther north, this fruit could be improved by developing cultivars with fruits that are larger, less seedy, and firmer than existing cultivars. University of Illinois Professor Joe MacDaniel (who, according to New Hampshire fruit breeder Professor Elwyn Meader, "knew the most about the American persimmon") and H. C. Barrett selected 'John Rick' and 'Florence' from only forty-five 'Killen' seedlings. Professor MacDaniel wrote that "amateurs . . . can probably do as well as Meader, Barrett, and I in breeding better American persimmon trees for their own particular areas. We got three excellent cultivars with an investment of time, some knowledge, and a little land." After all, wild kakis in China produce small, seedy fruits. Imagine what years of breeding could do for persimmons by comparing a diminutive, puckery, wild apple with a perfectly grown 'MacIntosh'. One amateur persimmon enthusiast who took up the torch from Meader and company is James Claypool, with over two thousand trees under evaluation.

One snag in breeding stems from the separate male and female trees: You can use a female clone that bears high-quality fruit as one parent, but how can you know what effect the nonfruiting male parent will have on the fruit? Fortunately, female trees sometimes bear male flowers. This characteristic is prevalent in some members of the 'Early Golden' family. And male clones occasionally bear female flowers when vigorous growth is encouraged. At the very least, development of cultivars with perfect flowers, cultivars bearing parthenocarpic fruits, and dwarfing rootstocks could increase productivity.

The search also is on for kakis that will fruit north of their present limit. Will this come from the selection of hardier existing cultivars, perhaps using hardiness-inducing rootstocks, or from the breeding of new hardier cultivars?

One route to follow in improving the persimmon is to have East meet West: combine the size and non-astringency of the kaki with the cold-hardiness and rich flavor of the American persimmon. And while at it, why not throw in the smaller stature of kaki trees and their fruits' thicker skin and greater tendency to parthenocarpy? Hybridization is potentially possible between the kaki, which has ninety chromosomes, and the ninety-chromosome race of American persimmons. One report of a successful marriage comes from the Ukraine with a cold-hardy cultivar named 'Rosseyanka', bearing three-ounce, seedless fruits. Generally, the seeds of such hybrids either do not germinate or, if they do, obviously contain genes of only the female parent.

Tasting fruit of persimmon seedlings can wreak havoc with the taste buds of any would-be persimmon breeder—all it takes is one astringent fruit. And some American persimmon seedlings never lose their astringency! Fortunately, there is a simple, though crude, chemical test for astringency. Moisten filter paper with a five percent solution of ferric chloride and hold it against the cut half of a persimmon. The more intense the color change of this indicator, the more astringent the fruit.

Cultivation

The American persimmon is not especially choosy about site conditions. The trees will tolerate almost any soil except those that are waterlogged, although given their druthers, they prefer warm, sandy soils. A kaki grafted onto an American persimmon rootstock is similarly unfinicky about soil. Full sunlight is required by the kaki and, possibly, the American persimmon. Trees of either kaki or American persimmon need ten to fifteen feet of space all around. One caveat: keep trees away from walkways. (Not that the trees dislike walkways, but any fruits that drop will splatter and be tracked indoors.)

Few fibrous roots and a long taproot make both the American persimmon and the kaki more difficult to transplant than most other fruit trees. Potted trees are easily transplanted, and bare-root trees also can be transplanted with success if they are dug in the spring with as many roots as possible. The roots of bare-root trees appear dead because they are black, but that is their natural, healthy color. Persimmon roots regenerate slowly, so do not let luxuriant top growth early in a tree's first season lull you into complacency when it comes to caring for the plant. Those lush leaves may suddenly flag, and the plant die, unless you coddle the plant with timely watering throughout that first season.

In common with many other tree fruits, a certain number of persimmon fruits drop following the initial fruit set. This is a natural thinning of fruits (for even up to seventy-five percent of kaki fruitlets!), though drop can become excessive especially on trees that are overly vigorous or too shaded. Once a tree has finished dropping its fruits naturally, further hand thinning may be needed to avoid overburdening the limbs, to increase the size of the fruit, and to diminish the tendency for a tree to bear prodigious crops in some years, then little or no fruit in alternate years. Especially with kakis that do not need pollination to set adequate crops, the presence of a male tree can cause overbearing.

Prune persimmon trees while they are dormant. The wood is brittle, so a sturdy framework must be built while the tree is young. Train trees either to an open center or a modified central leader form. Shorten or support with stakes long, willowy branches on young trees.

Once bearing has commenced, prune enough in winter to stimulate some new growth, on which fruit will be borne the following season. Also head back some one-year-old branches to decrease fruit load in the upcoming season and to keep bearing wood near the main branches. But do not cut off the ends of too many of these one-year-old branches or the crop will be too small. Where invigoration is needed, cut back some branches severely, then save some of the stoutest and most vigorous watersprouts that result for new, bearing wood; those angled up at about a forty-five-degree angle will bear best. The American persimmon naturally drops some of the branches that have borne fruits, so is somewhat self-pruning—what more could you ask for in a tree?

Persimmon trees, when young, are susceptible to sunscald in winter. Protect the trunk, especially its southwest side, with a coat of white latex paint or a commercially available plastic or paper tree-guard.

Pests rarely pose a problem, especially if there are no wild persimmon trees nearby. In some areas, the persimmon girdler can warrant action. To abate damage by the girdler, pick up and burn fallen twigs in the autumn. There also is a persimmon borer that can kill a tree as it tunnels into the roots. Various scale insects weaken trees by sucking the sap. Black spots on the leaves are signs of anthracnose, a disease the severity of which can vary greatly from one cultivar to the next. For example, 'Fuyu', 'Izu', and 'Fehrmann' are very susceptible, whereas 'Morris Burton' and 'Runkwitz' are very resistant. In some regions, such as the southeastern U.S., trees will suddenly die, the result of a persimmon wilt inadvertently imported from Asia in the 1930s; atypically cold winters or late spring freezes seem to trigger this calamity.

Propagation

Kaki, date plum (*Diospyros lotus*), and American persimmon have all been used as persimmon rootstock. Kaki is the least cold-hardy of the three rootstocks, so is suitable only where winters are mild, probably Zone 8 or warmer. The kaki cultivar 'Shakokushi' has been used as a rootstock to induce dwarfing and precocity in scion cultivars, as has diamond-leafed persimmon (*D. rhombifolia*).

The date plum is moderately cold-hardy (probably to Zone 6), has an easily transplanted fibrous root system, and tolerates a range of soil conditions. Unfortunately, this rootstock is incompatible with some PCNA kakis such as 'Fuyu', 'Jiro', 'Suruga', and 'Gosho'. The date plum is also more susceptible to diseases than is either the kaki or the American persimmon. (As you might guess from the name, date plum does produce an edible fruit, small, yellowish brown to bluish black, often dried, and tasting, of course, something like dates.)

American persimmon is a suitable rootstock for either the kaki or for other American persimmons and is the rootstock of choice in northernmost growing areas. Of the three rootstock species, this one tolerates the widest range in soil conditions. Its major drawbacks are that it is harder to transplant and that it sends up suckers, often a few feet from the mother plant.

Cleft grafting, whip grafting, and chip budding are suitable methods of joining stock and scion. Cleft and whip grafting are most successful if done when leaves on the rootstock start to unfurl (with the scion cut while fully dormant and kept so in a refrigerator until needed). The best scion wood comes from the base of vigorous one-year-old shoots, such as watersprouts. After making the graft, some gardeners completely cover the grafted scion and the graft union either with grafting wax or with a plastic bag. In the latter case, cover the plastic bag with a paper bag to prevent overheating in the sun. Once growth begins, take off the plastic bag but replace the paper bag, gradually tearing it open to admit air and light to the growing scion.

Seed can be used for raising rootstocks or developing new cultivars. Stratify seeds for two to three months immediately after extracting them from the fruit. Germination can be enhanced by removing the hard coating of each seed. Where sunlight is intense, shade seedlings during their first few weeks of growth. Seedlings begin to bear fruit when they are about six years old.

The persimmon also can be propagated from cuttings and, in the case of the American persimmon, by digging and transplanting suckers. Use hardwood or root cuttings for the American persimmon. Cut wood that is two or three years old for hardwood cuttings. Immediately after taking either root or hardwood cuttings, seal both cut ends with grafting wax. Softwood cuttings of kaki taken in spring will root under mist.

Harvest and Use

The fruit of most kaki cultivars does not separate easily from the tree even when ripe, so must be clipped off with a short piece of stem. American persimmons commonly drop from the trees when ripe, though some clones hold their ripe fruits into winter. A soft mulch beneath the trees cushions their landing. Fresh persimmons can be stored for about two months at a temperature just above freezing. The length of storage depends somewhat on whether and how the fruit was artificially ripened, a procedure discussed later in this chapter.

Where the climate is equable (in California for instance), a mature kaki tree yields about four hundred pounds of fruit. A semi-wild mature American persimmon tree at least a decade old will yield anywhere from fifty to a hundred pounds of fruit. The original tree of the 'Knowles' persimmon was eighty feet high and produced over one ton of fruit in 1956.

Unripe persimmons are "harsh and choakie, and furre in a man's mouth like allam [alum]" (William Strachey, *The Historie of Travaile into Virginia Brittanica* c. 1612). This "harsh and choakie" feeling in the unripe fruit is caused by a chemical tannin, leucodelphinidin, which bonds to proteins in the mouth. Correct harvesting and ripening are all-important to enjoying a persimmon, just as they are for enjoying European pears (except that an unripe pear is not nearly as unpleasant as is an unripe persimmon).

Leucodelphinidin is the potential source of another problem: the formation of a bezoar, an insoluble mass that can lodge in your gut. Trouble begins when stomach acids react with leucodelphinidin to form a sticky substance; add some persimmon skins and seed, and you have the makings of a bezoar. A bezoar is unlikely to form if you eat the flesh—not the skin or seeds—of only ripe persimmons and if you chew the flesh thoroughly. Don't be put off from enjoying a persimmon for fear of a bezoar. Bezoars are rare, frequently associated with decreased peristalsis that results from gastric surgery, and, if truth be known, they also can be caused by more common foods such as celery, coconut, and oranges.

Pick fruits of non-astringent kakis when they are fully colored and firm. Astringent kakis and American persimmons are not at their best until they are thoroughly ripe. At this point, the pulp is so mushy as to be barely contained by the skin, the skin is almost translucent, and the calyx—the green cap to which the stem is attached—separates readily from the fruit.

Contrary to popular myth, frost is not necessary to ripen a persimmon. Though fruits continue to ripen following light frosts, development is arrested when the mercury plummets to the mid-twenties—hence the importance of choosing a suitable cultivar, especially in areas with short seasons.

There are a number of ways to ripen a persimmon artificially, but the fruit must already be nearing ripeness on the tree. Artificial ripening is not as successful with the American persimmon as it is with the kaki. All these methods aside, near ripe persimmons will also ripen in due course if just left sitting on the kitchen counter. Artificial ripening of astringent kakis makes the fruit edible while it is still relatively firm.

The easiest way to accelerate ripening is to put the fruits into a plastic bag with a ripe apple. Ethylene gas given off by the apple will ripen kakis in three to four days, American persimmons in a slightly longer time.

In Japan at one time, kakis were stored in sake casks, where traces of alcohol vapor accelerated ripening. In the absence of old sake casks, equally good results can be achieved by spraying the fruits with thirty-five percent ethanol (whiskey, for example), then sealing them in a plastic bag for one to two weeks. Fruits still on trees have even been subjected to alcohol ripening by enclosing them individually in plastic bags along with a few drops of alcohol.

In China, persimmons have been ripened by immersing them in a ten percent (by volume) solution of lime water or a ten percent water solution of the juice of *hon laat liu* (a species of *Polygonum*). The main mechanism here is depriving the fruits of air, causing them to form acetaldehyde, which, in turn, reacts with the tannins to make them insoluble. Plain water and hot water (104 to 140 degrees Fahrenheit) have been similarly used. The alcohol, mentioned previously, caused a similar release of acetaldehyde in the fruit.

Kakis have also been traditionally ripened in jars with crushed banyan (*Ficus benghalensis*) leaves or with burning incense. The incense gives off carbon dioxide, a gas that is sometimes used to ripen persimmons in Japan, and perhaps some ethylene, the gas previously mentioned as being emitted by ripening apples.

Drying removes persimmon astringency naturally and preserves the fruit for winter use. Dried persimmons are a delicacy in Japan and were used as a sweetener there before cane sugar became available. The sugar that forms on the outside of drying fruits is sometimes collected and then pressed into molds to make ornamental tablets offered, for example, as wedding gifts. 'Hachiya' is the favored cultivar for drying. Other PCA cultivars are also suitable; non-astringent cultivars become tough when dried.

For drying, the fruits are picked when fully colored but still firm, then peeled, leaving just a small circle of skin at both the stem and the calyx ends. The Japanese hang each peeled fruit by a string attached to the stem, or spear a number of fruits together on a bamboo skewer. In dry weather, the fruits dry to a soft consistency in three weeks. These half-dry *ampo-gaki* are considered a delicacy, but will keep only for about two weeks. Left to hang another three weeks, the fruits become thoroughly hard and dry and then do keep well. Best-quality dried kakis have been massaged weekly during their first four to five weeks of drying.

Native Americans also dried their native persimmons for winter use. They extracted the pulp by rubbing the fruit through a sieve, then formed the pulp into finger-thick loaves that were dried in the sun or in an oven. Fruits of some late-ripening American persimmon clones can be left hanging in the trees late into fall, whence they turn sweet, dark, and dry, resembling dates in appearance and flavor.

Frozen persimmons are delicious as is, slightly softened like ice cream. American persimmon cultivars such as 'Morris Burton', 'John Rick', and 'Lena' are best at retaining their flavor when frozen. Once the fruit is ripe enough, slow freezing and thawing also removes the astringency from certain cultivars by rupturing the cells so the leucodelphinidin combines with proteins in the fruit and is inactivated.

Aside from being eaten fresh, persimmons may be cooked into delicious pies, cookies, and cakes. Native Americans used persimmon in gruel, cornbread, and pudding. 'Morris Burton', 'John Rick', and 'Beavers' are American persimmons especially good for cooking. Any astringency still lingering in the fruit is accentuated by cooking, but can be removed by the addition of half a teaspoon of baking soda for each cup of pulp. Also, never allow cast-iron cooking utensils to come in contact with persimmon pulp, or the pulp will turn black.

Like other sweet fruits, persimmons ferment. Native Americans made an alcoholic beverage from persimmons and honeylocust pods. In the American South persimmons have been mashed with cornmeal, then brewed into "'simmon beer." Across the Pacific in the early twentieth century, the American plant explorer Frank Meyer reported that the Chinese were fermenting kakis into vinegar and brandy. He also wrote of persimmon paste stuffed with walnuts and pressed into square cakes.

These are surely a goodly number of uses for a fruit that "has received more criticism, both adverse and favorable, than almost any other known species" (so wrote a U.S. Department of Agriculture horticulturalist in 1915). No doubt the adverse criticism would abate if this "food of the gods" were better understood by mere mortals.

Cultivars

Kaki (*Diospyros kaki*)

A fruit two and a half inches across is considered to be medium-sized; three inches across is considered to be large. No pollination is needed for fruit set, unless otherwise noted.

Abbreviations:

PCA = pollination constant, astringent
PVA = pollination variant, astringent
PVNA = pollination variant, non-astringent
PCNA = pollination constant, non-astringent

'Aizu Mishirazu': PVA; tree is small and spreading; round, yellow fruit is medium-large, but lacks sweetness and flavor.
'Eureka': PCA; does not need pollination; the medium-large, round fruits are deep red and of excellent quality.
'Fuyu' ('Fuyugaki'): PCNA; one of the leading market persimmons, selected in 1902; tendency to alternate-year bearing; bears better if pollinated; the large orangish red fruits have an excellent flavor; there is a nomenclature problem with this cultivar—'Fuyu' in Japan is evidently different from the cultivar with the same name that is grown in California. The Japanese 'Fuyu' is slightly four-sided, oval, and flattened, and incompatible with *Diospyros lotus* rootstock. California 'Fuyu' is rounded with a slight point, bears some male flowers, is

occasionally seedy, and is compatible with *D. lotus* rootstock. California 'Fuyu' seems to be a generic name applied to a few varieties.

'Gailey': PVA; male pollinator that bears some fruit; not reliably cold-hardy in Zone 7; fruits are small and of poor quality.

'Giboshi' ('Smith's Best'): PVA; one of the most cold-hardy; needs pollination for best yields; the delicious fruit is top-shaped; seeded fruit is the color of chocolate.

'Giombo': PCA; fruit is broad, conical, and yellow; good flavor.

'Gosho': PCNA; needs pollination for best yields, but produces some male flowers so can be used as pollinator; subject to preharvest drop; excellent fruit, though astringency is inconsistently lost on tree-ripened fruits, especially in cool seasons.

'Great Wall' ('Atoma'): PCA; orangish red fruits with very good flavor.

'Hachiya': PCA; the major market persimmon in the United States; tends to bear parthenocarpic fruit; the large, conical, orange-red fruits have an almost transparent skin and excellent, honey-sweet flavor.

'Hanafuyu' ('Winter Flower'): PCNA; tree is semi-dwarf; ripens two weeks before 'Fuyu'; fruit is large, orangish red, and of good quality.

'Hanagosho' ('Flower of the Imperial Palace'): PCNA; produces some male flowers; yellowish orange, round fruit is of good quality, but retains some astringency in cool regions.

'Hiratanenashi' ('Flat Seedless'): PCA; a vigorous grower; medium-sized, flat, brilliant red fruits are of good quality and ripen a week before 'Fuyu'; rarely forms seeds even if pollinated.

'Hyakume': PVNA; medium to large fruit, roundish, with a buff yellowish orange skin and dark cinnamon flesh.

'Ichikikei Jiro': PCNA; a bud sport of 'Jiro'; tree is dwarf; fruit is large, orangish red, and ripens three weeks before 'Fuyu'.

'Izu': PCNA; needs pollination; this cultivar was bred in Japan and named in 1970; low yields; fruit is burnt orange, of medium quality, and ripens three weeks before 'Fuyu'.

'Jiro': PCNA; ripens one to two weeks before 'Fuyu'; fruit is large, crimson-yellow, flattened and squarish from four shallow indentations in its side; crisp to tender, juicy; no male flowers; often sold as 'Fuyu'.

'Kawabata': PCNA; cold-hardy for a NA type kaki; tends to produce parthenocarpic fruits; the large, yellow fruits are of excellent quality.

'Kyungsun Ban-Si': PCA; needs pollination to set fruit; fruits are up to three inches across, orange, with good flavor.

'Lantern': male pollinator that bears some fruit, albeit of poor quality; more cold-hardy than 'Gailey'.

'Maekawa Jiro': PCNA; a weak grower; a bud sport of 'Jiro', maturing about two weeks earlier.

'Matsumoto Wase Fuyu': PCNA; a bud sport of 'Fuyu', discovered in 1935; ripens about the same time as or a bit earlier than 'Fuyu'.

'Niu Nai': PCA; tree has good red fall color, fruits are large and yellow, but lack sweetness.

'Okugosho': PCNA; late-ripening; inconsistent loss of astringency; the round, medium-sized fruit is orange-yellow with a good flavor; another variety that might be California 'Fuyu'.

'Peiping': PCA; fruits are medium-large, yellow, and of fair quality.

'Saijo' ('Very Best One'): PCA; the small, yellowish orange fruits are very sweet.

'Sheng' ('Etter'): PCA; moderate amounts of fruit set without pollination; the fruits are yellow and flattened, with lobes; flavor is delicious.

'Shogatsu': PVNA; needs pollination, but occasionally produces some male flowers; the large, orangish red fruit is late-ripening and of mediocre quality.

'Suruga': PCNA; needs hot summers; better yields if pollinated; the large fruit is orange, late-ripening, and of high quality.

'Tamopan' ('Large Grindstone'): PCA; large, flat fruit constricted near its top so it looks like it's wearing a cap; the skin is thin, tough, and orange; flesh is likewise orange, juicy but not rich.

'Tanenashi' ('Without Seed'): PCA; does not need pollination, although pollination results in increased yield, quality, and fruit size; fruit is large, orange, and conical.

'Tecumseh': PCA; large crops without pollination; good fall color; the yellow, square-lobed fruits are of good quality.

'Tsurunko' ('Child of the Stork', 'Chocolate Persimmon'): PVNA; a female that also produces many male flowers; medium to small fruit, cylindrical shape, orange-red skin over a dark brown flesh; flavor is sweet and rich. (Other varieties are called 'Chocolate Persimmon' as well.)

'Twentieth Century': PCNA; similar to 'Fuyu', but slightly smaller and flatter.

'Yamagaki': PVA; can be used for pollination because it produces male and female flowers; fruit quality is mediocre.

'Zenjimaru': PVNA; produces many male flowers so a good pollinator, but fruit is small, seedy, and of poor flavor.

AMERICAN PERSIMMON (*Diospyros virginiana*)

The following descriptions of American persimmon cultivars come from many sources, and, in reviewing what has been written about the cultivars, more than occasionally I was struck by a lack of consensus on fruit quality and ripening dates. The American persimmon seems to be an inconsistent fruit, varying from region to region and year to year.

'Beavers': fruit is button-shaped and small, with a red flesh dotted with dark specks; fresh flavor is mediocre, but tastes good frozen or cooked; does not ripen in northernmost growing areas.

'Blagg': tree is precocious and productive; fruits are flattened and large; won first prize at the 1961 Persimmon Festival in Mitchell, Indiana.

'Craggs': the large, pale fruit is late-ripening; excellent texture and flavor.

'Dollywood': from Claypool's breeding program; the red-blushed fruits are medium to large and borne mid- to late season; excellent flavor.

'Early Golden': sometimes produces a few male flowers, but not reliably enough for pollination every year; resists anthracnose disease; the thin-skinned fruits have good size and quality, and freeze well.

'Elmo': a seedling of 'Early Golden' from Claypool's breeding program; prolific production of large, orange fruits borne early to midseason and having good flavor.

'Ennis Seedless': a male tree that occasionally bears seedless fruits that taste good but are small; probably ninety-chromosome type.

'Evelyn': fruit is large, early, sweet, and seedless.

'Fehrmann': fruit flavor is medium to good; sometimes seedless; won first prize at the 1958 Persimmon Festival in Mitchell, Indiana.

'Festimoon': the small, soft fruits taste good and may be seedless.

'Florence': smaller seeds, but otherwise very similar to one of its parents, 'Killen'; occasional male flowers; usually excellent flavor.

'Garretson': a seedling of 'Early Golden', named in 1920; resistant to anthracnose; seedless if not pollinated; better than 'Early Golden' and 'Killen'; ripens one week earlier than 'Early Golden'; clear orange pulp is delicious and freezes well.

'George': a male tree, seedling of 'Killen'.

'Golden Supreme': one of the largest, but will not ripen far north.

'Hicks': red-cheeked yellow fruits ripen just before 'Garretson'; thin, tender skin; average flavor.

'John Rick': a seedling of 'Killen', named in 1958; tree is precocious; fruit is one of the largest and most attractive of American persimmons; ripens at same time as 'Early Golden'; the red pulp is delicious fresh and also good frozen or cooked (but not frozen and cooked!).

'Josephine': an old cultivar bearing some seedless fruits; tough skin; the bright yellow, medium-sized fruits are sweet and rich.

'Juhl': fruit is very early (earlier than 'Garretson'), ripening over a short time period; large, clear yellow with a red blush on the skin and black specks in the pulp.

'Kansas': tends to overcrop, so needs thinning; fruit is large and yellow, splashed with red; good flavor but watch out for delayed pucker.

'Killen': a seedling of 'Early Golden' named in 1915; occasional male flowers; differs from parent in being larger and ripening later, prolific bearer, healthy foliage; excellent flavor.

'Knowles' ('Owen'): good-tasting, seedless fruits that are small even if pollinated; late-ripening, sixty-chromosome.

'Lena' ('Mitchellena'): leaves resistant to anthracnose; fruit starts to ripen early and continues over a long period; the large, flattened fruit is reddish orange, with an almost transparent, tender skin; very soft, good flavor, and freezes well.

'Meader': seedling of 'Garretson'; one of the most cold-hardy, surviving to at least minus twenty-five degrees Fahrenheit; occasional male flowers; bears prolifically and wood is brittle, so fruits need thinning; adapted to regions with cool summers; occasionally produces a male flower; fruit ripens early, but loses its astringency slowly; average quality.

'Mike': a male tree, seedling of 'Killen'.

'Miller' ('Marion'): fruit is large, with translucent, tough, reddish yellow skin; many seeds; not as sweet as some other cultivars, but still good quality.

'Mohler': very early-ripening (beginning at the end of August in my garden) and very high quality; sweet fruit up to two inches across with a pale orange skin; drops as it ripens.

'Morris Burton': won first prize at the 1957 Persimmon Festival at Mitchell, Indiana; tree is slow to bear; leaves turn bright yellow in the fall; fruits are small and reddish orange, with few seeds and a tender skin; the honeylike flavor makes this one of the most delicious persimmons.

'NC-10': ripens early, a month before 'Early Golden', and has a long ripening period; needs pollination; fruit is small, sweet, and almost seedless.

'Penland': a sixty-chromosome cultivar that bears seedless fruits if not pollinated; fruit is long, conical, and small, but seeds also are small; fair flavor.

'Pieper': can be seedless; fruit is small and reddish yellow; good for colder regions.

'Runkwitz': tree is very cold-hardy and resistant to anthracnose; fruit has a tough skin, solid flesh, and good size and flavor.

'Szukis': extremely cold-hardy and prolific; bears some male flowers; fruiting is prolific; moderately early-ripening (beginning in late September in my garden); clear, orange-colored skin encloses delectable flesh that is sweet, rich, and without astringency; fruits are one and a half inches across; most fruits cling to tree after ripe, well after leaves fall.

'Wabash': good red fall color to leaves; the fruit is small, early-ripening, and seedless, with a dark red pulp having many dark specks; the flavor is excellent, but not retained in frozen fruit.

'William': a male tree that bears occasional fruits; a ninety-chromosome cultivar.

'Yates': fruit is moderately early, very large, seedless, and of good flavor. (Probably the same as 'Juhl'.)

HYBRIDS OF KAKI AND AMERICAN PERSIMMON

'Keener': a hybrid allegedly developed by Luther Burbank, although Burbank did state, at least once in his writings, that he had "not succeeded in effecting this hybridization." At any rate, the tree is vigorous and prolific, and produces an early crop of large, flat, nearly seedless fruits.

'Rosseyanka': a Russian hybrid from the Nikitsky Botanical Gardens of Yalta; a very cold-hardy tree bearing large, nearly seedless fruits that taste like kaki persimmons.

Elaeagnus
Gumi, Autumn Olive, and Russian Olive

BOTANICAL NAME
Elaeagnus multiflora, Elaeagnus umbellata,
and *Elaeagnus angustifolia*

PLANT TYPE
Deciduous shrubs or shrubby trees

POLLINATION
Partially self-fertile

RIPENING SEASON
Summer to fall, depending on species

Take your pick: amongst the three edible species of the genus *Elaeagnus* (pronounced el-ee-AG-nus) in this chapter, we find fruits that are sweet and mealy, as well as fruits that are sprightly and juicy. In all cases, each fruit contains a single, hard seed.

Dead-ripe gumi fruits (*Elaeagnus multiflora*) have a pleasant, tart flavor with a bit of astringency. Fruits of some seedlings, unfortunately, have more than a bit of astringency, but even those have an aroma that beckons me to keep picking and eating. Gumi fruits are the juiciest of the three species of this chapter. They also are the earliest to ripen, ready for harvest by mid-July. The plant's other common name, cherry elaeagnus, is fitting, for the half-inch- to one-inch-long fruits, scarlet red and speckled with silver, make a striking picture as they dangle on long stalks from the undersides of the branches.

An autumn olive bush (*Elaeagnus umbellata*) in fruit is just as attractive as the gumi. In the case of autumn olive, the adornment is a profusion of small berries (each about a quarter of an inch across) appressed all along the branches, brightening them, as the name implies, in autumn. Like gumi fruits, autumn olive fruits are red with silvery flecks, and sprightly in flavor. In fact, many of the fruits I have tasted have been too tart, to my taste, to eat out of hand. But my six-year-old niece, who usually exhibits a sweet tooth, shoves handfuls of these fruits into her mouth, and another grower assures me that whenever he sets out a bowl of autumn olive fruits after a dinner party, his guests always pick the bowl clean—sufficient testimonials to accord this fruit the title "dessert fruit."

Both autumn olive and gumi fruits are eaten in the Far East. In Japan, whole branches are cut off with their fruits attached and sold as such on the streets. The Japanese name for gumi is *daio-gumi*, meaning "rhubarb silverberry," and the name for autumn olive is *aki-gumi*, meaning "autumn silverberry."

More soothing to the taste buds are Russian olive (*Elaeagnus angustifolia*) fruits, which are silvery yellow, mealy, sweet, and about half an inch long. They ripen in late summer. A botanical variety with a red skin, *E. angustifolia* var. *orientalis*, is familiar in the markets of Turkey and surrounding countries. Fruits are eaten fresh, dried, stewed in milk, or boiled with sugar. When dry, the loose skin of *iğde*, as the fruit is called in Turkey, peels away easily to reveal a cream-colored, almost dusty, sweet pulp that practically dissolves in your mouth. (This red-fruited form has sometimes been referred to erroneously as the Trebizond date, which is in fact the date plum, *Diospyros lotus*, another small, dark, sweet, dried fruit eaten in that part of the world.)

All three species of *Elaeagnus* were introduced into North America over a hundred years ago. In North America, though, autumn olive and Russian olive are grown primarily as ornamentals or to provide wildlife with food and habitat. The Russian olive also finds use as a windbreak or living fence in cold, semiarid regions of the Midwest. Both Russian olive and autumn olive have found conditions in North America much to their liking, perhaps too much, so that the former is now listed as a noxious weed in some western states and seedlings of the latter frequently colonize abandoned roadsides and fields, especially of the eastern states. The gumi, though an attractive plant with tasty fruit, is largely unknown. Still, I grow all three species.

Description of the Plants

Gumi, autumn olive, and Russian olive are shrubby plants, often spiny, with leaves that are green on their uppersides and hoary below. A dark background—Norway spruce or some other evergreen, for example—highlights the silvery glow of these plants. In a breeze, the plants come alive, shimmering as their fluttering leaves show first one side, then the other. Russian olive

Gumi

leaves are willow-shaped; those of the two other species, and the red-fruited variety of Russian olive, are more oval.

Russian olive is the most treelike of the three species, developing with age a thick trunk usually bifurcating near the ground. As the trunk ages, the bark turns a rich brown color and shreds off. Under good conditions, this species will grow as large as forty feet high and wide. A full-sized, unpruned plant makes an impenetrable thicket—hence its use for wildlife cover or living fences. The botanical variety *orientalis* is especially attractive, "a glorious sight, the bright orange-red fruits contrasting beautifully with the silvery foliage," wrote U.S. Department of Agriculture plant explorer Frank Meyer when he came upon large hedges of the plant in western China in the early twentieth century.

Both autumn olive and gumi grow as rounded shrubs. Gumi typically grows to about eight feet high and wide. Autumn olive is not a plant for a small property for, though shrubby, a single plant can grow into a billowing mass as high and as wide as twenty feet.

In spring, all three *Elaeagnus* species bear cream-colored flowers that fill the air with a delicious scent. Individual flowers are unremarkable in appearance, but have a wonderful effect en masse as they blanket the plant in a pale yellow mist. The flowers are at least partially self-fertile (less so for Russian olive, more so for gumi) and seedlings come relatively true from seed.

Just a few cultivars have been selected of these three *Elaeagnus* species. From the Kiev Botanical Garden comes 'Sweet Scarlet' gumi. 'King Red' is a nearly thornless cultivar of Russian olive notable for its large red fruits, up to an inch long. Seed for 'King Red' was collected by a U.S. Department of Agriculture scientist in Afghanistan in 1958. 'Cardinal' autumn olive is usually grown as a soil and wildlife conservation plant, being especially tolerant of poor soils and a prolific producer of quarter-inch-sized fruits. The autumn olive cultivar 'Ellagood', from Georgia, was selected for its ability to hang on to its fruits late into winter, while 'Charlie's Golden' puts on a showy autumn display of yellow fruits, and 'Ruby' is notable for large, crimson fruits. 'Elsberry' autumn olive, which originated in Elsberry, Missouri, grows to be a very large bush, with fruits almost half an inch across. 'Elsberry' is not particularly cold-hardy. Among the best of the named cultivars of autumn olive for human consumption is 'Redwing', hailing from Michigan and with fruits that are especially large and sweet. The plant grows to about twelve feet high and is somewhat more cold-hardy than are other autumn olives. My current favorite for fresh eating is 'Brilliant Rose', which is quite sweet when caught at the right moment.

Except for the few named cultivars, little has been done to breed superior fruiting clones of any of the *Elaeagnus* species. The usual objective in breeding or selecting superior *Elaeagnus* plants has been yield rather than flavor, understandable since the targeted consumers were birds. Given the variability in yield, fruit size, and fruit flavor within each of the species, there is opportunity to create some tasty, ornamental garden plants. *Elaeagnus* species, and specifically the gumi, were among the "plants that await the breeder's attention" mentioned by fruit breeder Dr. George Darrow in the United States Department of Agriculture's *Yearbook of Agriculture, 1937*. These plants are still waiting.

Because these plants do come relatively true from seed, the would-be *Elaeagnus* breeder would do well to intervene in the self-pollination that occurs in order to draw from a wider genetic base. To hybridize two different clones or cultivars, snip the anthers off a few flowers from one plant before pollination takes place. Then dust the stigmas with pollen (a small paintbrush is handy for this) of another clone or cultivar. Bag the flowers in cheesecloth to prevent the possibility of insect pollination or, later on, a bird's eating your work.

Cultivation

The gumi, the autumn olive, and the Russian olive are all tolerant of conditions inimical to most other cultivated plants. In infertile soil, *Elaeagnus* species form a symbiosis with root-inhabiting bacteria that gather nitrogen from the air to feed the plants. Because of their ability to grow in nitrogen-poor soils, *Elaeagnus* are used to reclaim strip-mined land. Some of the nitrogen gathered by the roots of *Elaeagnus* might be available to feed other plant species growing nearby.

The plants also tolerate dry, salty, or alkaline soils. Russian olive requires a soil pH greater than 6, but autumn olive will tolerate a pH range between 4 and 8. These are tough plants—they also tolerate extremes of heat and cold. Russian and autumn olive are suitable for USDA Hardiness Zones 3 through 7. The gumi thrives in Zones 4 through 9. Except in areas with intense summer sun, where a bit of shade would do no harm, these *Elaeagnus* species do need full sun in order to fruit well.

All three species are medium- to fast-growing plants that are rarely affected by insect or disease pests. One exception seems to be the 'King Red' strain of Russian olive: I and at least one other grower in the eastern United States find that this plant reliably dies back or is killed in its youth. Considering this plant's origins, humidity could be the problem, which I may be able to ferret out by growing a number of seedlings in different microclimates. With that exception, the near weed status of *Elaeagnus* in some regions attests to its ease of cultivation and cosmopolitan tastes.

Propagation

Cultivars usually are propagated by seed, and plants grown from seed require five years or more to begin fruiting. Within any seedling population, a small percentage of plants will be substantially different from the parent plant. This is more of a problem with some of the seed-propagated cultivars—'Cardinal' autumn olive, for example—than with others.

Seeds of all three species generally need cold stratification before they will germinate. Gumi seeds need a one- to two-month stratification period. As expected of any weedy plant, autumn olive seeds germinate readily. Usually they need a two- or three-month stratification period, but germination immediately upon sowing, for some clones, at least, has also been reported.

Russian olive seeds do not germinate so readily, often waiting until their second season. Germination is delayed by inhibitors in both the endocarp (the outer covering of the seed) and the seed coat. If the endocarp is nicked with a file, softened for between thirty and sixty minutes in concentrated sulfuric acid, or kept warm and moist for four weeks, about fifty percent of the seeds will germinate even without cold stratification. If the endocarps are cracked open and the seed coats peeled from the embryos, almost all the seeds germinate even without cold stratification. A six-day washing in water also leaches inhibitors and so speeds germination. Intact seeds require two to three months of cool, moist stratification before they will germinate.

All three species can be propagated clonally by stem cuttings taken mid- to late summer, or by root cuttings and layering when plants are dormant. Do not expect a high percentage of Russian olive stem cuttings to root. With gumi, include a small "heel" of old wood at the base of cuttings taken from the current season's growth.

Harvest and Use

The yield reported for a mature 'Cardinal' autumn olive bush is thirty-six pounds of fruit. Russian olives yield between sixteen and twenty pounds of dried fruit per plant. Gumi, being a smaller plant, would be expected to yield somewhat less.

For fresh eating, allow gumi and autumn olive fruits to hang on the plants until dead ripe. During the final stages of ripening, the sweetness almost doubles and acidity and astringency decrease dramatically. Not rushing harvest also gives more fruit, because the pulp (but not the seed) almost doubles in bulk as the fruit ripens. For my tastes, the window in time when autumn olives are at their best, having lost their astringency but not yet shrivelling, is brief, too brief. That window, though, especially with the delectable 'Brilliant Rose', is well worth waiting for. Incidentally, autumn olives have been found to be an extremely rich source of lycopene, a natural compound that offers protection against certain types of cancers.

No need to rush harvest of Russian olive, for unharvested fruits hang on the plant through much of the winter, the pulp becoming drier and drier though the skin retains its shape. Of course, during that period, birds freely feast upon the fruits—more than fifty kinds of birds enjoy Russian olive.

The following information is perhaps too far afield from the heading "Harvest and Use," but in old Persia the delicious perfume of *Elaeagnus* blossoms was said to have a powerful effect on a woman's emotions. So much so that husbands reputedly locked up their wives while the trees were in bloom.

Gooseberry

Fruit with a Checkered Past

BOTANICAL NAME
Ribes uva-crispa and *Ribes hirtellum*

PLANT TYPE
Deciduous shrub

POLLINATION
Self-fertile

RIPENING SEASON
Midsummer

A fully ripened dessert cultivar of gooseberry is as luscious as the best apple, strawberry, or grape. In fact, the flavor of the gooseberry was considered more like that of grapes than of any other fruit in seventeenth-century England, to the extent that gooseberries were raised commercially for fermenting into a delicate summer wine.

Such comparisons do injustice to the gooseberry: the fruit has a flavor all its own, and there is a world of difference between a poor-quality cultivar and a good one. At one end of the spectrum are cultivars whose fruits have sour pulp and tough skins; at the other end are those whose tender skins envelop an aromatic, sweet pulp. There is similar diversity in appearance of the fruit. A gooseberry might be green, white, yellow, or shades of red from pink to purple to almost black. In size, the spectrum runs from cultivars producing pea-sized fruits to those whose fruits are almost the size of hens' eggs.

Though considered as English as fish and chips, the gooseberry originated in continental Europe. In *The Small Fruits of New York* (1925), U. P. Hedrick suggested that the fruit was ignored by ancient Greeks and Romans because it "requires a low temperature to bring it to perfection, and cold must sharpen the appetites of those who would relish the austere taste of the first garden gooseberries," which were not far removed from the small, tart, astringent fruits of wild gooseberries. The first mention of English gooseberry cultivation is in the thirteenth-century bills of purchase of the fruiterer of Edward I, for plants shipped over from France. By Elizabethan times, gooseberries were common in English gardens, and in 1548 William Turner even listed a few different sorts in his *Names of Herbes in Greke, Latin, Englishe, Duche, and Frenche wyth the commune names that Herbaries and Apotecaries use.*

Popularity of the gooseberry in England began to soar by the eighteenth century, when cottage gardeners, particularly in Lancashire, Cheshire, and the Midlands, began vying to see who could grow the largest fruits. Competitive spirit was organized into annual gooseberry shows, held usually in clubrooms of local inns. The gaiety of singing and refreshments at these shows was offset by the solemn weighing of fruits. Weights were recorded in pennyweights and grains, just as for precious metals. The *Gooseberry Grower's Register* (first published in 1786) reported at least 171 shows taking place in 1845.

Over the years, fruit sizes swelled as backyard gooseberry growers became backyard gooseberry breeders, and as growers learned to nurture their prized berries. Most of the fruits were picked off a bush, so the plant could channel all its energy into the few fruits that remained. Some growers encouraged the growth of chickweed under their bushes in order to maintain a cool, moist atmosphere around developing fruits. Perhaps the strangest practice (at least of those that are known) was suckling, whereby a saucer of water was perched beneath an individual berry just high enough to wet only the calyx. Mats, bedsheets, tablecloths, even sheets of iron, were readied throughout the season, in spring to protect the plants from late frosts, then later on as protection from wind and rain. Rumor has it that rain burst all the real giants just before the show!

Whereas wild gooseberries weigh only about a quarter of an ounce, a gooseberry show winner in 1817 weighed in at one and a quarter ounces; by 1852, a winning fruit tipped the scales at just under two ounces. This demonstration of the effects of "nature and nurture" caught the interest of Charles Darwin, who noted the relatively short period of time in which the gooseberry had swollen from the size of a pea to that of a small apple!

Gooseberry mania subsided by the end of the nineteenth century, leaving in its wake hundreds of gooseberry cultivars. Some of those cultivars, such as 'Crown Bob', 'Leveller', and 'Lancashire Lad', are still popular today. Other cultivars from that golden age of gooseberries are unknown today, and rightly so, for their fruits were large but tasteless. Gooseberries still are popular in England (and in other northern European countries). And yes, gooseberry clubs still hold their annual shows.

Gooseberry

European gooseberries were brought across the Atlantic by early settlers of the New World, but most cultivars quickly succumbed to a mildew indigenous to America. Native American gooseberry species, represented by the cultivar 'Pale Red', for instance, proved to be somewhat resistant to the mildew, but had small fruits. Therefore, European and American species were crossed, the first hybrid, 'Houghton', making its debut at the 1847 meeting of the Massachusetts Horticultural Society. Other cultivars with American "blood" soon followed, and gooseberry breeding in America continued into the early twentieth century. The promising career of the gooseberry in America was brought to an abrupt halt in the 1920s, when gooseberry growing was restricted by federal law because the plant was implicated in the spread of white pine blister rust, a serious disease of white pine trees but one only mildly bothersome to gooseberries (more on this in a bit).

Even in England, the gooseberry has had a checkered career, too often considered as a fruit for children or as a substitute for something better. Especially in America, the lack of popularity of the gooseberry can be traced to the almost exclusive use of unripe fruits and the predominant sale of poor-quality cultivars. The name "gooseberry"—possibly derived from the use of the fruit for sauce with goose, or from the plant's resemblance to the gorse bush— has not helped matters. The gooseberry probably would have fared no better with its older English name of "feaberrie," a corruption of "feverberry," referring to the reputed cooling properties of the juice for fever.

Description of Plant

The gooseberry bush has arching branches giving the plant a height and breadth of between three and five feet. The buds perk up early in the spring, dotting the stems with green when most other plants are still tawny. Leaves are lobed and an inch or two wide and long. John Parkinson pointed to a major deficiency of the plant when he wrote (in *Paradisi in Sole Paradisus Terrestris*, 1629) that the plant is "armed with verie sharpe and cruell crooked thorns."

The flowers, borne laterally on one-year-old wood and on short spurs of older wood, open early in the season, but are inconspicuous. They are self-fertile and pollinated by wind and insects, but usually not by honeybees. Each flower bud opens to yield from one to four flowers, depending on the cultivar.

Cultivated gooseberries are derived mostly from two species: the European gooseberry (*Ribes uva-crispa*), native to the Caucasus Mountains and

Gooseberry

North Africa; and the American gooseberry (*R. hirtellum*), native to the northeastern and north central United States and adjacent parts of Canada. So-called European cultivars are pure species, but virtually all so-called American cultivars are also infused with genes of the European species.

The only goal of those amateur gooseberry breeders of eighteenth- and nineteenth-century England was a gooseberry of gargantuan proportions; breeders since have been interested in imbuing the gooseberry with more useful characteristics.

Take those thorns, for instance. Thorns of American gooseberries are bothersome; thorns of European cultivars are daunting! Only a few European cultivars, such as 'Souvenir de Billard', 'Belle de Meaux', and 'Edouard Lefort', are spineless. Breeding of spineless, or nearly spineless, gooseberries has been successful, though fruit quality of these cultivars does not compare with that of the best thorny cultivars.

In the 1920s, plant breeders in South Dakota hybridized European gooseberries with native American species in an attempt to develop plants that could tolerate the rigorous climate of the upper Midwest. Numerous cultivars emerged, such as 'Sunset', 'Kabu', 'Kataga', 'Kapoza', and 'Kopa', all or most of which may be lost today.

All gooseberries are relatively cold-hardy but gooseberries have been bred cold-hardy enough to push limits of their cultivation even to within the Arctic Circle. Among the most cold-hardy (not necessarily to within the Arctic Circle, though) cultivars are 'Hinnonmaki Yellow', 'Houghton', 'Downing', 'Silvia', 'Poorman', and Russian cultivars such as 'Smena', 'Pjatiletka', and 'Rekord'.

The hypothetically ideal gooseberry would also be resistant to disease and bear prolific crops of delicious fruits. Large fruits, of course.

Cultivation

SITE AND SOIL   Like other members of the *Ribes* genus, the gooseberry is a plant of cool climates. It tolerates extremely cold winters (USDA Hardiness Zone 3) and performs best where summers are cool and moist. The gooseberry can be accommodated throughout much of the northern half of the United States if plants are mulched heavily to keep their roots cool, given some shade where summers are torrid (the Midwest, for example), and irrigated where natural rainfall is deficient (the western mountain states, for example). Summer weather seems to have some influence on fruit quality.

Choose a site for a gooseberry bush with care, for a plant can crop for thirty years or more. Then again, it is no large investment in money to just plant a new bush when the need arises; nor a large investment in time, for bushes begin production only a year after planting. Gooseberry plants are less finicky about soil acidity than are most other small fruits, and tolerate a wide range of soils, except those that are waterlogged. Where summers are hot, bushes will grow better and produce better fruit in heavier soils, which retain more moisture and stay cooler. Gooseberries thrive even in partial shade. In northern latitudes, where the sun takes a broad enough sweep around the horizon in summer, gooseberries can be trained against north-facing walls.

A gooseberry bush has a moderate need for nitrogen—excessive amounts promote disease, especially mildew—and a high requirement for potassium. Between four and eight ounces per square yard of actual nitrogen (between forty and eighty ounces if a fertilizer is ten percent nitrogen, for example) strikes a good balance between growth and disease tolerance. The symptom of potassium deficiency is scorching of leaf margins. Deficiency can be avoided with an annual dressing of half an ounce of potassium (supplied by half a pound of wood ash or seaweed meal, for example) per square yard. Gooseberry plants also have a fairly high requirement for magnesium, so if the soil is very acidic and needs lime, use dolomitic limestone, which supplies magnesium as well as calcium, and neutralizes acidity.

Plant gooseberry bushes between four and six feet apart, the precise distance depending on the vigor of the cultivar and the richness of the soil. Do not plant the bushes close to one another as a continuous hedge, or the arching, spiny branches of adjacent bushes will interlace, making pruning and picking a nightmare. Gooseberry plants become impatient to grow with the very first breath of spring, so set bare-root plants in the ground either in the fall (with plenty of mulch) or as early as possible in spring.

PRUNING   A gooseberry bush usually is grown on a permanent, short "leg," which is a trunk about six inches long, or as a "stool," where the bush is continually renewed with new shoots arising at or near ground level. The advantage of the leg is that it holds branches up off the ground, keeping fruits clean and facilitating weeding, picking, and spraying. The downside of the leg is the risk of losing the whole plant should that single leg be damaged. Stooled plants live longer and bear more (though smaller) fruit.

No matter how the bushes are trained, all wood on which fruit is directly borne should be less than four years old. Also, the shape of the bush should be consistent with the planting site: for instance, where summers are hot and dry, the many long branches of a stooled plant provide leaf cover to protect fruits from sunscald.

Plants grown on legs spend their first couple of years in training, the objective being a framework of permanent branches growing from the leg and giving the mature bush the shape of an empty ice cream cone on a stick. To develop this form, during the winter after a plant's first growing season, cut off all but three or four vigorous branches that point up and out off the leg. Head the three or four retained branches back to six inches in order to stiffen them and induce further branching. The following winter, similarly head those secondary branches that grew the previous season—there should be half a dozen to a dozen of these, and they will be the plant's permanent leaders.

In subsequent years, head back leaders each winter by about a quarter of the amount they grew the previous season, more where growth was weak and less where growth was vigorous. Fruiting and age will slow leaders' growth, so that eventually all that they will need will be a light tipping or nothing at all. Each of these leaders will be more or less permanent, though after a number of years, a leader might need to be replaced with a new, vigorous, young shoot. Always keep on the lookout for, and snap off (less chance of regrowth than with cutting off), any branches that form along or below the six-inch leg.

Lateral branches grow off the leaders and are pruned according to how neat you like your plants and how large you like your gooseberries. More severe pruning gives a neater bush with fewer, yet larger, fruits. At the very least, each winter cut away any laterals that are crossing, drooping, or otherwise misplaced. Very vigorous laterals can be left to fruit, if they are not overcrowding the bush, or cut away entirely.

If your goal is neat plants and large gooseberries, shorten all laterals in early July to about five inches. Then, during the winter, cut these shortened laterals further back, to about two inches. Tightly pruning a plant has the benefit of cutting away some mildew (discussed further on) and keeping the bush open to air, sun, and, if needed, sprays. Fruits of such plants also are easier to pick.

A gooseberry grown as a "standard," or small tree, is trained and pruned in the same way as a bush grown on a leg, except that a standard has a longer leg. Grow upright cultivars on their own legs; graft gangly cultivars onto special rootstocks.

Single-stemmed cordons carry the theme of tight pruning to its extreme. The single stem is treated the same as one leader of a tightly pruned bush growing on a leg. The advantage of cordons is that they permit many different cultivars to be grown in a limited area, as only about fifteen inches is needed between plants.

Turning now to the stooled gooseberry bush: In the winter following a plant's first season in the ground, cut away all but six of the previous season's shoots. Do the same after the second winter, so that the bush then has six one-year-old and six two-year-old shoots. Repeat after the third winter, and the bush will then have six each of one-, two-, and three-year-old shoots.

In the fourth and subsequent winters, pruning consists of cutting away all four-year-old shoots and all but six of the shoots that grew up from ground level the previous season. What is left, then, is a bush with half a dozen each of one-, two-, and three-year-old shoots. Except for lanky shoots, which need shortening, all pruning of stooled plants is done by cutting away branches at ground level.

PESTS American gooseberry mildew can be a serious disease, ruining the fruit overnight if weather conditions are conducive. The disease makes its presence first known as powdery white patches on new leaves, and these leaves subsequently become stunted and deformed. Fruits are similarly affected.

In many areas, plants that are disease-free when set in the ground will never get the disease (avoidance depends on the proximity of diseased wild and cultivated plants). Sappy growth and potassium deficiency encourage mildew, so correct fertilization, especially with nitrogen and potassium, helps limit the disease. Mildew also thrives in high humidity, which is decreased by pruning and by choosing a planting site with free air circulation. Disease spores overwinter in infected shoot tips, so pruning three inches off the ends of the branches (and removing the prunings!) in late summer also helps control the disease.

Much of the effort in gooseberry breeding in the twentieth and twenty-first centuries has been directed, successfully, toward the development of mildew-resistant cultivars. Generally, European cultivars are susceptible to the disease, so resistant genes have been garnered from wild species, such as *Ribes divaricatum*, and from American cultivars that are only mildly affected. German breeders, beginning in the 1950s, developed resistant cultivars such as 'Resistenta', 'Perle von Müncheberg', 'Robustenta', 'Remarka', 'Rokula', 'Risulfa', 'Ristula', and 'Reverta'. More recent disease-resistant introductions from Germany include 'Rixanta', 'Reflamba', and 'Rolanda'. From Russia came cultivars not only resistant to mildew, but also cold-hardy and large fruited: 'Russkij', 'Malahit', and 'Plodorodnyi' are examples. Some cold-hardy cultivars grown in Scandinavia, including 'Hankkijan Herkku', 'Hankkijas Delikatess', 'Hinnonmaki Yellow', and 'Pellervo', also are mildew-resistant. Resistance in one region has not always spelled out resistance everywhere, due possibly to the existence of differing strains of the mildew-causing fungus.

American gooseberry mildew can be controlled with spraying. The traditional spray is lime sulfur or elemental sulfur, applied just as the buds break in spring, just before bloom, then again two or three weeks after bloom. Both forms of sulfur should be used with caution, for they can damage plants when the temperature rises above eighty-five degrees Fahrenheit, and some cultivars are "sulfur shy." The latter cultivars include 'Leveller', 'Langley Gage', 'Bedford Yellow', 'Careless', and (ironically) 'Early Sulfur'.

Sprays made from washing soda or baking soda also have been used to control mildew. (Note that washing soda is sodium carbonate, different from baking soda, which is sodium bicarbonate.) Use one pound of washing soda and a quarter to half a pound of soft soap per five gallons of water. Alternatively, use baking soda at a rate of one tablespoon per gallon, also adding one tablespoon per gallon of soybean oil. Repeated applications of either "soda" spray are necessary, because rain readily washes them off plants.

Leaf spot is another common gooseberry disease, and it begins work on gooseberry plants in early summer, first spotting the leaves, then causing them to yellow and drop. (Actually, there are two leaf spot diseases, similar in effect and similarly controlled. The more common one also is called anthracnose; the less common one, *Septoria* leaf spot.) If defoliation occurs late enough in the growing season, plants bear well in spite of the disease. Because the disease overwinters in old leaves on the ground, one control, practical on a small scale, is to rake up the old leaves in the fall or to smother them under a mulch (which the bushes enjoy anyway). Copper sprays, such as Bordeaux mixture, beginning just after the leaves appear, are very effective in controlling leaf spots, and lime sulfur sprays less so.

As with mildew, cultivars vary in their susceptibility to leaf spot disease, though response is erratic. Most of the German and Russian cultivars previously mentioned as being resistant to mildew are also resistant to leaf spots.

Though most gooseberries are little affected by white pine blister rust, this disease has had a profound effect on gooseberry growing in America. White pine blister rust arrived in America around the turn of the twentieth century, at a time when gooseberries were becoming popular in gardens, but also at a time when white pine was an important lumber tree. Because the disease cannot survive unless both host plants—white pine and a susceptible species of

Ribes—are present, federal restrictions on growing *Ribes* were imposed in an effort to protect the pines. Many Civilian Conservation Corps crews were kept busy in the 1930s ripping wild *Ribes* out of forests and cultivated gooseberries and currants from backyard gardens.

Though there is a spectrum in susceptibility to white pine blister rust among gooseberry cultivars, the plants generally are resistant to the disease. *Ribes* eradication was not as effective as hoped for in controlling the spread of rust to pines because many wild, susceptible *Ribes* exist, spores can travel hundreds of miles from pines to *Ribes*, and up to a mile from susceptible *Ribes* back to the pines. The federal government got out of the *Ribes* eradication business in 1966, lifting the ban. State bans now run the gamut, with some states permitting the planting of any *Ribes*, others banning all *Ribes*, and still others limiting planting to certain species, township by township within the state. (I grow about three dozen cultivars of gooseberries, all of which would be illegal if my property were fifty feet north of its present location!) Unfortunately, the gooseberry has not as yet recovered from its fall into obscurity as a result of the federal ban.

Two insect pests that require attention if they find their way into a garden are the imported currantworm (currant sawfly) and the gooseberry fruitworm. I say "if" because I grew gooseberries for almost two decades without seeing either of these pests, or even mildew. All three pests eventually found their way into my garden as I expanded my collection of plants through exchanges with fellow enthusiasts.

First, let's do in the currantworms. They begin their work just as the leaves have expanded, chewing at and quickly stripping a plant of its leaves. One insecticide spray applied when damage is first noted—damage usually occurs down in the center of the bush—controls the currantworm. Thorough control at this time lessens the damage and may obviate the need for another spray when the second brood of currantworm comes around, just as fruit is ripening. (A third brood also may show up in some areas.)

The gooseberry fruitworm damages berries rather than leaves. Just before fruits ripen, these caterpillars burrow into the berries, eat the pulp, then exit and spin a silken web joining fruits and sometimes leaves together. Damaged fruits change prematurely to their ripe color. One insecticide spray, applied as soon as the webbing is evident, controls the gooseberry fruitworm. A spray containing the bacterium *Bacillus thurengiensis* (B.t. for short, and sold under such names as Thuricide and Dipel) is effective and lethal only to caterpillars.

Gooseberry

Propagation

The ease with which gooseberries propagate from cuttings depends on the cultivar. Generally, American cultivars are easier to root than are European cultivars. Take hardwood cuttings in early fall, even before all the leaves have dropped. The presence of a few leaves actually enhances rooting. Make the cuttings about a foot long, but do not include tip growth.

For bushes to be grown on legs, remove all except the top four or five buds to lessen the chance of shoots growing from near or below the ground on the resultant bushes. Alternatively, since the presence of buds enhances rooting, it may be advisable to leave all the buds on a cutting. Later, when the plants are lifted from the soil for transplanting, pull (do not cut) off all the bottom shoots and buds.

Tip layering is a surer method of propagation than cuttings, though a single bush furnishes far fewer layers than cuttings. Mound layering yields more plants, but sacrifices the crop that season. To mound layer, cut back the whole bush to the ground in winter, then in early summer pile up sawdust or light soil amongst the new shoots. In both types of layering, roots form where the stems are in the soil, and the small plants will be ready for transplanting either by the first fall or, with difficult-to-root cultivars, the following fall.

Clove currant (*Ribes odoratum*, and the closely related *R. aureum*, both uncommon fruits of this book), Worcesterberry (*R. divaricatum*, with edible fruit, incidentally), and *R. sanguineum* provide suitable rootstocks and trunks for tree-form gooseberries. Be warned that clones of clove currant vary in their compatibility with gooseberry scions and in the vigor, and hence yield, they confer to those scions. In a Hungarian study, clones named 'Fritsche' and 'Brecht' were best for rootstocks.

Would-be gooseberry breeders interested in developing new cultivars (strive for few spines, disease-resistance, large fruit, and good flavor, for starters) must sow seed. Seeds require moist stratification, just above freezing, for three to four months before germination can occur. Keep an eye on the seeds toward the end of this stratification period, for they commonly begin to germinate even in the cold.

Harvest and Use

Average yield from one gooseberry bush is between eight and ten pounds of fruit, though individual plants have been known to produce even twenty-five pounds of fruit. Single-stemmed cordons yield a pound or two per plant. To pick the fruit, first slide a thick leather glove onto your hand and with this hand hold a branch up or steady; then gingerly pick the berries from the branch with your other, ungloved hand. Keep harvested berries in the shade for they scald quickly in the sun. Many people top and tail gooseberries before eating them, though I see no reason for this as the short stem and little piece of dried calyx on opposite ends of the fruit are hardly noticeable when the fruits are eaten.

Gooseberry is one of the few fruits more usually picked underripe than fully ripe. Today, as for hundreds of years, the fruit is used in various stages of unripeness for cooking. "The berries of the ordinary Gooseberrie, while they are small, greene, and hard, are much used to bee boyled or scalded to make sauce both for fish and flesh of divers sorts, . . . as also before they bee neere ripe, to bake into tarts, or otherwise, after manie fashions, as the cunning of the Cooke, or the pleasure of his commanders will appoint" (John Parkinson, *Paradisi in Sole*, 1629). A classic gooseberry concoction is a fool, made by folding cream into the stewed fruit.

Perhaps it is all this cookery and fussing that has overshadowed the gustatory pleasure of eating the fully ripened fruit right from the plant. Once one gains an appreciation of dessert gooseberries, the goal becomes to seek perfection in flavor. Be forewarned though: just as grapes have their vintage years, gooseberry flavor also varies from season to season. And how do you know the prime moment to pick a green-ripe cultivar? Tickle the fruit—ripe ones drop off into your hand. Opinions differ on whether ripe gooseberries taste best early in the morning, still cool from the night air, or at noon after being slightly warmed by the sun, but no matter when you pick it, the fruit is at its best plucked straight from the bush into your mouth. As Edward Bunyard stated, in *The Anatomy of Dessert* in 1934, "the Gooseberry is of course the fruit par excellence for ambulant consumption."

Cultivars

Those gooseberry shows spurred the creation of numerous cultivars, some of which are listed here. Some of the cultivars listed may be hard or impossible to find, for the present, at least. They may resurface, however, if truly worthy, so are worth listing.

'Abundance': hybrid of *Ribes missouriense* with 'Oregon Champion', originating in 1932; bush has few thorns and bears prolifically; fruits ripen early, are borne in clusters, and are small, with tough, purplish red skins.

'Achilles': European type; fruit is very large with a green skin having a few hairs; very susceptible to mildew; excellent flavor.

'Bedford Yellow': European type originating in 1922; prolific bearer of large, hairy, golden-yellow fruits that are streaked with red and ripen midseason; good flavor.

'Black Velvet': a hybrid of gooseberry and Worcesterberry; lanky growth; fruit is small and dark red, with very good, rich flavor.

'Broom Girl': European type originating before 1852; productive bush; fruits ripen very early and are large and greenish yellow; good flavor.

'Canada 0-273': hybrid gooseberry; somewhat mildew-resistant; almost thornless; coppery red berries are medium to large in size with average flavor.

'Captivator': a hybrid introduced in 1952; plant is resistant to mildew and leaf spots and is almost spineless; fruits ripen midseason and are small with a purplish pink skin; very good flavor.

'Careless': European type originating before 1860; sprawling bush; fruit ripens midseason and is large with a thin, smooth, pale green skin; average flavor; 'Jubilee' is a virus-free selection of 'Careless'.

'Carrie': hybrid of 'Houghton' and, probably, 'Whinham's Industry', originating in 1893; plant is large and spreading with willowy branches having few spines; fruit is small and deep maroon and ripens midseason; good flavor.

'Catherine' ('Catherina'): upright bush is moderately resistant to mildew; heavy yields; very early-ripening; fruit is variable in size with a thin skin and very good flavor cooked or fresh.

'Chatatuqua': a European type originating in 1876 from seed sown in New York; very similar to cultivars 'Columbus', 'Portage', and 'Triumph'; bush is upright, compact, productive, and makes few suckers; more resistant to mildew than are most European gooseberries; the large, silvery green fruits ripen midseason; good flavor.

'Clark': a Canadian hybrid that is resistant to mildew but susceptible to leaf spots; fruits ripen midseason and are very large, with coppery red skins; excellent flavor.

'Como': a hybrid of 'Pearl' and 'Columbus', originating in Minnesota in 1922; bush is disease-resistant; fruits are large, green, and resistant to sunscald; average flavor.

'Crown Bob': an old English cultivar; bush is large and spreading, somewhat resistant to mildew but susceptible to leaf spot diseases; fruits ripen midseason and are large with claret red skins; good flavor.

'Downing': American type that was a seedling of 'Houghton', originating about 1860; the most widely grown cultivar in North America in the early twentieth century; plant is resistant to mildew; fruits are small and green, with a blush of red, ripening midseason; fruits must be picked as soon as they ripen, or else they rot; very good flavor.

'Early Sulfur' ('Yellow Rough', 'Golden Ball', 'Yellow Lion'): European type originating before 1825; bush is vigorous and spreading; very mildew susceptible;

fruit ripens early in the season and is medium-sized with a pale, golden yellow skin having long hairs; hangs well after ripe; excellent flavor.

'Fredonia': American type; defoliates early due to leaf spot diseases; not productive; fruit ripens late season and is medium-sized, with a pinkish red skin; good flavor.

'Glendale': a hybrid of *Ribes missouriense* with European gooseberry, originating in 1905; bush is rank growing; wine-red, medium-sized berries; resistant to mildew and leaf spots; best gooseberry for regions with hot summers but also grows well in cooler areas; good flavor.

'Glenton Green': fruits ripen early and are green, hairy, and medium-sized; excellent flavor.

'Golda': European type from Holland; fruit is yellow and large; excellent flavor.

'Golden Drop': European type originating in 1847; bush is upright and compact, susceptible to mildew; fruits ripen early to midseason and are small and dull greenish yellow; excellent flavor.

'Goudbal': European type from Holland; fruit is yellow and large; excellent flavor.

'Greenfinch': hybrid of 'Resistenta' and 'Whinham's Industry' followed by a further cross with 'Careless'; erect, compact plant yields well and is resistant to mildew, moderately resistant to leaf spots; medium-sized fruit is green with good flavor.

'Green Hansa': European type originating in 1802; bush is large and upright; mildew-resistant; fruit is large with a thin, white- to yellow-green skin; good flavor.

'Hinnonmaki Yellow' ('Hinnonmaen Keltainen'): hybrid from Finland; somewhat resistant to mildew; fruit ripens midseason with a smooth, yellow skin; fruit size is variable; excellent flavor, apricot-y and sweet.

'Hoenings Früheste': European type originating about 1900; not very productive; fruit ripens early, and is medium-sized with a thin, bright yellow skin; hangs well after ripe; very good flavor.

'Houghton': a hybrid originating from seed planted by Abel Houghton of Lynn, Massachusetts, in 1833; this cold-hardy bush is spreading and bears prolifically; fruits are very small, dark red, and ripen late season; good flavor.

'Howard's Lancer': European type originating in 1831; fruit ripens midseason, is medium-sized with a thin, green skin tinged yellow; very good flavor.

'Invicta': a hybrid of 'Resistenta' and 'Whinham's Industry' followed by a further cross with 'Keepsake'; vigorous bush with many large spines; very productive; mildew-resistant; the large, pale green, slightly prickly fruits ripen midseason; early-ripening; average flavor.

'Jahn's Prairie': a *Ribes oxyacanthoides* seedling; mostly upright plant with few, small spines; yields well; resistant to mildew, leaf spots, and rust; productive; fruit large and pinkish red with good flavor.

'Jumbo': upright American type; bush has stout branches and thorns; few fruits on one-year-old wood; berry is very large with a pale green skin having a slight tinge of yellow and prominent veins; long ripening season; very good flavor.

'Keepsake' ('Terry's Early Kent'): European type originating in 1841; bush is especially susceptible to mildew; also susceptible to late frost because of early bloom; fruit ripens midseason, is medium to large, with a slightly hairy, whitish green skin; good flavor.

'Lancashire Lad': European type originating in 1824; plant is relatively resistant to mildew; fruit ripens midseason and is medium-large and red; average flavor.

'Langley Gage': European type originating in 1896; plant is upright and resistant to mildew; fruit is silvery white and small, ripening midseason; excellent sweet and aromatic flavor.

'Lepaa Red' ('Lepaan Punainen'): a hybrid from Finland; bush is large and sprawling, with long, willowy branches; very resistant to mildew and leaf spot diseases; fruits are red and small; average flavor.

'Leveller': European type originating in 1851; spreading bush; very susceptible to mildew; fruit ripens midseason and is very large, with a yellowish green, almost hairless skin; excellent flavor.

'May Duke': European type originating in 1900; bush is upright; fruits ripen early and are among the first to size up (for picking green); fruit is medium large with a smooth, deep red skin; fair flavor.

'Mountain': a wild hybrid, probably of *Ribes cynosbati* and a European gooseberry, discovered by the Shakers in New York about 1846; bush is tall and sprawling with good fall color; not very productive; fruits have smooth, dull, brownish purple skins and green pulp; juicy and sweet.

'Oregon Champion': hybrid from cross of 'Crown Bob' with 'Houghton', originating about 1860; bush is small and dense, reputedly resistant to mildew (though not in my experience) and leaf spot diseases; very productive; ripe fruit is medium-sized and green; very good flavor some years, poor others.

'Pax': plant is vigorous, spreading, and spineless; yields well; resistant to mildew, moderately resistant to leaf spots; ripe fruit is large, dark red, and slightly bristly with a good flavor.

'Perry': hybrid of *Ribes missouriense* and 'Oregon Champion', originating in 1932; bush has few thorns and bears prolifically; fruits are borne in clusters and are small, with tough, purplish red skins; needs a pollinator.

'Pixwell': hybrid of *Ribes missouriense* with 'Oregon Champion', originating in 1932; bush has few thorns and bears prolifically; disease-resistant; fruits are borne in clusters and are small, with tough, purplish red skins; poor flavor.

'Poorman': seedling of 'Houghton' originating in about 1888; bush is productive and has few spines; very vigorous; resistant to mildew and leaf spots; fruit ripens midseason and is wine red, pear-shaped, and medium-sized; excellent flavor.

'Red Champagne': bush is tall and upright; productive; fruit is medium-sized, with slightly hairy, red skin; very good flavor.

'Red Jacket' (the original, originating in Britain before 1881): bush is cold-hardy, productive, and mildew-resistant; very thorny; fruit is large, with sweet, good flavor.

'Red Jacket' ('Josselyn'): a hybrid that is different from the European cultivar also named 'Red Jacket'; seedling of 'Houghton' crossed with 'Red Warrington', introduced in 1890; fruit is medium-sized, red, and ripens early season; resistant to mildew and leaf spots; very good flavor.

'Red Warrington': European type; ripens late; fruit is medium-sized with a dull red skin having reddish hairs; excellent flavor.

'Remarka': hybrid from Germany; resistant to mildew and leaf spots; fruits ripen early, and are large and red.

'Resistenta': hybrid from Germany; mildew-resistant; fruits ripen late, and are medium-sized and green.

'Reverta': hybrid from Germany; mildew-resistant, moderately erect plant, not productive; fruits are large and ripen early.

'Risulfa': hybrid from Germany; mildew-resistant; moderately erect plant; large fruit.

'Robustenta': hybrid from Germany; upright bush; mildew-resistant and very productive; fruits ripen late, and are medium-sized and green with very good flavor.

'Rokula': hybrid from Germany; mildew-resistant and moderately erect; fruits ripen early and are large.

'Silvia': hybrid from Canada; bush is spreading; fruit is medium-sized with a silvery green skin having a red blush; soft berry with tough skin; excellent flavor.

'Spinefree': a hybrid introduced in 1932; branches are completely spineless; bush is resistant to mildew and leaf spots; fruits are small and have a thick, red skin; average flavor.

'Welcome': a seedling of 'Poorman', originating in 1957; sprawling bush has long, willowy branches with few spines; fruits ripen early and are medium-sized and wine red; average flavor.

'Whinham's Industry': European type originating in 1835; upright growth habit; fruit ripens midseason and is medium-large with a brownish red, hairy skin; very good flavor.

'Whitesmith': European type originating in about 1824; bush is upright and allegedly resistant to mildew and leaf spots (not in my garden); fruits ripen midseason and are medium-large with thin, pale green skins tinged with yellow; excellent, vinous flavor.

Maypop

A Passionflower for the North

BOTANICAL NAME
Passiflora incarnata

PLANT TYPE
Herbaceous perennial vine

POLLINATION
Cross-pollination is necessary

RIPENING SEASON
Late summer into fall

Maypop is a species of passionflower whose aromatic fruits and breathtaking flowers may well inspire horticultural passion. But neither the maypop nor any of its *Passiflora* relatives will start anyone's blood boiling in erotic passion.

The "passion" in passionflowers and passion fruits refers to a religious passion, the passion of Christ. When Christian missionaries arrived in the Americas, they saw in wild passionflowers the symbolism of the crucifixion.

The plant became a seventeenth-century teaching tool for spreading the gospel. Passionflower "had clearly been designed by the Great Creator that it might, in due time, assist in the conversion of the heathen among which it grows," wrote a Christian scholar of the seventeenth century. The ten so-called petals (botanically, five petals and five petal-like sepals) were taken to represent the ten apostles present at the crucifixion. The threadlike rays of the corona were taken for symbols of the crown of thorns. The five stamens and three styles referred, respectively, to the five wounds of Christ and the three nails used in the crucifixion. Even the rest of the plant figures in, with the three-lobed leaves representing the Trinity and the tendrils representing the scourges.

Passionflowers are heavenly enough to bring on a religious devotion to growing the plants, and many species and cultivars are grown solely for their flowers. Passion fruits that are most commonly eaten are the purple passion fruit (*Passiflora edulis*) and its variant, the yellow passion fruit (*P. edulis* var. *flavicarpa*). Almost everyone is familiar with the flavor of passion fruit, perhaps unknowingly, from tasting Hawaiian punch. Purple and yellow passionflowers can be grown only in tropical regions or, farther north, in a greenhouse.

The maypop is a cold-hardy species of *Passiflora* whose flowers are indistinguishable to nonbotanists from those of the tropical species and whose fruit can be equally delicious. Why "can be"? Though a few enthusiasts might be growing maypops for fruit in their gardens—as did the Native Americans, according to Captain John Smith of the Jamestown settlement—maypop fruits are usually eaten from wild plants. As with many wild plants, individuals within the population vary. Though some maypop plants bear fruits that are unpleasant to taste or even smell, the best plants bear fruits that are aromatic, with a deliciously semisweet, melting taste similar to that of apricot.

Maypop fruits are yellow to yellow-green, oval, and one and a half to two inches across. Like a tropical passion fruit, the inside of a maypop fruit is filled with air and with seeds surrounded by a tasty gelatinous pulp. To quote seventeenth-century writer William Strachey, the maypop has "the bigness of a green apple, and hath manie azurine or blew kernels, like as a pomegranat, a good summer cooling fruit." If you squeeze the fruit it pops, just like a balloon; hence the name maypop. Alternatively, our common name for the fruit might be traced back to its Algonquin name, *maracock*, or to its Powhatan name, *mahcawq*.

Description of the Plant

The maypop, in common with tropical species of passionflower, is a climbing vine that clings to available support by tendrils growing from each leaf axil. Unlike the tropical species, the maypop is an herbaceous perennial that dies to the ground each winter. It is a native North American found growing from Virginia west to Nebraska and south to Florida, with occasional wild plants showing up as far north as Pennsylvania. Maypops start growth each season later than do most other temperate zone perennials. In northern areas, the first shoots do not poke through the ground until early summer. But when the shoots finally do show, stand back! Each shoot will divide into two to five branches and each branch might grow twenty feet in a season.

The maypop is every bit as vigorous underground as it is above ground. The roots, both the fine and thickened storage roots, push outward many feet

Maypop

from a plant's origin. And each season new shoots can arise from either type of root. Vigor is quickly evident even in seedling plants. Only eleven weeks after a seed has germinated, its taproot has probed a yard deep into the soil and shoot initials (the makings of a new shoot) are already present on roots. Maypop can become weedy, especially in warmer climates (USDA Hardiness Zones 8, 9, and 10). Before the widespread use of chemical weedkillers, maypop was a common weed clambering over roadside fences and along railroad beds from Virginia down to Florida and west to Oklahoma.

Each season, blossoms first appear when the shoots are about four feet long, which is about a month after the shoots have emerged. Since shoots do not appear until June in northern areas, blossoming may be forestalled until July. Once the flowers appear, they continue almost nonstop through the summer until fall, with one to a few new flowers opening each day.

The flowers, which are produced singly in the axils of the leaves, are one and a half to two inches across, with lavender or white petals and a purple or pink crown that has a darker halo toward its base. Pure white forms also exist. The open blossoms exude a delicious lemon musk aroma. Each flower lasts for one day only, opening in late morning then closing by nightfall.

Maypop flowers need cross-pollination in order to set fruit, yet even when pollinated not all flowers will fruit. The flowers are andromonoecious, which means that on every plant some flowers are perfect and some are functionally male. Functional males have female parts but are functionally male either because their stigmas are held upwards out of the way of insect visitors or because their female parts are atrophied. A maypop plant adjusts the types of flowers it has through the season to growing conditions. As more fruits set or light becomes limiting, fewer perfect flowers are produced. An increasing percentage of flowers are male as the season progresses, unless no fruits have set already. A fruit follows each successfully fertilized flower by two to three months.

In spite of the good flavor of the best maypops, no one has attempted to breed them to improve taste or productivity. 'Alba', the only cultivar of *Passiflora incarnata*, was selected for its white, extremely fragrant flowers.

Species of *Passiflora* hybridize freely, affording greater opportunities for improving maypop fruits or flowers than if selections had to be made by drawing solely from the maypop gene pool. Most hybrids have been developed for their flowers. The first was produced in 1825, when maypop was crossed with *P. caerulea* to produce a showy hybrid designated *P. ×colvillii*, hardy to Washington, D.C. It was not until about 150 years later that the second maypop hybrid was developed. This cultivar, named 'Incense', was the result of a cross between a maypop and the Crato passionflower (*P. cincinnata*). 'Incense' is semi-evergreen and has survived outdoors as far north as Connecticut. The vines produce fewer suckers than do species maypops and put out about twelve feet of growth each season. The flowers are deep blue, five inches across, and showier than those of the maypop.

'Incense' is pollen-sterile, so cannot be used to pollinate either itself or any other passionflowers. When pollinated by another clone, 'Incense' fruits are oblong, about two inches long, and drop when ripe. They are chartreuse, with a roselike fragrance and a sweet, sprightly flavor. Unfortunately, 'Incense' is very susceptible to a virus disease.

Both the tropical yellow and the purple passion fruits are already cultivated for their fruits, so are obvious candidates for hybridizing with the maypop to improve maypop fruits (or increase the cold-hardiness of the tropical species). Such hybrids have been produced, and plants grown from colchicine-treated seeds from some of the crosses have borne fruits of various colors that were juicier than those of either species. Such plants also were hardier than *Passiflora edulis*. 'Byron Beauty', one such hybrid that does not bear fruit, does have stunning blossoms that are over three inches across and are purplish blue, and is hardy as far north as Georgia.

Another possible candidate for hybridization with the maypop is *Passiflora lutea*. This species bears greenish yellow flowers, just under an inch across, in August, and the fruits are a third of an inch across and deep purple. *P. lutea* might be most useful in breeding because it is slightly more cold-hardy than the maypop and because its vines grow to a more manageable five to ten feet in a season.

THE FUTURE OF MAYPOPS? It's bright. Maypop fruits compare gustatorily with other passion fruits and the plants already are hardy quite far north. It's time to venture out into the wild to find the best plants and fruits. These plants could then be hybridized to create even better ones. Maypop's flower structure lends itself to controlled pollinations and the breeding cycle from sowing to fruit is short. Besides the usual quest for bigger, juicier, tastier, and more abundant fruit, a self-fertile plant would be nice. The last goal may be within reach because there exist self-fertile plants among the closely related *P. edulis*, which also is usually self-infertile.

Cultivation

Archeological digs in the southeastern U.S. offer evidence that humans were popping maypops into their mouths as far back as 5000 years ago, and increasing concentrations of plant remains over time suggest that the plants came to be cultivated or at least semi-cultivated. In the seventeenth century, William Strachey noted that "in every field where the Indians plant their corn be Cart-loades of them [maypops]."

Because of the genetic variation in maypop, any maypop grower would do well to plant a number of seedlings or different clones, especially in northern areas. Though maypops can be weedy in certain areas, getting plants started is sometimes tricky. Plants seem not to transplant well until they are old enough for their roots to have thickened and provide energy reserves. Even then, the roots are sensitive to desiccation. To assure successful establishment, grow young plants in containers for a few weeks. After transplanting to open ground, coddle the plants for another few weeks with water and fertilizer, as needed.

Maypops will grow in full sun or partial shade, but shade will reduce a plant's fruiting potential. At the northern end of its cultivated range (Zone 5, with about 150 frost-free days), choose a sheltered area, such as the south wall of a house or garage, which will be spared the full brunt of winter cold. A thick mulch, once again more important as one progresses north, offers additional protection to the dormant roots through the winter.

Established plants can spread above and below ground like weeds, especially in warmer climates. New shoots from underground roots have even been known to pop up on the far side of a sidewalk! The plant must be kept under control. The best way is to pull unwanted suckers with a quick jerk when they are three inches high. Maypops planted in beds surrounded by lawn are put in their place every time the lawn is mowed.

Training maypops on some sort of a support brings the flowers to eye level and facilitates harvesting the fruits. The curling tendrils grab on to a variety of supports, such as chain-link fencing, pieces of string stretched vertically, and wooden latticework. Allow between thirty and forty square feet of support per plant.

Maypops also can be trained to ramble over early-flowering shrubs, a method of training sometimes employed with clematis. The maypop, being a "late riser" in the spring, does not interfere with the spring show of the shrub. Then, from midsummer on, the shrub once again bursts into show—of maypop flowers this time. There is little chance of a maypop's choking most shrubs because by the time a maypop vine builds up steam, it is late summer and shrubs are winding down anyway. My maypop cohabits with a lilac in a small bed, with the surrounding lawn and its attendant lawnmower keeping maypop's spread in check.

Hand-pollination ensures best-quality fruits and, where natural pollinators (mostly carpenter bees) are not abundant or not sufficiently active, maximum yield per vine. Hand-pollination typically results in about fifty percent fruit set as compared with, sometimes, just a few percent when relying on natural pollinators. One way that hand-pollination increases set is by getting pollen to the stigmas of functionally male flowers with viable ovaries. Fruits are larger and juicier when the flowers are hand-pollinated.

Probably the best time to hand-pollinate is as soon as the flowers open in late morning. Remember, each flower is open for one day only and you need two different clones for cross-pollination. Because maypops spread underground, shoots growing out of the ground far apart could be mistaken for different plants when they might very well be one plant sharing a common root system (i.e. be the same clone).

As is true of corn, the pollen parent can influence the quality of the fruit. *Passiflora cincinnata* is one of the best pollinators for many species, yielding fruits that are often larger than those resulting from other pollinators.

No insect or disease pest worth mentioning affects maypop. Nectaries at the bases of the flowers attract ants, which have been shown to keep many insect pests at bay. Not larger animals, though: fruits of wild plants are frequently eaten even before they are ripe, in all likelihood by frugivorous mammals. Watch out.

Propagation

Maypops are easily propagated by seeds, shoot cuttings, and root cuttings. In common with other weedy plants, maypop seeds germinate under a wide range of conditions. For best germination, however, soak the seeds in water for twenty-four hours, then keep them in the dark after sowing until they germinate. Germination is quickest between eighty-five and ninety-five degrees Fahrenheit. Depth of planting is probably not important; maypop seeds have been known to germinate from almost half a foot deep within the soil. At temperatures of about ninety degrees Fahrenheit, seedlings planted an inch deep emerge in eight to nine days.

Tip cuttings and root cuttings need no special treatment. You can probably expect one hundred percent success from root cuttings two to three inches long that are planted just below the soil surface and kept between seventy and ninety degrees Fahrenheit.

Harvest and Use

A single plant might produce a dozen or so fruits through the season. Fruits, like flowers, are produced sequentially so plan to harvest frequently.

For best flavor, let a fruit mature, then drop to the ground before gathering it up. Handle it gently, for the skin is thin, possibly wrinkled. Wait, don't eat it yet! Instead, store it for a week or two in a cool, not overly dry, room to allow full flavor to develop. Then go ahead and eat it. Scoop out the pulp with a spoon, suck off the juice, then spit out the seeds. Or, scoop out the inside and eat it seeds and all, like a pomegranate.

The juice is easily extracted through a wire mesh. While a single fruit from a wild plant might yield only a quarter teaspoon of juice, each fruit from a cultivated, hand-pollinated plant might yield a couple of teaspoons.

Use of maypops need not end with the fruit. If you are willing to sacrifice some blossoms for beauty rather than for fruit, pick and float them indoors in a bowl of water. They should keep for several days if refrigerated each night.

Dried maypop vines are a mild, sedative drug. Native Americans used maypop vines to treat insomnia, and maypop is the ingredient of *tinctoriae passiflorae*, used for similar purposes. Several hundred thousand pounds of the plant are collected from the wild in America each year and shipped to Europe for processing into naturopathic medications. Smoking the tops reputedly induces a short, marijuana-like high.

Passionflower plants also find use as fodder on butterfly farms. Passionflower coevolved with zebra butterflies, whose larvae must feed on the plants. Some vines have evolved ruses to keep themselves from being chewed to death by the caterpillars: leaf shapes that disguise the plant, nectar-secreting glands to attract wasp and ant parasites of the butterfly larvae, and plant poisons.

Still other plants keep their leaves free of zebra butterfly eggs by growing egg mimics, broadcasting the message "this leaf is already full" to female butterflies fluttering about looking for places to lay their eggs. Passionflower plants evidently have some symbolism for butterflies as well as for humans.

Che

Chewy Dollops of Maroon Sweetness

BOTANICAL NAME
Cudrania tricuspidata

PLANT TYPE
Shrubby tree

POLLINATION
Unresolved; may not need pollination or may need
pollination from a male plant or the occasional male flowers
borne on female plants

RIPENING SEASON
Early to late fall

I wish that I had become better acquainted with che soon after our introduction. That first meeting was in 1979 at the home of renowned fruit breeder Dr. George M. Darrow, then ninety years old and retired from the U.S. Department of Agriculture. His dooryard che, unfortunately, had no fruits ripe for sampling. In the years that followed, I occasionally happened upon the plant again, on the printed page, where I found lukewarm descriptions of the fruit's flavor—"mild watermelon," for example. Almost twenty years after our introduction I decided, finally, to plant a che and evaluate the fruit for myself; a year later I tasted my first fruit. It was very good, and nothing like a "mild watermelon."

Were you to meld together all the characteristics of a fresh fig and a mulberry—both, incidentally, relatives of che—you would end up with something very close to a che fruit. To wit, che is an inch to an inch and a half across, round, and dull maroon with a rich red interior, a slightly chewy texture, and a few edible seeds. The flavor is most definitely fresh fig plus mulberry, although neither as rich as the fig nor as sweet as the mulberry.

Che, like mulberry and fig, is an aggregate fruit, the individual fruitlets more or less coalesced together. Actually the surface texture most closely resembles that of yet another relative, the osage orange (*Maclura pomifera*), whose four-inch-diameter, green-skinned orbs are completely inedible. Deliberate hybrids—with the euphonious and likewise hybrid name *Macludrania hybrida*—have been created between osage orange and che, the first in France in the latter half of the nineteenth century. Specific goals (a baseball-sized che fruit?) in creating such hybrids were not specified, but the original ones, using che as the male parent, most closely resembled their father in plant form. Hybrids derived from those French plants that were planted at the U.S. National Arboretum in 1960 were said to look like thornless osage orange trees. Their hybrid origin has since been questioned and, anyway, little mention has ever been made of their fruits.

Che fruit itself is likewise rarely mentioned in writings from China, where che is native. What che plants have been valued for by the Chinese are their leaves, as feed for silkworms. Although silk produced from such feed was said to produce lute strings whose sound was of particular clarity, che leaves usually were used only to supplement the usual feed of mulberry leaves, perhaps because thorny stems make picking che leaves more difficult.

It was in the latter half of the nineteenth century that che first made its way to the western world. Che has been grown in France since 1862 and in England since 1872 with no mention made of its fruit production or use. Che first arrived in America in 1909 among a few thousand other cuttings and live plants sent over from China by E. H. "Chinese" Wilson. By 1912, a tree, presumably from that introduction, at P. J. Berckman's Nursery in Augusta, Georgia, was twelve feet high and bearing a bushel and a half of fruit. The following year another shipment arrived from China, sixteen rooted plants sent over by U.S. Department of Agriculture plant explorer Frank N. Meyer for testing in drier regions as a hedge plant for gardens and a living fence for farms, and, in less arid regions, for bank stabilization.

Today, che remains relatively unknown as a fruit or a plant, despite the plant's early and reliable fruit production, its resistance to pests, and its probable (judging from the closely related osage orange) wide adaptability. It even lacks a more widespread common name, having been also called cudrang, mandarin melon berry, or silkworm thorn in English, and in China: *tcho sang* (wild mulberry), *tsa*, *tse-tsang* (thorny mulberry), *cha-shu*, *poh-hsi*, *shih*, *nu-che*, or, of course, che. Yet, given the quality and productivity of even unselected seedlings, che is surely an uncommon fruit worthy of attention, especially if some of that attention were directed to selecting or breeding plants that were thornless, bore well without pollination, and ripened earlier.

Che

Description of the Plant

Che has been variously described as a large shrub or a small tree usually growing to a height of about twenty feet, occasionally soaring to sixty feet. Some suckers are produced at the base of the plant and, with age, the tree develops a spreading, flattened top and a bark that ripples with deep furrows. A sprawling, almost vinelike habit has been ascribed to some of the shrubbier sorts. But morphological changes beyond the capacity to flower accompany many kinds of plants as they transition from juvenility to maturity. As examples, citrus lose their thorns and English ivy changes from a vine to woody shrub. Vining behavior and increased thorniness could merely be descriptions of juvenile che plants.

Che's thorns are a thorny issue. Although the plant is typically thorny, branches higher up in older plants frequently are thornless. Dr. Darrow propagated two plants from thornless branches, and, while one of the two remained thornless, the other eventually grew some thorny new shoots. The question arises, then, whether we have here a chimera, a plant made up of two kinds of genetically dissimilar cells; new plants propagated from one set of cells may be thornless, from the other set they would be thorny. Or perhaps it is merely a question of juvenility versus maturity, with juvenile stems, as in citrus, being the thorny ones. Plants propagated from vigorous stems near the base of a seedling tree will be juvenile and thorny while those propagated from stems higher in the tree will be mature and thornless. Cytological studies and observation of seedling plants as they mature would resolve this issue.

The shape—or, I should say, "shapes"—of che's leaves are similarly variable. In 1877, a Dr. Hance, who had assigned to che the botanical name *Cudrania triloba*, wrote that it was "an unfortunate specific name, as the foliage seems highly variable." The plant's specific name was later changed to *tricuspidata*, although the leaves are sometimes entire or indistinctly lobed, and sometimes three-lobed. Increased lobing of leaves, incidentally, is another characteristic of plant juvenility that might be lost with maturity, another change exemplified in maturing English ivy plants. Che leaves remain healthy and green throughout the growing season, then drop without fanfare.

Che flowers are as hard to pin down morphologically as are the leaves. Mostly, plants are either male or female (dioecious), but male trees frequently bear some fruits (which only follow female flowers) and female trees frequently yield good crops without male pollinators. Like some varieties of persimmon, male or female che plants might bear a few flowers, perhaps whole branches, of flowers of the opposite sex. This explanation seems more likely than parthenocarpy because ripened fruits typically have a few seeds in them, which indicates that pollination did occur—unless che is among the few plants capable of producing seeds solely from mother plant tissue, without pollination (i.e. it is apomictic). The waters are further muddied by a possible link between thorniness and gender; Dr. Darrow observed that, on one plant at least, thorny stems acted like males: they were fruitless but their presence made female stems fecund. Gender questions could be answered with close observation and controlled pollinations.

Che flowers are reliably borne, either singly or in small groups, in the axils of leaves on growing shoots. Fruiting is equally reliable because the flowers open late, about the time that mulberry fruits are just starting to ripen. Plant a che tree and it will not have you waiting long for those first flowers or fruits; my plant yielded both the year after planting.

Cultivation

The etymological meaning of "che" is "stony ground," indicating its natural habitat. Just because it tolerates drought and poor soil does not mean that it would thrive best and yield the most luscious fruits on such ground. I give my che the same good soil—moderately fertile, humus-rich, and having good tilth —enjoyed by my other fruits. Good drainage is important.

Che is said to prefer a warm soil. This requirement probably has basis, especially if a warm soil infers also a warm site, because in northern regions such a site would be needed to ripen the relatively late-ripening fruits. The plant itself is hardy to USDA Zone 5 and also grows well into subtropical regions, although individual clones might better tolerate either end of this climate spectrum.

Che is a plant that performs well with little or no regular pruning. Prune the young plant so that each of its main branches has plenty of room, then, when the plant matures, do nothing more than cut off any dead, broken, or out-of-place branches that you might find. Drastic shortening of any branches that become decrepit will stimulate vigorous, new shoot growth on which flowers and fruits are borne.

You may want to prune the tree more heavily if you are feeling regal, in order to extract a reddish yellow dye from the pruned stems. The Chinese used so-called "che yellow" for coloring imperial garments.

Propagation

Che is easy to propagate by any one of a number of methods. Seeds germinate readily if sown immediately upon removal from the fruit, or, if stored, after a period of cool, moist stratification. Be forewarned, though: seedlings may take up to a decade to bear fruit.

As previously mentioned, cloned plants bear at a very young age. Take semi-hardwood cuttings after midsummer, ideally treating them with rooting hormone and then putting them under mist. Root cuttings are another method of clonal propagation.

Che takes well to all sorts of grafting techniques. Grafting seedlings onto mature plants is one way to shorten the juvenility period and so more quickly evaluate their fruits. Create more robust and treelike specimens by grafting che on osage orange rootstock.

Harvest and Use

Although che fruits ripen late in the growing season, be patient with their harvest because they are tasteless until softened and dead ripe. Do not expect the fruits to drop into your hands at that time; each che has to be plucked individually (which makes a case for parthenocarpy). Likewise, do not expect to pick the fruits all at once, because they have a long ripening season, a month or more. Here in New York, my che fruits begin ripening about the middle of October, about the same time as has been reported from the mountains of Virginia and a couple of weeks after times reported from near Washington, D.C. Reports of first ripening in November in California and August in Georgia possibly highlight different ripening seasons for different clones.

Che bears heavily, with Darrow reporting hundreds of pounds on a mature female tree. What fruits you cannot eat at one sitting will keep for several days under refrigeration. Still more than you can eat? Blend the fruits, then strain out the seeds, for a delicious nectar.

Black Currant
Fruit from Fragrant Bushes

BOTANICAL NAME
Ribes nigrum, Ribes odoratum, and *Ribes americanum*

PLANT TYPE
Deciduous shrub

POLLINATION
Most European black currants are self-fertile; clove currants set
more fruit with cross-pollination; no pollination information is
available on the American black currant

RIPENING SEASON
Mid- to late summer

What all these black currants—one European and two American species—have in common are small, black berries and robust flavor. The European black currant and the American black currant have the same strong resinous flavor, attenuated and offset by sweetness in the best dessert cultivars. The flavor of clove currant, the other black currant of North America, is markedly different: still intense and somewhat resinous, but more fruity.

The European black currant is a relative Johnny-come-lately among cultivated fruits. Written references first turn up in the sixteenth century, but early on it was frowned upon for eating though lauded for medicinal use. In the 1633 edition of Gerard's *Herball*, the fruit is described as being "of a stinking and somewhat loathing savour, the leaves also are not without the stinking smell." The fruit is extremely high in vitamin C and, even before vitamins were known, the fruits were called "squinancy berries" for their soothing effect on sore throats.

Admittedly, the robust flavor of the European black currant will not please everyone's palate, but I take exception with jibes against the smell of the leaves (the branches, too). I have yet to meet anyone who has smelled the fragrance and not considered it a virtue of the plant. The aroma makes pruning or even brushing against the European black currant a pleasurable experience.

The native American black currants—the American black currant and the clove currant—were eaten by the Native Americans and then received a passing flurry of attention from plant breeders in the early twentieth century. The clove currant became fairly well known primarily as an ornamental shrub planted near homes, where the delicious fragrance of its flowers could waft indoors. But today both American species are virtually unknown for either their gustatory or ornamental qualities.

Black currants—any currants, for that matter—are unrelated to the small raisins sold as dried or black currants. These raisins are called "currants" because they are made from 'Black Corinth' grapes, a small grape that has been dried and shipped for centuries from the Greek port of that name. The *Ribes* fruits that are the subject of this chapter—and that resemble the raisins in appearance only—came to be called *bastardes corinthes* and *corans*, either of which is just a step away from "currants." To further complicate the nomenclature, in Italy the small *Ribes* fruits have been called *uvetta*, meaning "small grape."

Description of the Plants

European black currant (*Ribes nigrum*) is a cold-climate plant (USDA Hardiness Zone 4 or colder) native to northern Europe and north and central Asia. Stiff, upright branches, growing five or six feet high, and a raiment of large, forest-green leaves make this plant an attractive specimen shrub or hedge. The leaves appear early, making European black currant one of the first plants to welcome in each new growing season.

European black currants flower mostly on one-year-old wood and to a lesser degree on tiny spurs on wood that is two years old or older. The flowers open early in the season but are relatively inconspicuous. Fruits are borne in strigs, or chains, much like those of the red currant, except shorter. The fruit averages about three-eighths of an inch in diameter.

European black currant cultivars do not exhibit a wide range of attributes in either plant or fruit, in part because so many of them have similar ancestry, being derived in most part from the cultivars 'Baldwin' and/or 'Boskoop Giant'. Breeders have more recently been looking to other *Ribes* species for new "blood." For example, *R. bracteosum* has been used to develop hybrids

European black currant

with longer strigs of berries ('Jet' is one such cultivar). *Ribes nigrum* var. *sibiricum* and *R. dikuscha* infuse their offspring (such as 'Primorskij Cempion') with high levels of vitamin C, disease-resistance, and cold-hardiness, even to the point of pushing black currant cultivation to within the Arctic Circle. *Ribes ussuriense* has been used to develop plants resistant to white pine blister rust (the cultivar 'Consort', for example).

Like a taste for artichokes and dark beer, a taste for European black currants must be acquired. Enthusiasts of this fruit will enjoy almost any cultivar out of hand; for fresh eating, novices should perhaps begin with cultivars whose fruits are mild and sweet, such as 'Blackdown', 'Brodtorp', 'Goliath', and 'Silvergieters Zwarte'.

The clove currant (*Ribes odoratum*), sometimes known as the Missouri, buffalo, or golden currant, or pruterberry, is a five- or six-foot-high bush with small, bluish green leaves that turn purplish red in autumn. Floppy branches and numerous suckers popping out of the ground—even two feet from the mother plant—give the plant an unkempt air that fits well in informal settings. The bush is native to the rigorous climate of the American Midwest as far north as Minnesota and as far south as Texas, so is very tolerant of cold (to Zone 4, at least), heat, and drought.

Flowers appear early in the season on wood that is one year old and older. The flowers are red-tinged yellow trumpets, two or three inches long and dangling in profusion from the branches like charms on a bracelet. But this show is eclipsed as the flowers play on another of the senses. I have gotten lightheaded as the flowers' heavy fragrance of clove and vanilla drifted even thirty feet across the garden to me.

Clove currant fruits are borne singly or in small clusters, which is well enough since the fruits are large (for currants) and ripen unevenly from midto late summer. The fruit ranges in size from one-quarter to three-quarters of an inch across. Usually the fruits are smooth, shiny, and blue-black, though some plants bear yellow or orange fruits.

Ribes aureum is a closely related plant, sometimes considered the same species as clove currant. They are almost identical except that *R. aureum* is more diminutive in all aspects and has less fragrant flowers. The clove currant has sometimes been sold as *R. aureum*.

The most widely grown clove currant was found in the wild by R. W. Crandall of Newton, Kansas, in 1888. 'Crandall', as it was called, had the virtue of bearing tasty fruits up to three-quarters of an inch in diameter. Unfortunately, many plants sold as 'Crandall' were seedlings, so plants were variable, leading some writers to report the flavor as good, others to report "tough skin, unpleasant flavor" (fruits on my plants have tender skins and a very nice flavor). In 1867, 'Deseret' was selected. This clove currant cultivar was productive and bore large, dark fruits, "pleasant and slightly tart." 'Jelly', another cultivar, had a tough skin, but an "agreeable" taste, and 'Vermillion', 'Golden Prolific', and 'Amber' evidently were cultivars with brightly colored fruits.

The American black currant (*Ribes americanum*) is native from New Mexico to Virginia, and north into Canada (USDA Hardiness Zone 2). Growth habit is similar to that of the clove currant but the inconspicuous flowers and black fruits are borne on drooping chains like those of the European black currant. Fruits, leaves, and shoots of the American black currant have the same pungent aroma as the European black currant. The leaves turn crimson and yellow in autumn.

Very few selections were made of *Ribes americanum*, and these probably do not exist today. 'American Black', selected in 1832, reputedly was better than the European black currants of its day. 'Sweet Fruited Missouri', with large fruit and a sweet musky flavor, was supposed to be an improvement over 'American Black', though another writer of yore reported that 'Sweet Fruited Missouri' was small and of poor quality.

There was some formal breeding of both the clove currant and the American black currant, mostly in the early twentieth century. Thousands of seedlings were planted by university plant breeders in the Dakotas in an effort to find fruit plants that were drought-tolerant, cold-hardy, and productive. 'Tonah', 'Atta', 'Mato', and 'Wanka' were some of the cultivars that were derived from wild black currants. At the New York Agricultural Experiment Station, the clove currant was hybridized with red and white currants.

More recently, Russian plant breeders have shown interest in breeding the clove currants. Cultivar names, such as 'Uzbekistanskaya Large', 'Beefsteak', and 'Uzbekistanskaya Sweet' hopefully are indicative of fruit quality.

Cultivation

The European black currant is native to and thrives in regions where summers are moist and not too hot. In America, plants grow best in the Northeast and the Pacific Northwest; in cool regions with dry summers, supplemental summer watering is needed. With mulch and partial shade, my plants thrived even in the sultry climate of Washington, D.C., which shows how limits of cultivation can be extended with site selection and modification. In very cold areas, avoid less cold-hardy cultivars such as 'Mendip Cross', 'Cotswold Cross',

'Baldwin', 'Silvergieters Zwarte', and 'Wellington XXX'. Plant instead 'Black-smith', 'Consort', 'Brodtorp', or one of the cold-hardy Russian cultivars (if you can get them) such as 'Altaj', 'Minaj Smyrev', 'Primorskij Cempion', 'Zoja', and 'Lenskaja'. 'Tifon' and 'Troll' are two cultivars suitable for regions (such as coastal California and parts of France) having cool summer areas but little of the winter cold needed to fulfill most other black currants' dormancy requirement.

The American species are both heat- and drought-tolerant, so can be grown wherever there is sufficient winter cold to give the plants an annual rest.

To grow any of the black currants as individual bushes, space them six feet apart. These currants also can be planted as hedges, in which case set them only three feet apart in a row. Because currants flower early, the planting site should not be prone to late frost. Full sun or partial shade is suitable.

Currants leaf out very early in the spring, so set out bare-root plants either in the fall (with a thick mulch to prevent heaving during the winter) or very early in the spring. Set plants slightly deeper than the depth at which they grew in the nursery so that plenty of buds and, hence, new shoots will arise at and below ground level. Unless plants are going to be given first-class growing conditions their first season, cut all branches right after planting to within an inch of the ground. This seemingly brutal treatment will prevent cropping the first season, inducing the plant to put its energy into growing strong shoots and roots instead.

Clove currants need cross-pollination; most European black currants (not *Ribes nigrum* var. *sibiricum*, though) do not, and no information is available on the American black currant. In a few cultivars of European black currant, the flower structure prevents ready self-pollination, so in these cases yields are increased if another cultivar is planted nearby.

All currants thrive best in soils that are rich in organic matter and slightly acidic. Take care of a plant's nitrogen needs with a yearly mulch of strawy manure or some fertilizer that supplies about four ounces of nitrogen per square yard (two-thirds of a pound of soybean meal, for example). Potassium, another important nutrient for black currants, is needed at the rate of half an ounce per square yard (supplied by, for example, half a pound of wood ash). Black currant bushes also enjoy a thick organic mulch to keep the soil cool and dispense with the need for hoeing, which can damage the shallow roots.

For bountiful crops, currant bushes need pruning every year. The aim of pruning the European black currant is to leave a good supply of one-year-old wood going into each growing season—this is the wood on which most fruit is borne—and to stimulate new shoot growth for fruit the following season. Each winter, cut away between two and five of the oldest branches at ground level; also shorten tall, old branches to vigorous, young side shoots. Prune clove currants less severely because this species bears many fruits on spurs on two-year-old wood. On both species, also remove branches that are broken, trailing on the ground, or diseased. (Little is known of the pruning requirements of the American black currant.)

As an alternative to winter pruning of the European black currant, prune during the growing season, at harvest time. Cut off branches with fruits attached, then make yourself comfortable in the shade and pluck off the fruits.

If production declines as a plant ages, rejuvenate the whole bush by lopping all the branches off at ground level in winter. This will sacrifice the crop for the following season, but after that, there should once again be a good load of fruit on vigorous one-year-old wood.

In some parts of the world, one of the most serious pests of black currant is the gall mite, a small creature that is especially hard to control because it spends much of its life living inside currant buds. Infected buds appear swollen, a condition called "big bud," and do not bear fruit. Worse, the mites spread reversion disease, and the resulting weakened plants, having deformed leaves and sometimes deformed fruits, should be destroyed to prevent further spread of the disease.

The mite becomes amenable to control early in the season as it hitchhikes from plant to plant on other insects and with the help of wind. Three pesticide sprays—the first just before the flower buds open, the next a fortnight later, and the final spray one more fortnight later—will do in the mite. Lime sulfur (a two-percent solution) is a traditional remedy, but should be used with caution on sulfur-shy cultivars, such as 'Boskoop Giant', 'Cotswold Cross', 'Goliath', 'Laxton's Giant', 'Seabrook's Black' (though this cultivar is resistant to the mite), and 'Wellington XXX'. Handpicking swollen buds also gets rid of the mites. Gall mite has not yet established itself in North America, and American species of black currants are resistant to it as are some of the Russian cultivars.

In some years, developing fruits drop from the bushes about three weeks after flowering, a bad habit known as "running off." The cause is not known, although poor pollination, low (but not freezing) temperatures right after flowering, even drought following harvest the previous year have been implicated. As with so many of the other potential problems in growing black currants, resistance to running off is found in genes from Scandinavian and other far northern kinds of black currants (e.g., *Ribes dikuscha*).

Of the cultivated *Ribes*, European black currants are most culpable for the spread of white pine blister rust, a disease that is devastating to white pines but not very debilitating to the currant. The disease needs both plants—white pine and a susceptible *Ribes* species—to complete its life cycle, so black currants are banned wherever white pines have been considered more important. Check with your state agriculture department for restrictions. The Canadian cultivars 'Consort', 'Crusader', and 'Coronet' and Russian cultivars such as 'Bzura', 'Ner', 'Warta', 'Koksa', 'Primorskij Cempion', 'Zoja', and 'Odra' are among those resistant to the rust. Due to varying strains of the rust fungus, a cultivar might not be considered universally resistant or susceptible: for example, 'Mendip Cross', usually considered highly susceptible, was not so in one study in Oregon.

Both the clove currant and the American black currant show a range in susceptibility to white pine blister rust from plant to plant. Many individuals show no signs of the disease. American black currants are generally less susceptible than are European black currants, and clove currants even less so.

Species of black currants also can be afflicted with the mildew and leaf spotting diseases that attack gooseberries and red currants. American species of black currant are generally immune, but the afflictions may also be inconsequential on European black currants if cultivar and site are suitable and if the bushes are pruned for good air circulation.

Propagation

Hardwood cuttings of any of the black currants root readily so long as each eight- to twelve-inch-long piece is set deep enough in the ground so that only the topmost bud is exposed. Set cuttings in early spring, autumn, or even at the end of the summer while leaves are still attached. In the latter case, make sure plants have moist soil and some shade.

Softwood cuttings also root easily. Three-inch tip cuttings, given shade and a clear plastic tent or mist, grow roots in three or four weeks.

Drooping branches of black currants often layer themselves. If only one or two new plants are wanted, this layering habit can be encouraged by bending a low branch to the ground and covering it with some soil and a stone.

Currant seeds germinate readily if sown immediately after being extracted from the fruit, or if the fresh fruits are just mashed onto the soil. Alternating cool and warm temperatures help, unless the seeds were slightly scarified or chilled before sowing. Once dried, the seeds need three to four months of cool, moist stratification before germination can occur. Seedlings begin to bear in their second or third year, depending on how much growth they make their first season.

Harvest and Use

Pick black currants while they are dry and still firm. An average yield for a European black currant bush is ten pounds of fruit. Yields of the American species usually are less, and variable, though breeders in Russia have reported yields of ten pounds, even thirty pounds, per bush on selected clones of clove currant. Pick European and American black currants by the strig, unless the fruit is to be used immediately. Clove currant fruits ripen unevenly, so are picked individually. Make sure the berries are fully ripe.

If you like their flavors, all these currants are delicious out of hand ('Kirovchanka' is—pun intended—my currant favorite), but even people who do not like the fresh flavor enjoy black currant juice, jams, tarts, and wines. In contrast to the European black currant, the American black currant loses much of its strong flavor when cooked.

Fruits of the European black currant, the most genteel of the black currant species, have been used many ways over the centuries. In the Bordeaux region of France, it is made into a liqueur called *cassis*. 'Ribena' is a black currant juice first promoted in Britain during the Second World War. Besides using the fruit fresh, I make black currant juice by covering the berries with water in a saucepan, bringing the water to a boil, then turning off the heat and letting the mixture sit a few minutes. The dark blue, strained juice is delicious and undoubtedly also good for "squinancy."

Cultivars: European black currant (Ribes nigrum)

'Amos Black': hybrid of 'Goliath' and 'Baldwin' raised in 1927; bush compact; production variable; frost-tolerant blooms; fruit is very late season; medium-large, and of good flavor.

'Baldwin': an old English cultivar, possibly the same as 'Black Naples', which was described in Britain in 1826; susceptible to leaf spot, rust, mildew, and late frosts; fruit ripens evenly and is late season; tough skin; large, sweet, firm fruit that is very high in vitamin C.

'Ben Alder': vigorous bush is resistant to powdery mildew and leaf spot, susceptible to rust; high-yielding; ripening fruit sometimes splits the thin skin; late-flowering and -ripening; particularly high in vitamin C; fruits are small, good for juice.

'Ben Connan': compact plant yields well; resistant to mildew and leaf spot; fruit is early-ripening, large, and hangs well.

'Ben Lomond': resistant to winter cold and late spring frosts; resistant to leaf spot; somewhat resistant to mildew; susceptible to rust; particularly high in vitamin C; very large fruit has tough skin and good flavor.

'Ben Sarek': originated in Scotland in 1985; bush is compact, high-yielding, resistant to mildew and leaf spot, and somewhat resistant to rust; good flavor; fruit is large and soft, drops readily.

'Blackdown': hybrid of 'Baldwin' and 'Brodtorp', raised in 1960; bush is large and spreading, resistant to mildew; berries are large, firm, and among the best for fresh eating; low in vitamin C; easy to pick.

'Blacksmith': raised in 1916; bush is large, spreading, and prolific; fruits are mid-season, of variable size, and have good flavor.

'Boskoop Giant': originated in Holland before 1885; mildew-resistant; bush is large; ripening fruits sometimes split the thin skin; fruits are early season, large, sweetish, and easy to pick; early-ripening.

'Brodtorp': A Scandinavian cultivar; bush is large and spreading; resistant to mildew and somewhat resistant to leaf spot; though the plant is cold-hardy, the flowers open early so are susceptible to frost; the fruit is early season and small, but with a mild, sweet flavor that is among the best for fresh eating; early-ripening.

'Consort': bush is resistant to rust; frost-tolerant blooms; fruit is of average quality.

'Coronet': bush is resistant to rust and slightly susceptible to mildew; fruit is large and of average quality; needs another cultivar nearby for good yields.

'Cotswold Cross': hybrid of 'Baldwin' and 'Victoria' raised in 1920; bush is moderately vigorous but tends to alternate-year bearing; fruits are midseason, medium in size, slightly sweet, and hang well on bush once ripe.

'Crusader': bush is resistant to rust and slightly susceptible to mildew; fruit is large and of average quality; needs another cultivar nearby for good yields.

'Goliath': bush is large, erect, and somewhat resistant to leaf spot; fruits are large and ripen midseason; a mild, sweet flavor makes 'Goliath' one of the best dessert-quality black currants.

'Golubka': hardy and disease-resistant; particularly high in vitamin C.

'Jet': raised in 1973; fruits are very late season, small to medium in size, acidic flavor, and low in vitamin C; the fruits hang down on long strigs.

'Kirovchanka': I have little information on this Russian variety except my own observations that the bush seems relatively compact and the berries taste great!

'Kristin': vigorous, erect bush resistant to mildew and leaf spot, but susceptible to rust; early-flowering; productive; fruits are large with good fresh flavor, hang well in fairly long strigs.

'Laxton's Giant': raised in 1946; bush is very large and prolific; fruits are very large, early season and have very good flavor.

'Malvern Cross': hybrid of 'Baldwin' and 'Victoria' raised in 1920; tends to bear biennially; fruits are late season, medium large, and hang well on the bush after ripening.

'Mendip Cross': hybrid of 'Baldwin' and 'Boskoop' raised in 1920; highly susceptible to rust; bush is vigorous and bears prolifically; fruits are early season, large, and sweet, but ripen unevenly and slow to pick.

'Minaj Smyrev': robust bush that is very cold-resistant; rust-resistant; large berries are borne heavily and early in the season.

'Narve Viking': vigorous erect plant that is late-flowering and ripens fruits late; resistant to mildew and leaf spot, but susceptible to rust; moderately acidic fruits are medium-sized with a tough skin, fairly good fresh, and very good for juice.

'Ojebyn': a Scandinavian cultivar selected from among wild plants; hardy to winter cold and late-flowering.

'Seabrook's Black' ('French Black'): raised in 1913; bush bears prolifically; fruits are midseason, medium in size, and tart with a strong flavor.

'Silvergieters Zwarte': a seedling of 'Boskoop Giant' raised in 1926; plant is tall and moderately susceptible to rust; fruits are borne midseason, are easy to pick, and are among the best for fresh eating.

'Titania': Scandinavian cultivar; very vigorous, the branches often breaking from snow or under its load of fruit; rust- and mildew-resistant; high yield, in midseason, of large berries with mild, average flavor.

'Wellington XXX': hybrid of 'Boskoop' and 'Baldwin' raised in 1913; highly susceptible to rust; bush is vigorous and spreading, bears prolific crops; especially early bloom; fruits are midseason, large, and sweet, but sometimes split and ripen unevenly; high in vitamin C; slow to pick.

'Willoughby': bush is prolific and resistant to rust; fruits are large but have a poor flavor when raw.

Nanking Cherry

Cherries on a Bush

BOTANICAL NAME
Prunus tomentosa

PLANT TYPE
Deciduous bush

POLLINATION
Requires cross-pollination

RIPENING SEASON
Early summer

Just as the last of spring's strawberries are ripening in my garden, I turn my attention to the Nanking cherry bushes. Or, I should say, the cherry bushes grab my attention as their fruits, ripened to a brilliant red, visually jump out from amongst the soft, green leaves. The ripe fruits are about half an inch across, with a meaty texture and a sprightly, true cherry flavor (and a single cherrylike pit).

This description fits fruit of most seedlings of Nanking cherry. But the species is variable. Occasional plants produce fruits even an inch across, and there are plants that bear pink, or almost white, rather than red fruits. Fruits of some plants ripen in late, rather than early, summer. The flavor also varies: some seedlings produce fruit close in flavor to that of cultivated tart cherries; the fruit flavor of other seedlings is more akin to that of cultivated sweet cherries. I have tasted some Nanking cherries that are better than others, but never have I tasted one whose flavor I did not enjoy.

Nanking cherry is cultivated in the cold, semiarid regions of Asia—in fact, it is the most common fruit plant in gardens of the Russian Far East. In Manchuria, the plant has been grown as a hedge, a windbreak, and for its fruit even in drifting sand dunes.

The introduction of Nanking cherry to North America began in 1882, and right away the plant was met with enthusiasm. In just one of his shipments around the beginning of the twentieth century, U.S. Department of Agriculture plant explorer Frank Meyer sent off a box of forty-two thousand seeds from China to the U.S.

Through the beginning of the twentieth century, prominent pomologists spoke highly of the plant's potential. Ulysses P. Hedrick, horticulturalist at the New York State Agricultural Experiment Station, wrote in 1915 that the Nanking cherry was "a promising plant for domestication and of particular merit for small gardens and cold regions." In 1929, Dr. George Slate, also of the New York station, wrote that "characters exist which if combined in one individual will make a worthwhile addition to our list of cultivated plants." The Nanking cherry was one of a handful of fruits highlighted by U.S. Department of Agriculture plant breeder George Darrow (a strawberry, a blackberry, and a blueberry carry his name) in his chapter entitled "Unusual Opportunities in Plant Breeding" in the *Yearbook of Agriculture, 1937*. An issue of the *National Nurseryman* in the 1930s was devoted largely to the Nanking cherry, and the editor summed up current sentiment, saying "there is a future ahead for *Prunus tomentosa*. Just who is going to take the final credit, it is hard to say."

What happened? Today, the Nanking cherry is occasionally planted as an ornamental, more rarely for its fruit. Thus far, the genetic potential of the Nanking cherry has remained untapped. Perhaps the plant's tolerance for inimical climates has caused it to be overlooked where climates are more congenial. Perhaps the plant's relative anonymity results from a lack of identity— aside from Nanking cherry, the plant has been called Manchu cherry, downy cherry, mountain cherry, Mongolian cherry, and Chinese bush cherry.

Description of the Plant

The Nanking cherry is native to central Asia, but has become naturalized from Japan and Korea west across China to Turkestan and the Himalayas. The plant is a spreading shrub or small tree, usually wider than its nine- to fifteen-foot height, and dense with twigs. Hardy is a word aptly applied to the Nanking cherry, for the plant will grow under semiarid conditions, and endure in the same year a snowless winter of minus forty degrees Fahrenheit, then scathing summer heat six months later.

In Nanking cherry, hardiness is married to another quality: beauty. This plant is a visual delight in three out of the four seasons (autumn color is unspectacular). Let us begin in winter, when the bark is no longer hidden

Nanking cherry

beneath the plant's dense, leafy raiment. That bark is lustrous and orange brown and becomes more engaging with age when occasional warty lenticels dot the smooth surface and paper-thin strips of older bark peel away in vertical curls.

Nanking cherry is one of the first "hounds of spring . . . on winter's traces," with flowers festooning bare branches at a time when most other plants still appear lifeless. What a season to watch pretty pink buds unfolding to cheery white petals (in some plants, the petals still tinged with pink)! Flowering is usually profuse as each bud on a one-year-old stem yields two flowers, and stems two and four years old produce flowers in clusters. Couple all these flowers with the plant's closely spaced nodes and you have branches looking like wands of cotton candy.

The plant flowers regularly and the flowers are very frost-tolerant, a desirable trait in such an early bloomer. (I have lost only one part of one crop to frost in a quarter century of growing this plant.) Nanking cherry commonly sets full crops, unlike apricots, which bloom the same season, but whose flowers too often succumb to spring frosts. Though some self-fertile clones have been identified, Nanking cherries generally require cross-pollination.

Early summer brings the fruits, borne in profusion and ornamental in their own right. In 1924, Dr. Darrow wrote that "in the rougher portions of Manchuria [the Nanking cherry] occurs only on hillsides where the bushes usually are three or four feet high and, in early summer, are red from the abundance of fruit."

Summer also clothes the plants in soft, green leaves. One of the plant's common names, downy cherry, derives from the downy hair that covers the plant in summer—the leaves, the new shoots, and, if you look very closely, even the fruits.

A plant with such merit has not been entirely overlooked by breeders, but has not been given its due. Most efforts have been directed toward developing the plant for fruit production in semiarid climates having extremes of heat and cold. To that end, there has been a limited amount of breeding of the Nanking cherry in Russia and in North America.

Early in the twentieth century, Russian fruit breeders introduced a number of good-flavored cultivars with moderately large fruits (about five-eighths of an inch across): 'Amurka', 'Ogonek', 'Pionerka', 'Samaya Rannaya', and 'Kabarovchanka'. More recent cultivars include 'Alisa', 'Chereshnevaya', 'Detskaya', 'Natali', 'Okeanskaya', 'Smuglyanka', and 'Vostochnaya'.

Besides working with the pure species, Russian breeders developed hybrids between the Nanking cherry and apricot, plum, and other species of cherry. Among the most promising hybrids were crosses between Nanking cherry and another very hardy cherry, western sand cherry (*Prunus besseyi*). Cultivars of these hybrids with good flavor range in color from the light red fruits of 'Leto' (with fruits three-quarters of an inch across), to the deep cherry-red fruits of 'Damanka' and 'Karamelka', to the almost black fruits of 'Smuglyanka'.

Most cultivars from North America were developed to withstand the climate of the upper Midwest. From Canada, in 1938, came 'Drilea', so named because of its adaptation to the dry leas. 'Eileen' was another cultivar from Canada, a hybrid with the western sand cherry that proved to be very susceptible to brown rot and a poor yielder. 'Baton Rouge' was a similar hybrid that produced large fruits, but these fruits were of poor quality and yields were low. In 1949, the Minnesota Agricultural Experiment Station introduced 'Orient', notable mostly for being self-fertile, but also for its tasty, fairly large fruits. Also around the middle of the twentieth century, Dr. George Slate introduced two superior clones, 'Slate' and 'Monroe', from the New York Agricultural Experiment Station.

Even if they still exist at all, none of these cultivars is readily available. Fortunately, most seedlings produce tasty fruit, often better than named selections of tart cherry (*Prunus cerasus*). I remember a tall hedge of seedlings bordering a bicycle path along which I once rode almost daily; each July, this hedge presented me with a wall of fruit upon which to feast.

Cultivation

Nanking cherry will grow in almost any place that has sun and well-drained soil. Full sun is best but I have seen plants bear in the shade, even if the plant was dwarfed and the yield not abundant. The degree of drought a plant can tolerate is influenced by the manner in which the plant is propagated. A seedling or a plant grafted onto a seedling rootstock develops a taproot that reaches deep within the soil, but a plant grown from a cutting has no taproot. The limits of cultivation are from the colder portion of USDA Zone 3 to the warmer portion of USDA Zone 6.

Nanking cherry is a vigorous plant. Growth in a single season can amount to several feet for a young plant afforded good growing conditions. Plants in Russia reportedly have two growth flushes each season—one in spring and the next after fruit ripens—but I have not observed this growth habit. Plants can live for fifty years or more, but if left completely on their own, become ungainly after about twenty-five years. Commercial plantations in Russia last about fifteen years.

Annual pruning, though not a necessity, brings out the best in any Nanking cherry in terms of yield and fruit quality. Prune in late winter with the aim of keeping a bush open so that all branches are bathed in sun and quickly dried by breezes. Accomplish these goals by shortening some branches, removing others entirely, and leaving still others untouched. This pruning also will stimulate a steady supply of young, fruitful branches each year. Old plants on commercial plantations in Russia are rejuvenated by being lopped completely down to the ground.

In lieu of the detailed pruning described here, a row of Nanking cherry plants can be sheared as a hedge. Or you can occasionally lop back an old branch or, as I stated earlier, not prune at all.

Plants often thrive for years and produce abundant crops without any attention at all to pest control. The Nanking cherry is reputedly subject to the usual pests of *Prunus* species, most notably plum curculio, peachtree borer, and brown rot, but in all my years of growing this plant in various regions where these pests are prevalent, this damage has been hardly worth noting. Dieback of one or a few branches occasionally happens, perhaps due to brown rot, especially on certain seedlings; just prune off these dead branches.

Propagation

Sowing seeds is a good method for propagating Nanking cherry, because most seedlings bear flavorful fruit and begin bearing by their third season. Seeds germinate readily so long as they are not allowed to dry completely before being sown. Wash the ripe pulp from the seeds (or eat the fruits and spit out the seeds), then slightly air dry the seeds and keep them cool until fall.

In the fall, stratify the seeds either outdoors or in a bag with moist vermiculite in the refrigerator. The seeds are attractive to animals, so outdoor stratification is chancy unless the seeds are protected in a wire mesh enclosure. About ninety-eight percent of the seeds should germinate after three months of cool, moist stratification.

Nanking cherry can be cloned by the standard methods used for other plants. Softwood cuttings root best if taken at about the time the fruit is ripening, treated with a rooting hormone (8000 ppm IBA in talc), and kept under mist. Hardwood cuttings should be prepared from dormant, one-year-old wood cut into eight- to twelve-inch lengths. Plunge the cuttings up to their top buds in a well-drained soil either in fall or early spring. Young branches can also be layered, drooping ones often doing so themselves.

Grafting methods such as budding and chip budding, which cause the least amount of bleeding, are the most suitable. Nanking cherry can be grafted on rootstocks of many different species of *Prunus*. The following have been used with success: *P. cerasifera*, *P. communis*, *P. hortulana*, *P. institia*, *P. munsoniana*, *P. nigra*, *P. persica*, and *P. ussuriensis*. A drought-tolerant, easily transplanted, and vigorous rootstock that has been used in Asia and even in the United States is *P. davidiana*, but this rootstock may not be as cold-hardy as the Nanking cherry itself. Western sand cherry is also compatible, but it is more difficult to bud than are other species and has the bad habit of suckering. One of the most satisfactory rootstocks is Nanking cherry itself, grown from seeds or cuttings. The following species do not make satisfactory graft unions with Nanking cherry: *P. avium*, *P. cerasus* 'Montmorency', *P. mahaleb*, *P. serrulata*, and *P. serotina*.

Harvest and Use

Average yields for plants cultivated for their fruits in Russia are fifteen pounds per bush, with maximum yields of up to fifty pounds per bush.

Ripe Nanking cherry fruits are poor commercial fruits because they are too soft for shipping and have a short shelf life. Baskets or branches laden with the fruits have been sold in markets in Manchuria, however. Nanking cherries would make superb cherry pie if the fruits were not so small as to make pitting tedious. Well, at least you do not have to pull off the stems, which remain attached to the bush at harvest (and leave a small hole in the detached fruits, contributing to their short shelf life).

The best way to enjoy Nanking cherry fruits, in my opinion, is to walk out into the garden and strip off the ripe fruits into your mouth right then and there. Or, perhaps pick a few into a bowl to bring inside for dessert. Then, whether the fruit is soft, perishable, or tedious to pit is of no consequence. For those who insist on bringing Nanking cherries into the kitchen for doctoring up, the fruits make a refreshing summer drink or a beautiful, clear jelly.

Cornelian Cherry

From the Shores of Ancient Greece

BOTANICAL NAME
Cornus mas

PLANT TYPE
Small, deciduous tree

POLLINATION
Partially self-fertile

RIPENING SEASON
Summer to fall, depending on clone

One summer day as I happened upon and ate cornelian cherries from a tree in New York City's Central Park, I had to assure a concerned passerby that I was not experimenting with a possibly poisonous new food. Instead, I was partaking of a fruit that has been enjoyed by humankind for the past seven thousand years! At a site in northern Greece, early Neolithic peoples left traces of their meals of cornelian cherry, along with remains of einkorn wheat, barley, lentils, and peas.

Cornelian cherry was well known to the ancient Greeks and Romans, and references to the plant abound in their literature. Speaking of the Golden Age in *Metamorphoses*, Ovid wrote:

> And Earth, untroubled,
> Unharried by hoe or plowshare, brought forth all
> That men had need for, and those men were happy
> Gathering berries from the mountain sides,
> [Cornel] cherries, or blackcaps, and edible acorns.

The plant was grown in monastery gardens of continental Europe through the Middle Ages and was introduced to Britain in about the sixteenth century. The great herbalist Gerard wrote in 1597 that "there be sundry trees of the cornel in the gardens of such as love rare and dainty plants, whereof I have a tree or two in my garden." By the eighteenth century, the plant was common in English gardens, where it was grown for its fruits that were sometimes called cornel plums. The fruit was familiar enough to be found in European markets even up to the end of the nineteenth century. Cornelian cherries were especially popular in France and Germany, and reputedly were a favorite with children.

Cornelian cherry is native to regions of eastern Europe and western Asia and, in certain parts of these regions, is appreciated for its fruit even today. Baskets of *kızılcık*, as the Turks call the fruit, are found in the markets of Istanbul. The fruit is a backyard tree in Moldova, Ukraine, and Crimea. Though cornelian cherry is not native to the Ukraine, the plant reached that region about nine centuries ago and became established in monastery gardens there. A former monastery garden (now a botanical garden) near Kiev has trees that are 150 to 200 years old and still bear regular crops of fruit. In spite of the long history of use in some regions of the world, and the recognition of superior fruiting types, just about all cornelian cherry plants that are cultivated are seedlings rather than propagated clones.

Over most of Europe and North America today, the cornelian cherry is admired solely as an ornamental plant. Even so, the bright fruits do not go unnoticed as they festoon a tree in summer. The fruits are generally cherrylike: oval, fire-engine red, with a single, elongated stone. Even the flavor is akin to that of a cherry, a tart cherry, somewhat austere when the fruit first colors, but developing sweetness and aroma with full ripeness.

Botanically, cornelian cherry is a species of dogwood, unrelated to grocers' cherries. The word "cornelian" refers to the fruit's similarity in color to cornelian (or carnelian) quartz, which has a waxy luster and a deep red, reddish white, or flesh red (*carnis* is Latin for flesh) color.

Description of the Plant

Cornelian cherry grows to a maximum height of about twenty-five feet, becoming a large shrub or an oval-headed tree usually branching near the ground. In full sun the stems are mostly upright; in shade they spread wide, as if to better embrace what limited light is available. Though the cornelian cherry never grows large, it is a long-lived plant that produces bushels of fruit even in old age. In *Arboretum and Fruticetum*, John Loudon wrote that, while traveling in Germany in 1828, his party

Cornelian cherry

stopped at the gardens of the ancient Chateau of Maskirch; and in a small enclosure close to the chateau, we found a labyrinth, the hedge of which consisted entirely of *Cornus mas*, with standard trees of the same species at regular distances, which were at that time bearing ripe fruit, which we tasted, and found of very good flavour. Later in the same year, we were shown, in the grounds of the Castle of Heidelberg, the famous cornelian cherry trees which were planted there in 1650.

Cornelian cherry has the pattern of leaf attachment and leaf venation characteristic of other members of the dogwood genus: Leaves oppose each other at each node, in contrast to most other trees, on which leaves alternate along the stem; and the major veins of a dogwood leaf trace out almost to the leaf margin, then join together and parallel the margin to the apex of the leaf. Cornelian cherry's leaves are satiny green in summer, often turning mahogany red in the fall. (Fall leaf color is not wholly reliable, however, for in some climates—probably in the warmer parts of the plant's range— and with some clones, the leaves drop to the ground while they are still green.)

In winter, the plant is notable from a distance for its rounded form. Step a bit closer to appreciate the bark, flaking off in muted shades of tan and grey. Get right up to the plant to see the distinctive flower buds, perched atop short stalks at the nodes of branches that grew the previous season and on spurs of older wood.

Flowers appear on leafless branches early in the season, blooming with the "first breath of west wind" (in Italy, at least, according to Pliny, writing in the first century A.D.), which is well before forsythia, around the first day of spring in my relatively northern garden. Individual flowers are tiny, but are born in such profusion that the whole tree appears swathed in a yellow veil, an effect that is all the more striking against a backdrop of a dark wall or evergreen plants. Despite the early bloom, fruit production rarely suffers because the trees have an extended flowering period and the blooms tolerate some frost. The flowers seem not to be completely self-fertile, because cross-pollination sometimes increases fruit production.

The few named cultivars of cornelian cherry available from nurseries reflect the plant's use as an ornamental rather than a comestible. 'Golden Glory' is an upright, columnar plant with especially dark green leaves, and 'Nana' is a cultivar diminutive in stature and leaf size. 'Spring Glow' is a cultivar that blossoms a couple of weeks earlier than the rest of the species generally, and has large fruits and glossy, thick, leathery leaves. Variegated leaves of 'Elegantissima' and 'Variegata' make for brighter-looking plants throughout the summer. Occasional leaves of 'Elegantissima' are completely yellow or tinged pink. 'Variegata' has irregular, creamy white leaf margins.

As mentioned previously, cornelian cherry fruit always has been considered decorative. 'Macrocarpa' is notable for its large fruit and 'Alba' for its white fruit. The fruit of 'Flava' is large and yellow, and a whit sweeter than those of most other cultivars.

If you were to wander into a Macedonian or Bulgarian forest, you would find that not all the wild cornelian cherry trees there would be bearing fruits resembling the common cherry. Within the wild population are plants with barrel-shaped or pear-shaped fruits and some that bear fruits even over an inch long. In color, the spectrum runs from cream colored, to yellow, orange, and fire-engine red, to dark red-violet and almost black. Were you to taste fruits from a number of trees, you would find a similar variation in flavor. The sugar content of the fruit might range from four to twelve percent, and acidity might range from one to four percent. The vitamin C concentration of cornelian cherries commonly averages twice that of oranges.

As it now stands, fruits of run-of-the-mill seedlings are quite good, and some superior wild plants from western Asia that have been earmarked as having better fruit are now available through nurseries elsewhere. If fruit qualities such as large size and a congenial blend of sweetness and acidity could be bred into a single plant, the result would be a highly ornamental plant bearing especially delectable fruit.

Cultivation

Cornelian cherry is easily transplanted and, once established, grows at a moderate rate. Calcareous soils are particularly suitable, though the plant is not particularly choosy about soil, tolerating even those that are somewhat dry. For best fruiting, plants need full sun, or almost so. Cornelian cherry survives in shade, but fruit production suffers.

Grow cornelian cherry as a specimen tree or shrub, or even as a large, sheared hedge. Space specimen plants between twenty and twenty-five feet apart. For a hedge, space plants twelve feet apart.

Cornelian cherry will grow in USDA Hardiness Zones 4 through 8, but languishes somewhat in the southern part of this range. At its extreme northern limit, fruiting is unreliable because the flower buds are hardy only to the colder regions of Zone 5.

Cornelian cherry is a plant from which you can expect annual harvests with little or no attention to pruning or spraying. The plant is rarely subject to insect or disease pests, but do expect some competition for the fruit from birds and squirrels.

Propagation

Cornelian cherries are usually propagated from seed. This is unfortunate because seedlings must be at least six years old—some wait until they are in their teens—before bearing, and the fruit is of variable quality. Seed germination usually is delayed until the second season, though this defect may be overcome by subjecting the seeds to warmth and moisture for four months prior to a one- to four-month period of cool, moist stratification. Nicking the seed coat should suffice in lieu of the four-month warm, moist treatment.

Do not be disappointed if no fruits set when seedlings finally do first flower. Ancient writers referred to the cornelian cherry as the "male cornel" because those first flowers are male flowers. This habit is the source of the specific epithet *mas*, meaning male in Latin. (The "female cornel" of the ancients was *Cornus sanguinea*, a shrubby, precocious species whose fruit is neither prominent nor palatable.) With time, cornelian cherry seedlings produce perfect flowers.

If only cornelian cherry cuttings rooted as easily in reality as in legend. Plutarch wrote that

> Romulus, once, in trial of his strength, cast hither from the Aventine Hill a spear, the shaft of which was made of cornelwood; the head of the spear sank deep into the ground, and no one had the strength to pull it up, though many tried, but the earth, which was fertile, cherished the wooden shaft, and sent up shoots from it, and produced a cornel trunk of good size.
>
> *(Parallel Lives: Romulus)*

Ovid's version (in *Metamorphoses*) is even more fantastic: "No less amazed was Romulus when he saw the spear he planted suddenly put forth leaves." With optimum conditions fifty percent of softwood cuttings might take root.

The best time to take softwood cuttings is in late July or early August. Make each cutting about ten inches long, remove all but the top two leaves, and provide partial shade and high humidity, preferably with mist. Rooting hormones (a modern horticultural aid unavailable to Romulus) greatly facil-itate rooting of hardwood and softwood cornelian cherry cuttings. Use IBA in talc, at concentrations in the range of 0.3 to 0.8 percent. The percentage of cuttings that root varies from clone to clone—softwood cuttings of the culti-var 'Flava' rooted one hundred percent under ideal conditions.

Opinions differ about the ease with which cornelian cherry may be prop-agated by root cuttings and layerage, but no matter, for the easiest way to propagate a superior clone is by any common method of grafting. Use seed-lings as rootstocks and graft low. Because the cornelian cherry branches low to the ground, take care that all the branches on a grafted plant arise from the scion rather than from the rootstock.

Harvest and Use

Cornelian cherries ripen from summer through fall, the time varying from clone to clone. Average yield of fruit from a single tree is between thirty and seventy pounds, although there are trees that bear more than two hundred pounds of fruit.

Fruits from a single tree ripen over an extended period. The simplest way to harvest in quantity is to give the branches a gentle shake periodically once the fruit has colored, then collect fallen fruit from the ground. Ripe fruits left to hang on the tree become more concentrated in flavor and sweetness. Some people prefer to allow harvested fruit to sit at room temperature for a day or more, in which case the flavor becomes sweet, but more sedate.

When the fruit was popular in Britain, it was rarely eaten out of hand, probably because better-tasting clones were unknown there. The fruits were held in high esteem for the delicious tarts they made, and shops commonly sold *rob de cornis*, a thickened, sweet syrup of cornelian cherry fruits. The juice also added pizzazz to cider and perry.

In regions of Europe where cornelian cherry is still a popular comestible, the fruit finds uses other than for just fresh eating. Since ancient times, the unripe fruits have been pickled as a substitute for olives.

> Cornel-berries, which we use instead of olives . . . should be picked while they are still hard and not very ripe; they must not, however be too unripe. They should then be dried for a day in the shade; then vinegar and must boiled down to half or one-third of its original volume should be mixed and poured in, but it will be necessary to add some salt, so that no worms or

other form of animal life can be engendered in them, but the better method of preservation is when two parts of must boiled down to half its original volume are mixed with one part of vinegar.

(Columella, *On Agriculture*, first century A.D.)

Cornelian cherry is a favored ingredient of Turkish *serbert*, a fruit drink sold in stores and from portable containers carried like knapsacks on the backs of street vendors. (Another common English name for cornelian cherry is "sorbet," though cornelian cherry is not the only fruit used for the Turkish *serbert*.) In Ukraine, cornelian cherries are juiced, then bottled commercially into soft drinks. There, the fruits are also made into conserves, fermented into wine, distilled into a liqueur, and dried.

The generic epithet, *Cornus*, is derived from the Latin word for "horn," alluding to the hardness of the wood, a quality I confirm from my experience in grafting this plant. Pliny wrote that cornelian cherry wood was used for making "spokes of wheels, or else for making wedges for splitting wood, and pins or bolts, which have all the hardness of those of iron." The wood's hardness also lent it a more menacing use in the making of spears. From the many gory passages relating this use by ancient writers, the following lines from Virgil's *Aeneid* serve as example:

> Through the yielding air
> The Italian cornel wings, and piercing through
> The gullet 'neath his deep chest passed right on;
> The cavern of the dismal wound gives up
> Its foaming tide . . .

Returning to beneficent uses of cornelian cherry, we find many parts of the cornelian cherry plant applied in folk medicine. The fruit is allegedly beneficial in the treatment of gout, anemia, skin diseases, painful joints, and disrupted metabolism. Fruit, leaves, or bark have been employed for gastrointestinal disorders and tuberculosis. The Russians report that the fruit contains components that leach radioactivity from the body.

But I digress—our primary interest here is with the gustatory pleasure afforded by the fruits, especially the fresh fruits of a superior clone plucked straight from the tree. The fruit is as worth cultivating today as it was three centuries ago when John Parkinson wrote of the cornelian cherry (in *Paradisi in Sole*) that "by reason of the pleasantnesse in them when they are ripe, they are much desired . . . also preferued and eaten, both for rarity and delight."

Cultivars

'Black Plum': very dark red, medium-sized fruits with good fresh flavor somewhat akin to guess-what; seedling tree selected by George Slate of Cornell University.

The following cultivars were selected for their gustatory value by Svetlana Klimenko of the Main Botanical Garden in Kiev, Ukraine.

'Elegant': bright red, long, pear-shaped fruits ripen early and are good for fresh eating.

'Pioneer': dark red, pear-shaped fruits are up to one and a half inches long and ripen early.

'Red Star': dark red, oval fruits are one-and-a-quarter inches long and ripen late to a sweet-tart flavor.

'Siretski': a vigorous plant bearing large, cylindrical, bright red fruits having a sweet-tart flavor.

'Vavilov': the large, oblong fruits have a deep red color and sweet-tart flavor that is good fresh also.

'Yellow': yellow fruits are an inch long with sweet-tart flavor that is good for fresh eating.

Currants, Red and White

Sprightly, Translucent Jewels

BOTANICAL NAMES
Ribes petraeum, Ribes rubrum, and *Ribes sativum*

PLANT TYPE
Deciduous, woody shrub

POLLINATION
Self-fertile

RIPENING SEASON
Midsummer

R ed and white currants are perhaps the most beautiful of fruits, hanging from the branches like shiny, translucent chains of beads. When the delicate spheres are backlit by the sun, you can see the seeds floating within. The color of currants ranges from dark to light red, on to pink, yellowish, and off-white. There are also cultivars with salmon or red-and-white-striped fruits.

Currants are known mostly for the beautiful jelly they make, but certain cultivars become delicious for eating out of hand if left hanging on the bush for some time after first turning color. The flavor of red and white currants at this point is still sprightly—just what is needed in the hot summer season during which currants ripen.

Red and white currants are relative newcomers to gardens because they are natives to the cooler regions of Europe and Asia, where agriculture arrived late. The plant was not pictured until 1484, in a German publication, *Mainz Herbarius.* But by the next century, Jean Ruel, a French author, was praising red currant bushes as ornamental shrubs and the fruits as appetizers. The first written reference to red currants in English was made by Gerard, who described, in *The Herball* of 1597, gooseberries "altogether without prickles, whose fruit is verie small . . . but of perfect red color" (i.e., red currants, which are close relatives of gooseberries).

Less than a handful of different sorts of red and white currants were grown until the nineteenth century. The popularity of red and white currants in Holland was evidenced by names of two of the most widely grown cultivars: 'Great White Dutch' and 'Great Red Dutch'. The fruit was an early arrival in America, for plants were ordered from Europe for the Massachusetts Colony in 1629. Popularity of the fruit increased in both Europe and North America through the nineteenth century. Introduction of the large-fruited cultivar 'Cherry' in 1840 spurred development of new cultivars. Downing, in his book *Fruits and Fruit Trees of America*, published in 1857, described twenty-five different cultivars, all of them of European origin.

The first red currant to be bred in America was 'Fay's Prolific' (later renamed 'Fay'). It originated in 1868 and was the culmination of fifteen years of experimentation by Lincoln Fay of Portland, New York. Mr. Fay died soon after introducing the fruit, but his heirs had reaped $22,000 in royalties for this plant by 1887. Other cultivars were subsequently bred in America, among them 'Wilder', 'Red Cross', 'Diploma', and 'Perfection'. These, along with 'Fay', were the leading cultivars being grown in America in the early part of the twentieth century.

Early in the twentieth century, the number of cultivars, both of European and American origin, continued to increase. In 1925, Ulysses P. Hedrick described 125 cultivars of varied origin in his book *The Small Fruits of New York*. Today, red and white currants are still popular in northern Europe, but are virtually unknown in America largely because of the plants' alleged culpability in the spread of white pine blister rust (a circumstance discussed more fully in the gooseberry chapter). In fact, cultivated red and white currants are generally resistant to the disease, though some states still have planting restrictions.

Description of the Plant

Red and white currants are, for all practical purposes, the same fruit, differing only in color. Cultivars are drawn primarily from combinations of three species of *Ribes*. The first species is *R. rubrum*, a very cold-hardy, upright shrub native from northern Europe across to Siberia and Manchuria. The second species, *R. sativum* (*R. vulgare*), is a spreading shrub of the cool, temperate regions of western Europe. The cultivar 'Cherry' is a large-fruited form of *R. sativum*. The third species is *R. petraeum*, a native of high mountain areas of North Africa and Europe. This vigorous grower, although the most disease resistant of the three species, bears the tartest fruit; it is represented by such cultivars as 'Prince Albert' and 'Goudouin'.

Currant flowers are borne toward the bases of one-year-old stems and on spurs on older stems. Each flower bud opens to a number of flowers, joined together on a delicate, drooping stem stalk that is called a strig. Individual flowers are not showy, but joined together on the strig they give the branches the appearance of having been draped with lace. Most currants have self-fertile flowers, but a few cultivars are partially self-sterile so set more fruits with cross-pollination. Depending upon the cultivar, fruits ripen between seventy and a hundred days after blossoming.

The best cultivars in terms of size and flavor of fruits are generally those in the 'Versailles' group, derived largely from *Ribes sativum*. Included in this group are such cultivars as 'Fay', 'Wilder', 'Laxton's Perfection', and 'Red Cross'. Instead of clothing their stems with fruits from top to bottom, this group does have an unfortunate tendency to leave areas of "blind" wood along their stems.

Taste aside, currants are easier to pick if their strigs are long and have "handles" (clear lengths at the bases) for holding on to while harvesting. Some cultivars, such as 'Maarse Prominent' and 'Laxton's No. 1', drop too many fruits toward the distal end of each strig, a habit to be frowned upon.

Cultivation

A nineteenth-century horticulturalist wrote: "The currant takes the same place among fruits that the mule occupies among draught animals—being modest in its demands as to feed, shelter, and care, yet doing good service."

Red currants do not need full sun to bear well, so American orchardists in the early part of the twentieth century planted currants in the partial shade between apple trees. In England currants are sometimes espaliered against north walls, but such walls may be too dark at more southerly latitudes, where the summer sun embraces less of the horizon.

Currants are plants of cold regions, best adapted to USDA Hardiness Zones 3 through 5. They will not tolerate hot weather, especially hot, dry weather. At the southern limits of currant cultivation, give the plants some shade or a site on a north slope.

Currants are not finicky about soil but, in keeping with their proclivity for cold, prefer heavier soils (those richer in clay), especially in warmer regions. A thick mulch of some organic material such as straw, hay, or leaves also keeps the soil cool in summer, at the same time enriching it with humus. Nitrogen, at the rate of four ounces per square yard, can be supplied with yearly additions of fertilizer (two-thirds of a pound of soybean meal, for example) or a mulch of strawy manure. Do not get too heavy-handed with nitrogen, though, or plants become more prone to disease. Potassium deficiency, evidenced by marginal scorching of the leaves, is averted with about half an ounce of potassium to the square yard (supplied by half a pound of wood ash, for example). Do not use muriate of potash (potassium chloride) to supply potassium, because currants are sensitive to chloride ion toxicity.

Though currant plants tolerate neglect, annual pruning increases yields and keeps plants manageable. Prune so that most fruits are borne on spurs of two- and three-year-old wood, even though younger and older wood also bear some fruit. Plants can be trained to a number of utilitarian and decorative forms. No matter what the form of a plant, if you want to increase both fruit size and number, clip off part of the free ends of the strigs while the bushes are flowering.

Most commonly, currants are grown as bushes spaced five feet apart each way. A renewal method of pruning maintains a continuous supply of two or three each of one-, two-, and three-year-old stems. In the winter of a plant's first season, remove at ground level all but two or three stems. The following winter again remove all but two or three of the stems that grew the previous season, at which point the bush will have two or three each of one- and two-year-old stems. Continue this each season, but by the fourth winter start cutting away at their bases any stems more than three years old; some growers remove stems after their second year. Each winter also shorten long stems that have grown too scraggly.

Cordons are a tidy way of growing currants. These are plants grown as a single stem. You can squeeze a number of cultivars into a small space with cordons, as each plant can be within eighteen inches of its neighbor. Cordons trained against a wall require a bed only a foot deep and, if birds are a problem, such plants are easily protected by a net draped down the wall.

When developing the cordon, shorten the single upright stem each winter to six inches of new growth and any laterals to two buds. When you shorten the leader each year, cut it to a bud on the opposite side of the plant from the previous year's cut. This will keep the leader straight. During the summer, cut developing laterals (not the leaders) back to five leaves just as the berries are beginning to color. When the leader reaches its allotted height, shorten it each winter to one bud of the previous season's growth and prune the laterals each winter and summer as before.

I've used essentially the same pruning technique to maintain a red currant espaliered to the form of a T: Once the trunk and two side arms are formed, each summer I shorten all laterals to about five inches just as berries color up, then go back in winter and cut back the laterals again, this time to about an inch. With the shiny, translucent berries dangling from the arms, the only problem with these espaliers is that they are too pretty to be ruined by eating the berries!

Currants can also be trained as small trees, a form that is ornamental and easy to manage, though with some sacrifice to longevity and productivity of the plant. To make a tree, maintain a single stem skyward and, when it reaches the requisite height (your choice), pinch back the top bud to induce branching. Cut the main branches of the tree back to four to six inches each year to induce further branching. Once the head is fully formed, cut the branches back to two to three buds each winter.

Red and white currants are subject to a few insect and disease pests, though it is possible to grow them with little or no spraying. Commonly, the plants are attacked by aphids, which cause leaves to blister and redden. Aphids can usually be ignored and the cosmetic damage tolerated. In my garden they come and then go with little intervention on my part. If you or your plants cannot tolerate such damage, spray the plants in spring with dormant oil or, during the growing season, with an insecticide (such as insecticidal soap), making sure to douse the undersides of the leaves.

Another insect pest is the currant borer, which makes its presence known when a stem wilts. Currant borers lay their eggs on the stems in late spring. The larvae hatch and bore into the stems, where they remain until the following season. Control this pest by cutting any infested stems off below the borer in residence. The borer obviously poses some risk to growing currants as trees or cordons, where you rely on a single stem.

The imported currantworm (currant sawfly) is a pest that quickly strips the foliage from the plant just as the leaves open fully, then comes back again to attack newly formed leaves at about the time the fruit is ripening. In spite of its name, this insect seems to relish gooseberry leaves much more than those of currant. If control is necessary, spray with insecticide as soon as damage is first noticed. A hundred years ago, a writer in the Kalamazoo, Michigan, *Telegraph* told of an alternative to spraying for the imported currantworm. He trapped the pest in a piece of woolen rag placed in each bush. The insects had to be removed daily, and the woolen rag replaced. Since the insect attacks new growth near the ground first, training plants to tree form was also suggested as a means of avoiding the problem.

Two diseases, leaf spot and anthracnose, can cause currants to lose their leaves in summer. Symptoms—spots on leaves—and control are similar. Both diseases spend the winter on old leaves, so they can be limited by cleaning up these leaves in autumn. The plants also can be sprayed just after their leaves unfurl, then again after harvest. Bordeaux mixture or lime sulfur (not as effective) are traditional sprays.

Powdery mildew sometimes strikes red currants just as it does other *Ribes*. Control with sprays, as described for gooseberries, or by planting a resistant cultivar such as 'Fay's Prolific', 'Houghton Castle', ' Jonkheer van Tets', 'Minnesota', 'Red Lake', 'Rondom', or 'Versailles'. Don't be surprised, though, if neither powdery mildew nor any of the other potential insect or disease pests ever rear their ugly heads on your red currants.

Propagation

Currant seeds germinate if stratified for three to four months at temperatures just above freezing. Keep an eye on the seeds toward the end of their stratification period, for they germinate even at low temperatures and then will need light. Bushes grown from seed bear when two to three years old.

Currants are easily propagated by hardwood cuttings of one-year-old wood. If the plants are to be grown in tree form or on short "legs," remove all but the top three buds from the cutting so that sprouts do not grow from below ground. Currants leaf out early in the spring, so set cuttings in the ground either in the fall (and mulch to prevent heaving) or very early in the spring.

Harvest and Use

There is no need to pick currants as soon as they color, for most cultivars hold well on the plant. For fresh eating, let the berries hang for about three weeks after they turn red. If the fruits are to be stored at all, they should be picked dry. To avoid damaging the fruits, pick a whole strig by its stem, taking care not to damage the spur.

Yields vary greatly, depending on growing conditions and cultivar. Anywhere from three pounds to over ten pounds might be harvested from a single bush.

Currants are unsurpassed, of course, for jelly, for which the fruits should be picked as soon as they turn red. Currants are also good in pies and sauces, especially when mixed with fruits such as mulberries and juneberries that have body but lack sprightliness. The crushed fruit makes a refreshing summer-ade.

Currants have also been used for wine. "The wine made from white currants, if rich of fruit, so as to require little sugar, is, when kept to a proper age, of a flavor similar to the Grave and Rhenish wines; and I have known it preferred as a summer table wine," wrote Henry Phillips in his *Pomarium Brittanicum* (1820).

The summer harvest of red and white currants was not enough to satisfy enthusiasts of this fruit in eighteenth-century England. Dormant bushes were forced under glass for early production and some outdoor bushes were covered with shade cloth so that ripe fruits would be available from March to the end of November.

And if that were not a long enough currant season, the aforementioned Henry Phillips also wrote that the fruit could be picked perfectly dry—but not too ripe—and packed into bottles that were corked, then buried upside down in a chest of sand. Under such conditions, the fruit would reputedly keep for years.

Cultivars

Currants have a history of being mislabeled because of the numerous synonyms of some cultivars and the relatively subtle differences among them. In the following list, characteristics given for each cultivar are those for which the cultivar is notable. For example, flavor is not mentioned unless it is especially good or especially poor.

'Albatross': a white currant originating in Holland in 1975, probably a hybrid of 'Red Lake' and 'Fay'; moderate yield; early-flowering and -ripening; easy-to-harvest pale yellow fruits have excellent flavor.

'Blanka': vigorous plant from Slovakia is high-yielding and somewhat disease-resistant; fruit is large, late-ripening, and on long strigs.

'Champagne' ('Couleur de Chair' or 'Pink Champagne'): a very old cultivar listed in the catalogue of William Prince's Long Island nursery in the early eighteenth century; fruit is pale red, with delectable flavor (the best I've tasted).

'Cherry': first noted in Italy in 1840; blind wood is a problem; bush is very vigorous but not productive; flowers early in the season; short stems are hard to pick; fruit is very large but rather tart.

'Diploma': A cross of 'Cherry' and 'White Grape' originating in New York in 1885.

'Erstling aus Vierlanden' ('Earliest of Fourlands'): resistant to leaf spot disease; bush is erect; very productive but slower to pick than are most cultivars; early-ripening.

'Fay' ('Fay's Prolific'): originated in New York in 1868; bush sprawling, with brittle branches that may break in strong winds; susceptible to leaf spot; blind wood is a problem; not very productive; flowers early in the season; fruit is large, easy to pick, early-ripening, with excellent flavor fresh.

'Goudouin': firm, white fruit; late-ripening.

'Heinemann's Röte Spätlese': bush is very productive; resistant to leaf spot disease; firm fruit; late-ripening; very tart.

'Houghton Castle': introduced about 1826 and one of the most popular cultivars for the next hundred years; one of the most cold-hardy red currants; very productive but more difficult to pick than most cultivars.

'Jonkheer van Tets': a seedling of 'Fay', originating in Holland in 1941, that has become a leading Dutch cultivar; bush is very productive and erect; fruit is tender, large, and easy to pick but very tart; in some years immature fruits drop prematurely; early-ripening.

'Knight's Sweet Red': bush has distinctive incised foliage; fruit is dark red on long strigs; a trace of sweetness to counterbalance the tartness.

'Laxton's No. 1': one of the leading English cultivars, originating in 1925; susceptible to leaf spot; bush is vigorous and very productive; fruit is especially easy to pick and early-ripening; tender fruits are among the best for eating fresh; immature fruits drop in some years; early-ripening.

'Laxton's Perfection': another of England's leading cultivars, originating in 1909; branches are brittle, so bush needs shelter from wind; susceptible to leaf spot; the tender, large, sweet fruits are produced on long strigs; one of the best for eating fresh.

'London Market' ('Scotch'): bush is vigorous, upright, and productive; withstands hot, dry weather, and is resistant to disease and borers; short strigs; fruit is large and very tart.

'Maarse Prominent': susceptible to leaf spot; bush is erect; fruit is large; immature fruits drop in some years; early-ripening.

'Minnesota 71': bush is upright and vigorous; fruit is large and late-ripening; good flavor.

'Mulka': bush is productive; fruit is late-ripening.

'Perfection': a hybrid of 'Fay' and 'White Grape' originating in New York in 1887; bush is of moderate vigor, but productive; few new canes are produced from below the soil; blind wood a problem; fruit is larger than 'Fay'; easy to harvest; long strigs; good flavor.

'Primus': White currants borne on an upright, vigorous bush, similar to 'Blanka' but with red young shoots and reddish leaves; good yields; the creamy white berries have excellent fresh flavor.

'Prince Albert': leaves distinctively folded and sharply serrated; resistant to leaf spot but susceptible to mildew; late-flowering and ripening; very tart.

'Raby Castle': introduced about 1826 and one of the most popular cultivars for the next hundred years; one of the most cold-hardy red currants; susceptible to mildew; late-flowering.

'Red Cross': A cross of 'Cherry' and 'White Grape' originating in New York in 1885; bush is large and spreading; especially susceptible to leaf spot; good flavor; berries may crack during rains.

'Red Dutch': one of the oldest currants known, first mentioned in 1665 in *Flora, Ceres, and Pomona* by John Rea, who described the cultivar as "greatest dark red Dutch curran" (but more than one clone has picked up this name); one of the most cold-hardy red currants; resistant to leaf spot diseases; very productive; long strigs; fruit very good, but small.

'Red Lake': bred in Minnesota in 1933 and now widely planted in America and Europe; one of the most cold-hardy red currants; bush is very productive and erect; fruit is large and borne on long strigs; good flavor.

'Redstart': moderately vigorous, erect plant originating in Britain in 1982; very susceptible to mildew; late-ripening fruit is born on moderately long strigs and has a very tart flavor.

'Red Versailles': originated in France in 1835; susceptible to leaf spot; blind wood a problem; fruit is large; very similar in all respects to 'Fay'.

'Rondom': a leading Dutch cultivar; bush is very productive; resistant to leaf spot disease, susceptible to mildew; fruit is especially easy to pick; firm skin; late-ripening and hangs well after ripe; very tart.

'Stephens No. 9': bush is very cold-hardy and productive; the fruit is large and mild-flavored.

'Victoria' ('Wilson's Long Bunch'): one of the most cold-hardy red currants; susceptible to mildew and anthracnose; low productivity; fruit is small but of good flavor; there has been some confusion in nomenclature among 'Houghton Castle', 'Raby Castle', and 'Victoria'.

'Viking': resistant to leaf spot but susceptible to mildew; not good fresh.

'White Dutch': an old cultivar, probably the "well-tasted" white currant described in 1665 in *Flora, Ceres, and Pomona*; sprawling bush susceptible to leaf spot; fruit milky yellow, small, and not uniform, but of excellent flavor; very similar to 'Red Dutch' except in color of fruit.

'White Grape': bush is somewhat spreading and irregular in form; the fruit is large and produced in long bunches; very cold-hardy; flavor good.

'White Imperial': bush semi-upright and small; excellent flavor, among the best tasting of all currants.

'White Versailles': bush upright; large fruit produced on long strigs; too tart for me.

'Wilder': a seedling of 'Versailles' originating in Indiana in 1877; needs heavy pruning; blind wood a problem; resistant to anthracnose; fruit large.

Asian Pear

The Crunch Pear

BOTANICAL NAMES
Pyrus pyrifolia, Pyrus ussuriensis, and *Pyrus ×bretschneideri*

PLANT TYPE
Deciduous tree

POLLINATION
Better fruit size and shape with cross-pollination

RIPENING SEASON
Late summer and fall

The first time you bite into an Asian pear, expect a different experience than you are accustomed to when you bite into a European pear (*Pyrus communis*), the pear most familiar to Westerners. A European pear is buttery; an Asian pear has a crisp flesh that explodes with juice in your mouth with each bite. European pears are pear-shaped; many Asian pears are round. Flavors of Asian pears range from sweet with just a hint of perfume to sweet with a strong, floral aroma. The skins of some Asian pears are smooth and clear yellow; others have skins that are russeted and light brown.

To differentiate them from European pears in the marketplace, Asian pears go under a number of names: apple pear, crunch pear, salad pear, sand pear, and *nashi* (Japanese for "pear"). Such names invite comparisons. But Asian and European pears are so different in taste, texture, and appearance that the comparison is almost like comparing apples and oranges. And "apple pear?" Though Asian pears (some, at least) and apples are similarly round and crisp, in flavor they are very different—once again, it's like comparing apples and . . . er, pears.

One more distinguishing feature of Asian pears is their price tag on grocers' shelves. But don't worry—the three dollars a pound that these pears sometimes fetch reflects supply and demand rather than difficulty of cultivation.

The Chinese have been growing and eating Asian pears for the past twenty-five hundred to three thousand years. By the time of the Han dynasty, two thousand years ago, there even were large orchards planted along the Huai and Yellow rivers. A chronicler of the first century B.C. in China wrote that "those who grow a thousand pear trees are as rich as those barons who possess a thousand families of tenant farmers." Currently, over three thousand cultivars are grown in China. These pears were first cultivated in Japan in the eighth century, but there were no commercial orchards there until the end of the nineteenth century.

Asian pears have been in America for about two hundred years. They were introduced into the American West during the gold rush by Chinese miners who grew the plants along streams of the Sierra Nevada. Subsequent waves of Chinese and Japanese immigrants to the West Coast planted Asian pears in their backyards and in small commercial orchards. The pears arrived via Europe to America's east coast in the early 1800s, where the plants were valued first as ornamentals and then for conferring resistance to fire blight disease in hybrids with European pears. The first of these hybrids, 'LeConte', originated in 1846 and was followed by 'Kieffer' in 1873, then others. These hybrids made pear growing more of a possibility in the southeast, where fire blight can be severe, but their eating quality was poor. The ussurien pear, a cold-hardy species, was introduced to the Midwest (Iowa) in 1867 in an attempt to breed cold-hardier pears.

Although the genes of Asian pears are dispersed in hybrids, the fruits themselves still are relatively unknown outside Asia.

Description of the Plants

So-called Japanese varieties of Asian pears are mostly derived from the sand pear, *Pyrus pyrifolia* (previously known as *P. serotina*), a native of Japan adapted to warm, humid climates. (The "sand" in "sand pear" refers to small, hard cells called stone cells, which make the fruit gritty just beneath the skin; these cells are few or lacking in the best cultivars.) Generally, sand pears are not very cold-hardy. The round or flattened fruits usually are russeted and have sweet and juicy flesh. 'Nijisseiki' and 'Chojuro' are well-known cultivars, but there are hundreds of others.

From colder growing regions of the Far East come the so-called Chinese varieties of Asian pears. These are complex hybrids of the ussurien pear (*Pyrus*

Asian pear

ussuriensis), the Chinese white pear (a hybrid, sometimes designated *P.* ×*bret-schneideri*), and perhaps other species of Asian pear.

The ussurien pear is extremely cold-hardy, native to regions of Korea and northern China where the mercury might plummet to as low as minus sixty degrees Fahrenheit. The species generally does not produce high-quality fruits —they are usually juicy with some tartness and sweetness, but lack aroma and have many stone cells. The fruits are small and round. There are some good-tasting cultivars, though, such as 'Ta-Shian-Sui-Li', 'Chien-Pai-Li', 'Sian-Sui-Li', and 'An-Li'.

Chinese white pears, with cultivars numbering in the thousands, are among the best as far as flavor and texture. The fruits generally are crisp, sweet, and juicy, with few stone cells. 'Ya Li', 'Shi-Hua-Li', 'Lai-Yangtz-Li', and 'Dong-Guo-Li' are some good-tasting cultivars. Many Chinese varieties of Asian pear are pear-shaped. Chinese white pears are cold-hardy to about minus ten degrees Fahrenheit and have green or yellow skins.

Asian pear trees can live a long time and grow very large. In China, bearing trees one hundred, two hundred, even three hundred years old are not unknown. Such trees are over fifty feet high and wide.

Asian pears flower laterally on (and sometimes on the tips of) one-year-old shoots and on spurs. Spurs are stubby growths elongating less than an inch each year. Each flower bud opens to produce half a dozen or more white flowers. Asian pears are only partially self-fruitful, so fruits are larger and have a better shape when the flowers are cross-pollinated. A European or another Asian pear is a suitable pollinator.

Cultivation

Although their fruits differ, cultivation of Asian and European pears is similar. Asian pears need a soil that has a neutral pH and retains moisture (or is irrigated). The trees grow large, so give them plenty of space, at least ten feet between trees. Trees can be dwarfed by being grafted on dwarfing rootstocks and to some degree by bending their branches down toward the horizontal, perhaps in conjunction with some summer pruning. Asian pear trees are precocious, commonly fruiting by their third season, and early fruiting also helps to dwarf the trees.

For effective cross-pollination, different cultivars must bloom at the same time and produce good pollen. Chinese cultivars such as 'Ya Li', 'Tsu Li', and 'Seuri' bloom earlier than do most other pears, so should be planted together for cross-pollination. Other Asian pear cultivars bloom late enough to be cross-pollinated by one another or by European pears. Exceptions include 'Niitaka', 'Kumoi', Seigyoku', and 'Ishiiwase', all of which are poor pollinators. And 'Kikusui' and 'Nijisseiki' cannot pollinate each other.

Asian pears produce their best fruits on spurs that are two to three years old. Each bud could set half a dozen or more fruits, but so great a fruit load would decrease fruit quality. When the trees are in bloom, or right after the small fruitlets form, clip off all but one flower or fruitlet per bud or leave enough so that remaining flowers or fruitlets are about five inches apart. Even then, remove excess so that fruits are no closer than four inches apart along the branches. Be bold! Only one percent of the blossoms need to set fruit for a full crop. Thinning the fruits even as late as a month after bloom helps improve the size of those that remain. Fruit thinning, especially when done early in the season, also helps ensure a good bloom the following year.

Young trees are generally trained to an open center form. About a month into their second growing season, cut back the limbs to eighteen inches to induce secondary branching. About a month into the following growing season, the secondary branches should be cut back to about thirty inches. Pruning after growth has commenced is a technique that ensures that many buds grow out along the branches and that the shoots growing from these buds come out at wide angles to the branches. The result: a sturdy tree, well supplied with branches.

Even after the tree has been trained to a sturdy framework, Asian pears, like European pears, need annual winter pruning. Remove watersprouts, those vigorous, upright shoots, because they are unfruitful and shade the tree. Remove shoots that grow from the undersides of branches, for these shoots bear inferior fruits. Shorten branches where invigoration is needed (mostly lower in the tree) and completely remove branches where growth is too dense (mostly higher up in a tree). Finally, thin out decrepit, old spurs to stimulate growth of, and make room for, young spurs. With pruning and fertilization, a mature tree should push out about eighteen inches of extension growth each season.

Asian pears are prone to deficiencies of iron and magnesium. Both cause areas between leaf veins to yellow, the younger leaves in the case of iron deficiency and the older leaves in the case of magnesium deficiency. Iron deficiency is usually not caused by insufficient iron in the soil, but by poor uptake because a soil is too alkaline (sulfur helps acidify the soil) or waterlogged. Avert magnesium deficiency by adding magnesium to the soil as dolomitic limestone or Epsom salts, and by avoiding over-fertilization with potassium.

Fire blight disease can be as devastating to some Asian pear cultivars as it is generally to European pears. As implied by the name, infected plants look as if they have been singed with fire: The leaves turn black and remain attached, and the tips of succulent new stems curl over like shepherds' crooks. One line of defense would be to plant disease-resistant cultivars such as 'Shinko', 'Seuri', and 'Ya Li', or almost any of the ussurien pears. Unfortunately, popular cultivars such as 'Nijisseiki', 'Chojuro', 'Shinseiki', 'Okusan-kichi', 'Seigyoku', and 'Kikusui' are susceptible.

Fire blight also can be controlled by increasing a plant's resistance and by pruning away any infection. Because overly succulent shoots are most susceptible, avoid stimulating growth too much with excessive pruning and/or excessive nitrogen fertilizer. Grass grown right up to the trunk of a mature tree provides a convenient safety valve for absorbing excess nitrogen and water. Let the grass compete better, that is, grow longer, if the tree is growing too vigorously.

During the growing season, keep an eye out for symptoms of fire blight and cut off any infected branches eighteen inches into healthy wood. Sterilize your pruning shears between each cut with alcohol. In winter, look for cankers, which are sunken, dark areas on the branches where the bacteria that cause this disease overwinter. Prune off branches below these cankers.

Fire-blight bacteria can travel within a plant toward the roots. A fire blight–resistant rootstock will not confer resistance to a scion. But if infection occurs in a tree grafted on a resistant rootstock, at least the whole tree will not be killed. If the framework of a tree—the trunk and the main scaffold branches—is of a blight-resistant rootstock, the disease is not able to travel from one branch to the next within the tree. Some blight-resistant rootstocks for Asian pears include *Pyrus betulifolia*, *P. calleryana*, and certain hybrids of *P. communis*.

Another disease, *Pseudomonas* blight, has symptoms very similar to fire blight. Wet weather favors both diseases, but *Pseudomonas* blight thrives in the cool temperatures such as occur in autumn, whereas fire blight prospers in warm weather. Fire blight cankers ooze in the spring; *Pseudomonas* blight cankers do not. *Pseudomonas* blight is controlled by pruning, as for fire blight, and by spraying bactericides.

Pear psylla is a small insect that causes symptoms sometimes mistaken for those of fire blight. Psyllas suck sap from plants and then exude a honeydew that drips on the leaves. A superficial black mold that grows on this honeydew might at first glance look like fire blight, but the mold can be rubbed off the plant. The real damage is the weakening effect of the psyllas' feeding and, eventually, shading from the black mold. Control pear psylla with a spray of dormant oil just before bloom or, during the growing season, of insecticidal soap or a kaolin clay formulation known as "Surround." In California, at least, psyllas seem less fond of Asian than of European pears, with 'Hosui' being especially resistant.

Asian pears are sometimes attacked by codling moths, whose handiwork is a large hole in the fruit. You also might find a resident caterpillar near the core. The codling moth is more likely to lay her eggs at the point where two fruits are touching, which gives yet another good reason for careful fruit thinning. (Unfortunately, the moth also likes to lay her eggs where a leaf touches a fruit.) Insecticide sprays are sometimes needed for this pest; that benign kaolin formulation is also effective against Ms. Codling.

Birds in some regions like to take pecks at Asian pear fruits. Netting is one solution, but difficult on large trees. How about enticing birds away from the pears with mulberry and juneberry trees?

Propagation

Asian pear cultivars, like European pear cultivars, are propagated by grafting scions onto suitable rootstocks. Two of the most satisfactory rootstocks are *Pyrus betulifolia* and *P. calleryana* because the root systems of both species are resistant to fire blight and tolerant of wet or dry soils. Both rootstocks are moderately cold-hardy, but tend to reduce the cold-hardiness of grafted scions. Therefore, these rootstocks are most suitable where winter lows are not too cold: about minus fifteen degrees Fahrenheit for *P. betulifolia*, about plus five degrees Fahrenheit for *P. calleryana*.

Seedlings of *Pyrus pyrifolia* and *P. ussuriensis* are also possible rootstocks. *Pyrus pyrifolia* tolerates a wide range of soils and *P. ussuriensis* has an especially strong root system, although it is sensitive to wet soils. Both species are cold-hardy so long as the temperatures stay cold. In milder climates, where winter temperatures fluctuate, these rootstocks awaken the buds on grafted scions too early, and cold damage results. Another problem with these two rootstocks is that they are susceptible to a viruslike disease, called pear decline, that is common in many of the major pear-growing regions of the world.

Why not turn to European pears as rootstocks for Asian pears? The response of an Asian scion to a European rootstock depends on the cultivar. Some trees make good growth ('Ya Li', 'Tsu Li', 'Seuri', and 'Ishiiwase', for example); others become severely stunted.

At present, there are no thoroughly tested rootstocks that will make Asian pear trees dwarf and productive. Quince, which is used to dwarf European pears, is unsatisfactory; the resulting trees are too stunted or the grafts may prove incompatible. Hope lies with some of the rootstocks that are hybrids of the European pear cultivars 'Old Home' and 'Farmingdale' (designated 'OH × F'), especially 'OH × F 217' and 'OH × F 333'. These hybrids also have the advantage of being resistant to fire blight, so at least those parts of grafted trees cannot be killed. Dwarfing can also be achieved by first grafting an 'OH × F' stem on a quince rootstock, then grafting the Asian pear on top of the 'OH × F' interstem.

Asian pears grow readily from seeds that have been stratified for two or three months. The trees grown from seed will bear fruits that will be different from, and probably inferior to, the fruit the seeds came from and will take many years to bear. The sixth-century A.D. Chinese text *Tsee Ming Yau Su* gives the following instructions to hasten fruiting: At the end of the second year, "after leaf fall in winter, prune off the stem near the ground level and scorch the cut surface with hot wood coal. In this way, the tree can begin to bloom and set fruit after two years." I would not bank on it.

Harvest and Use

Large Asian pear trees bear prodigious quantities of fruit. A full-grown 'Nijisseiki' yields, on the average, four hundred pounds of fruits. Very old pear trees in China have been known to produce over a ton of fruit each—three tons in one recorded case!

In contrast to European pears, which have good flavor only if the final stages of ripening occur while the fruit is off the tree, Asian pears must ripen thoroughly on the tree before they are picked. Watch for a color change, from green to light brown or orange on russeted cultivars, and from green to greenish yellow on smooth-skinned cultivars. The color change on the smooth-skinned cultivars is often subtle. Taste a fruit if in doubt.

Handle the fruit gently, for bruises quickly show up as brown marks on the skin. At room temperature, the fruit will keep for a week or two, then begin to wrinkle and dry. At just above freezing, most cultivars keep at least until Christmas, but the ability to keep well varies with cultivar. Cultivars such as 'Nijisseiki', 'Seigyoku', 'Okusankichi', and 'Shinseiki' may be stored for substantially longer. 'Pingo-Li', a popular variety in China, keeps for a year in nothing more than a root cellar.

Asian Pear

Cultivars

'Chojuro': originated in Japan in 1895; productive; fruit has a strong flavor enjoyed by some people, not by others (I like it); skin is slightly astringent; stores for about five months.

'Hosui': introduced in 1972; tree is a strong grower with almost a weeping form; fruit is golden brown, large, with a sweet, aromatic, rich flavor; stores one to two months.

'Ishiiwase': a seedling of a 'Nijisseiki' and 'Doitsu' hybrid introduced in 1921; tree is very vigorous; fruit is large, dark brown, and mediocre in quality.

'Kikusui': a productive seedling of 'Nijisseiki', was introduced in 1915; fruit is flat, small, with a yellow-green, slightly bitter skin and a flesh that has a hint of tartness; excellent flavor; stores well.

'Kosui': tree is vigorous; fruit is small and flat with a tender, bronze-colored skin covered with russet and enclosing a sweet flesh; early-ripening; stores moderately well.

'Kumoi': introduced in 1955; the large, orange-brown, russeted fruit has fair flavor and a tough, thick skin; pollen-sterile so cannot be used to pollinate other cultivars.

'Niitaka': tree is very upright, but stunted if grafted onto European pear; fruit is very large, brown-russeted, with average flavor; pollen-sterile so cannot be used to pollinate other cultivars; does not keep particularly well in cold storage, but keeps well for a couple of weeks at room temperature right after harvest.

'Nijisseiki' ('Twentieth Century'): originated in Japan in 1898; productive; the small, round, yellow fruit has a thin, tender, bitter skin; bland flavor; stores six months.

'Okusankichi': the very large brown-russeted fruit has only fair flavor but stores well.

'Seigyoku': a seedling of a 'Nijisseiki' and 'Chojuro' hybrid that originated in 1922; the small tree has a flat or weeping form; the large, yellow fruits are mediocre in quality; keeps well.

'Seuri': tree is very productive; fruit is perhaps the largest of all Asian pears; pleasant flavor, hinting at walnut, but does not store well; late-ripening.

'Shinko': introduced in 1932; very productive; fruit is golden-russeted, with a thick skin and a neutral flavor; stores only about two months.

'Shinseiki' ('New Century'): a seedling of a 'Nijisseiki' and 'Chojuro' hybrid that originated in 1945; very similar to, but not quite as good as, 'Nijisseiki'; tree has a spreading growth habit that makes training easy; matures early; the fruit is large, pale yellow, and sweet; stores moderately well.

'Shinsui': tree is upright growing and vigorous; fruit is small to medium in size, brown-russeted, very juicy and sweet; introduced in 1965 and now the most popular cultivar in Japan.

'Tsu Li' ('Tzu Li'): an old Chinese cultivar; fruit is pear-shaped, large, and has a thick skin; keeps long in storage, during which time the flavor improves. The

'Tsu Li' cultivar described here is the one available in the United States; 'Tsu Li' grown in China is different.

'Ya Li' ('Duckbill Pear'): an old Chinese cultivar, still the most important one in China; very productive but slow to come into bearing; late-ripening; fruit is pear-shaped, sweet, and aromatic; stores well.

Jostaberry

The Gooseberry and Black Currant Hybrid

BOTANICAL NAME

Ribes nidigrolaria

PLANT TYPE

Deciduous bush

POLLINATION

Self-fertile, with exceptions

RIPENING SEASON

Summer

Gooseberries and currants are related species within the genus *Ribes* and each has its devotees, so it is inevitable that hybridization would be attempted to combine the best of each species into a single plant. At the very least, hybrids were sought that lacked the thorns of the gooseberry and the susceptibility to white pine blister rust disease of the black currant, yet had large, flavorful fruits.

The first hybrids between black currant and gooseberry were produced in 1883 by W. Culverwell of Yorkshire. These hybrids, designated *Ribes ×culverwellii* in honor of Mr. Culverwell, formed with relative ease so long as black currant was the female parent. Most such hybrids that were produced both in Europe and North America were similar in that they lacked the thorns of the gooseberry and the characteristic aroma of the black currant plant.

But the story does not end there. Although the hybrids grew vigorously and flowered profusely, they bore no fruit—a case of mule sterility. Black currant and gooseberry are in the same genus, but are in different subgenera into which *Ribes* is divided.

Efforts to produce fertile hybrids between black currant and gooseberry continued into the twentieth century, most notably in Germany. In the 1920s, Professor Erwin Baur at the Max Planck Institute in Germany crossed gooseberry with *Ribes ×succirubrum* and produced a fruitful hybrid to which he gave the common name *Jochelbeere* (jochel berry), from the German names for currant, *Johannisbeere*, and gooseberry, *Stachelbeere*. This was progress, but still not a hybrid of black currant and gooseberry.

The real breakthrough came in the late 1950s, when the German scientist Rudolf Bauer overcame the mule sterility of hybrids of black currant and gooseberry by treating their buds with a chemical called colchicine. A few branches flowered and fruited. Seeds from these fruits resulted in plants that evidently were double hybrids (from cross-pollination between two different black currant–gooseberry hybrids) with two different black currants and two different gooseberries in their lineage.

Professor Bauer, like his predecessor, Professor Baur, combined the common German names for currant and gooseberry to come up with a common name for this new fruit, except this later Bauer used the beginning letters of *both* common names. The resulting name is the more euphonious prefix "josta." He similarly made up a new species name, *Ribes nidigrolaria*, by combining *R. nigrum* (black currant), *R. divaricatum* (Worcesterberry, another ingredient of the original jostaberry hybrid), and *R. grossularia* (sometimes used instead of *R. uva-crispa* as the botanical name for gooseberry).

There was a brief flurry of interest in hybrids of gooseberry and black currant at the U.S. Department of Agriculture and Oregon State University in the 1960s. George Waldo, stationed in Corvallis, named his most promising hybrids as numbered selections of ORUS (Oregon State + USDA.).

Jostaberry has a flavor that is reminiscent of, though different from, both black currant and gooseberry. Fruit size averages about five-eighths of an inch across—larger than a black currant, but smaller than a large gooseberry. Jostaberry gets its black color from black currant, and from the gooseberry a persistent calyx (a tiny bit of dried flower that remains attached, opposite the stem end). Like the black currant, the jostaberry is extremely high in vitamin C.

Description of the Plant

Jostaberry is a tetraploid (a plant with double the chromosome number of the parents), and shows vigor with increased plant and flower size. The bush has strong, upright branches, each growing over six feet tall, and begins growth early in the season. The glossy, dark green leaves are a couple of inches across, intermediate in size between those of the black currant and the gooseberry, and are held on the plant late into the fall.

Jostaberry plants bear fruit laterally on one-year-old wood and on spurs of older wood. Fruits are formed in clusters of three to five berries and ripen in summer as do black currants and gooseberries.

The first jostaberries were second-generation hybrids containing genes of 'Silvergieters Zwarte' black currant, 'Green Hansa' gooseberry, and Worcesterberry. Each Jostaberry seedling differed somewhat from its siblings, giving a range in fruit quality. A subsequent hybrid of the black currant cultivar 'Schwarze Traube' with Worcesterberry resulted, in 1980, in the cultivar 'Jostaki'. More recently introduced, and reputedly the best, hybrids are 'Jostagranda', appropriately named—its fruits are one inch in diameter—and 'Jostina', with fruits three-quarters of an inch in diameter. These latter two cultivars evidently need cross-pollination: it is suggested that they be planted as a pair.

Cultivation

Allow about six feet square of ground area to accommodate the vigor of each jostaberry plant. Plants probably tolerate winter cold to USDA Hardiness Zone 4, perhaps colder, but blossom early in spring so need a site not subject to late spring frosts.

An unpruned jostaberry can bear prolifically—too prolifically, in fact, with a resultant loss in fruit quality. On the other hand, some jostaberry plants seem to grow rampantly yet yield just a handful of berries. "Jostaberry" represents a number of hybrid plants, and the problem of low yield could possibly be indicative of a poor-yielding clone. Self-sterility or lack of pollination are other possibilities.

Where a bush is bearing well, one use of annual pruning is to thin out potential fruits so that those that remain are of higher quality. Annual pruning also stimulates and makes room for new growth. Each winter prune a mature plant by removing at ground level one or two of the oldest shoots. When I prune my jostaberry, I am thankful the hybrid lacks the thorns of its gooseberry parent. But I do miss that black currant aroma, sadly missing in this hybrid offspring.

Jostaberry is little affected by pests. Besides resistance to white pine blister rust, the hybrids also are resistant to gall mites, which attack black currants in Europe, and the leaf-spot and mildew diseases that attack gooseberries and black currants everywhere.

The imported currantworm, which strips leaves just after they open, can be a problem, though not in my experience. Control this pest, when necessary, with an insecticide spray as soon as damage is first noted. If the first spray was not sufficiently thorough, a second spray may be needed when the pest resurfaces again just after harvest.

Propagation

Jostaberries are easily propagated by hardwood stem cuttings set in the ground either in fall or very early in spring. The stems of the plants also layer readily, sometimes even without assistance from the gardener.

Harvest and Use

Average yield from a mature jostaberry bush is about twelve pounds of fruit. There is no need to rush the harvest, for ripe berries adhere firmly to the bushes.

Cultivars

'Josta': introduced to Europe in 1977; vigorous, thornless plant is resistant to American powdery mildew, white pine blister rust, leaf spot, and gall mites; fruit color and size similar to black currant but with milder flavor; high in vitamin C and stores well.

'Jostina': introduced to Europe in 1985; vigorous, thornless plant is resistant to American powdery mildew, white pine blister rust, leaf spot, and gall mites; medium to large berries are borne in clusters of two or three; fruits keep well on bush; uneven ripening; very good flavor.

'Jostaki' ('Jostagranda'): introduced in 1987; moderately vigorous plant with slightly drooping stems that need trellising; high-yielding; vigorous, thornless plant is resistant to American powdery mildew, white pine blister rust, leaf spot, and gall mites; fruits are larger than those of 'Josta' and borne in clusters of two to four; fruits keep well on bush; very good flavor.

'ORUS 1': vigorous, spreading plant resistant to American powdery mildew and white pine blister rust; productivity about the same as 'Josta' and ripening about a week later.

'ORUS 10': vigorous, spreading, thorny plant resistant to American powdery mildew and white pine blister rust; less productive than 'Josta' and ripening about the same time; fruits small and dark.

Lowbush Blueberry

More American Than Apple Pie

BOTANICAL NAME
Vaccinium angustifolium

PLANT TYPE
Low-growing, deciduous, woody shrub

POLLINATION
Partially self-fertile, so better yields and larger berries
with cross-pollination

RIPENING SEASON
Midsummer

Bountiful harvests provided by wild lowbush blueberry plants may be one reason that this fruit is not planted along with strawberries and raspberries in backyard gardens. I can remember childhood summers hiking sun-drenched slopes of the White Mountains in New Hampshire, picking the frosty blue fruits from the twiggy, small bushes. As many of the sweet berries found their way into my mouth as into the bucket of berries destined for pies. I still enjoy lowbush blueberries, but now pluck them from my front yard, or from plants growing in the Shawangunk Mountains, which rise up behind my backyard.

Acres and acres of commercial lowbush blueberry fields cover the landscape in those regions where the plant is indigenous, but even those commercial fields consist of tamed wild plants. The lowbush blueberry is a plant that tolerates fire, and for decades commercial fields have been maintained with deliberate, periodic burning to get rid of competing vegetation. Native Americans cultivated lowbush blueberries in much the same manner in prior centuries.

There may not have been the ghost of a sign
Of them anywhere under the shade of the pine,
But get the pine out of the way, you may burn
The pasture all over until not a fern
Or grass-blade is left, not to mention a stick,
And presto, they're up all around you as thick
And hard to explain as a conjuror's trick.

(Robert Frost, "Blueberries")

In contrast to their highbush counterparts (*Vaccinium corymbosum*), lowbush blueberry fruits are sweeter, though less aromatic. The highbush blueberry, incidentally, is also a latecomer as a cultivated crop. Early in the last century, blueberries caught the fancy of Dr. F. V. Coville, a plant breeder for the United States Department of Agriculture, who selected and bred superior clones and studied the special soil requirements of the plants. Ironically, 'Russell', the second superior clone selected by Dr. Coville (in 1909), was a lowbush blueberry.

Whereas growers of highbush blueberries dig holes and plant the bushes therein, commercial growers and lovers of lowbush blueberries still content themselves with harvest from wild plants.

Description of the Plants

If "lowbush" is arbitrarily defined as a blueberry bush that never grows more than a yard tall, then there are perhaps eight species that can bear both this label and good-tasting fruits. Most commonly, "lowbush blueberry" refers to *Vaccinium angustifolium*. This plant is native to rocky uplands, dry, sandy pine barrens, and bogs of the upper northeast of the United States and a stretch of Canada from Manitoba across to Newfoundland. Over this range, abandoned farmland or timberland that has been logged or burnt over is likely to become naturally colonized by *V. angustifolium*.

Another blueberry likely to be found mingling amongst these plants is the sourtop, or velvet-leaf blueberry (*Vaccinium myrtilloides*), especially in what was once forest. Sourtop plants have a wide natural range, cutting a broad swath from the Pacific Northwest east to Labrador and down to West Virginia. The plants are more shade-tolerant than *V. angustifolium* and bear light blue, pleasant tasting, slightly tart berries.

Lowbush blueberry

Not quite as far north are found two species—*Vaccinium lamarckii* and *V. brittonii*—so similar to *V. angustifolium* that they are considered by some botanists to be the same. *Vaccinium brittonii* (or *V. angustifolium* var. *nigrum*, as it is sometimes designated) is commonly called a huckleberry and has shiny black berries and blue-green leaves. Another good-tasting "huckleberry" is *V. alto-montanum*, whose dull, glaucous fruits are borne on plants that inhabit the woods of Kentucky, Virginia, Alabama, and Georgia. (The botanists' huckleberry is related to blueberry, but is in a different genus, *Gaylussacia*. How do you tell them apart? Eat the fruit: If you feel seeds crunching between your teeth, the fruit is a true huckleberry; otherwise it is a blueberry.)

As long as we've ventured off into huckleberries—or, rather, blueberries called huckleberries—two other low ones also deserve mention. Blue huckleberry or big whortleberry (*Vaccinium membranaceum,* possibly the same or at least very close to globe huckleberry, *V. globulare*) ranges in size from a one-foot lowbush to a six-foot highbush. It is native to the northern mountains of the American West, where the black fruits are very popular and gathered from the wild. The Cascade or blue huckleberry (*V. deliciosum*), native to wet sites of the Pacific Northwest, is a one- to two-foot-tall shrub yielding bright blue berries that are, as the botanical name says, delicious. Berry size of both western natives is a quarter- to a half-inch, and the plants are hardy from Zones 4 through 8.

Lowbush blueberries spread by underground stems called rhizomes. These rhizomes eventually form an interlacing network just beneath the surface of the ground. By means of this network, plants spread outward from as little as a couple of inches to more than a foot each year. Rhizomes on young plants tend to grow more than do those on older plants. Unlike the highbush blueberry, the lowbush blueberry has a taproot, which probably accounts for the latter's greater tolerance of dry soil.

Each spring new shoots arise both directly from rhizomes and from buds on stems above ground. The shoots grow rapidly, almost reaching their full length by the time blossoms open in spring.

Buds at the ends of the previous season's shoots burst into clusters of flowers, each flower a nodding white or pinkish bell that looks very much like lily of the valley. Insects, mostly bees, pollinate the flowers and, for fruit production, cross-pollination is important. Some clones are apparently self-fertile, but even these set more fruit if cross-pollinated.

As the height of summer approaches, two things happen. Fruits ripen one to two months after bloom. Also, the tips of all the growing shoots suddenly die, leaving the remains of a small withered leaf. There is no cause for alarm; this is a natural event, and just the tips, not whole shoots, die.

As summer wanes, shortening daylight hours trigger changes in the plants at once obvious to the naked eye. The one or two distal buds on new young shoots become round and plump flower buds, and buds lower on the stem become long and pointed shoot buds. Flower buds are produced only on new shoots (so flower blossoms open on one-year-old stems), but those buds that form on new shoots growing directly from rhizomes are more winter-hardy and produce more flowers than those produced on laterals of above-ground stems. (An exception is the velvet-leaf blueberry, which yields more on new shoots growing off existing stems.)

As plants go into autumn, the small leaves turn crimson. Even after the leaves have fallen, cold weather causes the stems of some clones to turn a bright red that almost rivals the color of the leaves. There also are evergreen species of lowbush blueberry whose leaves stay green throughout the year.

Lowbush blueberry plants show great variation in plant characteristics. Fruit color ranges from white (rare) to shades of pink and red, to dark blue. Leaf size varies somewhat from clone to clone, and autumn color, at its best, rivals that of sugar maple, euonymous, and other plants valued for their autumn foliage. Couple these characteristics (do not forget the nodding white flowers) with the red or yellow winter stems of certain clones, and you have a plant as pleasing to the eye as to the palate. In fact, cultivars such as 'Burgundy' and 'Claret' are among those selected solely for their beauty, in these two cases the red color of the autumn leaves and winter stems. That the lowbush blueberry is so attractive should come as no great surprise considering its kin: mountain laurel, azalea, andromeda, heather, and rhododendron.

Given the range in characteristics—fruit flavor included—one can only wonder why more selection has not been done for superior plants. One could view this anomaly as a testimonial to the quality of fruit on even the average lowbush blueberry plant.

The dearth of lowbush blueberry cultivars leads one to believe that this plant has been ignored in breeding. Not true! Genes of the lowbush blueberry have been incorporated into many highbush blueberry cultivars. To these hybrids, the lowbush blueberry has added soil tolerance, winter-hardiness, low stature, and sweetness of fruits.

Cultivation

Lowbush blueberry can be grown where winter cold is severe, in part because the plants are low enough to avail themselves of the protection of snow cover. In commercial blueberry growing areas, winter lows regularly plummet below minus twenty-five degrees Fahrenheit. USDA Hardiness Zones 3 through 7 are suitable for the plant.

Although lowbush blueberries often grow wild in the dappled shade of the forest, for best production plants need full sun, or nearly so. With handsome leaves, stems, and flowers, and a low, spreading growth habit, the lowbush blueberry is ideally suited as an edible and attractive groundcover. For more serious fruit production where you want to avoid trampling plants during harvest and pruning, grow the plants in a matted row in much the same manner as garden strawberries are grown, allowing plants to spread to fill a two- or three-foot-wide bed. Keep the rows to this width by hand-pulling errant plants or by rototilling along the edges of the bed.

Lowbush blueberries are slow to establish themselves; six years are required before the ground is completely covered when plants are set at a two-foot spacing. Potted plants establish themselves more readily than do bare-root plants. To hasten the spread of rhizomes and minimize plant heaving in winter, set potted plants three inches deeper than the ground level of the pots (unless, of course, the stems are less than three inches tall). Pegging aerial stems down to the ground will also increase the rate of spread. A mulch two inches thick covering the ground increases the rate of plant spread and decreases weeds, soil water loss, and winter heaving.

In common with other heath plants, the lowbush blueberry revels in a soil that is well-drained, acidic, and high in organic matter. Elemental sulfur can be used to bring the pH to the required range of 4.2 to 5.2. In sandy soils add three-quarters of a pound of elemental sulfur per hundred square feet for each pH unit the soil is above 4.5. Use three times this amount of sulfur for loams. Sulfur must be added the year before planting.

Enrich the soil with organic matter by mixing a bucketful of peat moss into the soil of each planting hole at the time of planting. (The peat moss will also help acidify the soil.) A mulch of sawdust, pine needles, or leaves, renewed yearly as needed, continually enriches the soil with organic matter as well as conferring the other benefits of mulching.

A walk through many forests of the Northeast attests to the productivity of wild lowbush blueberry plants that receive no care at all, but cultivated plants that are fertilized and pruned can do even better. Especially in humid climates, supplemental watering is usually unnecessary for the relatively drought-tolerant *Vaccinium angustifolium*, although it would be of benefit to other moisture-loving "lowbush blueberries," such as the Cascade huckleberry.

As far as nutrients go, what the plants need most is nitrogen, applied at the rate of one-third to one pound per hundred square feet. Use the lesser amount if annual stem growth is more than six inches and the larger amount if it is less than four inches. Organic and ammoniacal forms of nitrogen are better than nitrate forms (look for "acid plant" fertilizer); I use soybean meal, seven percent nitrogen and sold as an inexpensive animal feed. Be careful not to add too much nitrogen, though, or the plants become more susceptible to blight and powdery mildew.

Do not prune lowbush blueberry plants at all for their first four years. After that, prune when the plants are dormant and do it severely. Use either hand pruners, hedge shears, or a lawnmower set to cut low to lop the stems off to one inch above ground level. Cutting this low stimulates growth of new shoots directly from the rhizomes. (Remember, these shoots produce the best fruit buds.)

The plants can be pruned every other year, in which case the planting also bears every other year (the season after the season following pruning). For fruit every year, prune a different half of the planting each year.

Alternatively, prune the plants every three years. The result will be no fruit in the season following pruning, a large crop in the second season, and a smaller crop (typically thirty percent of first crop) in the third season. To get continual production from a planting pruned this way, divide it into thirds, and prune a different third each year.

Lowbush blueberry is susceptible to certain nutritional and pest problems evident in the appearance of the leaves. When the oldest leaves start turning pale green, then take on red, purple, or yellow tints, this is an indication that plants lack sufficient nitrogen. Phosphorus deficiency causes leaves to be undersized and dark green, then to develop purple patches that progress inward from the margins. Red margins on leaves that eventually die indicate potassium deficiency. When drought strikes, the leaves turn tan or brown and dry up but remain attached to the plant.

A disease called mummyberry causes watersoaked splotches along the mid-veins of leaves, wilting of twigs, and browning of blossoms—symptoms not unlike those of frost damage. The fruit, as one might surmise, shrivels to a dried mummy in which the fungus spends the winter. One way to control mummyberry is to apply a thick mulch each year, which buries the mummies enough so that they cannot send spores up to new shoots in the spring.

A greyish brown mold on leaves, blossoms, or twigs indicates botrytis blight, a disease, like mummyberry, most prevalent in cool, wet weather. The infected blossoms remain stuck to the plant. A mulch such as sawdust (but not peat) that presents a dry surface creates a microclimate less favorable for botrytis. Clones vary from those that are inherently very resistant to the disease to those that are very susceptible. Overfertilizing plants increases susceptibility.

Red leaf disease causes beet-red blotches on the leaves in early summer. Later on, a feltlike fungal mat becomes evident on the undersides of infected leaves. Red leaf affects *Vaccinium angustifolium* var. *nigrum* more than it does other lowbush blueberries. The only cure is to rogue infected plants.

The blueberry maggot will be evident in the fruit rather than on the leaves. This pest is notably absent on the West Coast and, after warm winters, south of Virginia. Control it by thoroughly harvesting all the fruit and by trapping it on ersatz fruits—sticky red spheres (available from organic pest control suppliers such as Gardens Alive!, 5100 Schenley Place, Lawrenceburg, IN 47025, 812-537-8650). Hang one trap per several plants before the first berries turn blue.

No need to wring your hands in worry every time a blueberry leaf changes color. Sometimes the leaves change color for no apparent reason. And the pests mentioned rarely appear or warrant control in small backyard plantings and often even in commercial plantings. My planting gets an annual mulch, soybean meal, and nothing else.

Propagation

Lowbush blueberries can be propagated by seeds, or by softwood or rhizome cuttings. The latter two methods have the advantage of producing plants identical to the mother plant, though seedlings do tend to resemble their parents and have a more spreading habit than do plants grown from cuttings. The outstretched branches are easily covered with mulch to stimulate rapid spread of plants.

Seed germination is erratic. Some researchers report that a high percentage of seeds germinate if sown right after being taken out of the fruit and kept at seventy degrees Fahrenheit. Other investigators suggest chilling the ripe fruit at fifty degrees Fahrenheit for several days before the seeds are extracted and sown. If the seeds are dried before they are sown, they will germinate best if stored dry in a refrigerator for five or six months before sowing. Refrigerated, dried seed stays viable for up to twelve years.

A good germination medium for blueberry seeds is equal parts sand and peat. Separate the seeds from the fruit before sowing or merely mash whole fruits on the surface of the medium. Then cover the seeds with a quarter-inch or less of milled sphagnum moss.

Softwood cuttings root readily, almost one hundred percent for some clones, if taken correctly. The best time for taking these cuttings is before the shoot tips die, while the shoots still are actively growing (late June to early July in Maine). Cuttings taken from shoots growing from rhizomes root better than those taken from shoots growing off above-ground stems. Cut off four inches of terminal growth, making the basal cut just below a node. Strip the leaves from the lower half of the cutting and stick it in a mixture of equal parts peat and sand. Rooting hormones offer no benefit.

For rhizome cuttings, dig the rhizomes either in early spring or in early fall and cut them into four- to six-inch pieces. Refrigerate the pieces, keeping them moist, for between five and nine weeks. Then plant the cuttings in vermiculite in warmth (seventy degrees Fahrenheit is ideal), moving them to bright light as soon as sprouts appear.

Harvest and Use

A good yield of lowbush blueberries is from ten to fifteen pounds of fruit per hundred square feet of plants, though average yields can be half or less than this amount and top yields can double it. Low-growing, nonspreading hybrids of highbush and lowbush blueberries, such as 'Northblue' and 'North Country', yield between three and seven pounds of fruit per plant.

Commercially, lowbush blueberries are hand-harvested with a blueberry rake, which resembles a dustpan with tines instead of a flat bottom. (Sources for these rakes include Hartmann's Plant Company, Inc., 310 60th Street, Grand Junction, MI 49056, 616-253-4281; The Hubbard Rake Company, RR1 Box 3115, Mason's Bay Road, Jonesport, Me 04649, 207-497-5949; and Raintree Nursery, 391 Butts Road, Morton, WA 98356, 360-496-6400.) As the rake is combed through the plants, the stems and leaves slide through the tines and the berries pop off into the "dustpan." This is another reason for pruning blueberries right to the ground: the branched shoots from unpruned stems above ground are harder to comb through the rake than are the unbranched stems that grow directly from the rhizomes.

Native Americans had a deep enough appreciation of lowbush blueberries to preserve the fruits, by drying them in the sun, for winter use. For authentic New England fare, cook dried blueberries in corn bread and enjoy it along with wild rice and venison or with dried sweet corn and maple sugar.

Cultivars

'Augusta': a six-inch-high clone from Maine that is especially easy to propagate; needs cross-pollination; the fruits ripen together and are just under half an inch across with a heavy bloom and fair flavor.
'Blomidon': the first lowbush blueberry cultivar that was bred rather than selected from the wild population; dark leaves; the plants grow about ten inches high and are prolific and easily propagated; fruits ripen uniformly but their flavor is only fair.

'Brunswick': a clone selected in New Brunswick in 1965; the plants grow a foot high and the leaves cover the fruits; needs cross-pollination; the fruits ripen together and are half an inch across, with medium blue color; the fruit flavor is excellent, though production is erratic.

'Chignecto': a clone selected from the wild in Nova Scotia in 1964; less productive, more vigorous, and easier to propagate than 'Augusta' and 'Brunswick'; fruit clusters are held above the pale green foliage; fruits are powdery blue and uneven ripening, and their flavor is excellent.

'Cumberland': a clone selected in Nova Scotia in 1964; needs cross-pollination;. fruits on the ten-inch-high plants ripen together and have very good flavor fresh or frozen.

'Fundy': selected in 1969 in Nova Scotia; needs cross-pollination, but not a good pollinator for some other clones; vigorous grower; fruits on the eighteen-inch-high plants are almost as good as those of 'Cumberland'.

'JonBlue': a selection of *Vaccinium darrowii*; the plant grows three feet tall and has tiny, evergreen leaves; the fruit is small, dark, and sweet; cold-hardiness is untested north of North Carolina.

'Northblue': a hybrid of highbush and lowbush blueberries (twenty-five percent *Vaccinium angustifolium*) that grows about two feet tall and does not spread by rhizomes; the dark blue fruits are as large as a nickel and are slightly acid with good flavor.

'North Country': another highbush-lowbush hybrid (also twenty-five percent *Vaccinium angustifolium*), growing just under two feet high, also not spreading by rhizomes; the fruits are sky blue and have a mild, very good flavor.

'Northsky': another highbush-lowbush hybrid (also twenty-five percent *Vaccinium angustifolium*); plant grows just over a foot tall; fruits are small with a dusty bloom and good flavor.

'Tophat': this cultivar does not spread below ground, making instead an individual bush twenty inches high and two feet across; best used for ornamental purposes; the fruit flavor is only mediocre.

Jujube

The Chinese Date

BOTANICAL NAME
Ziziphus jujuba

PLANT TYPE
Deciduous tree

POLLINATION
Partially self-fertile, but yields better with cross-pollination

RIPENING SEASON
Late summer on into fall

If this book were written in China, this chapter would be omitted. The Chinese have been growing and eating jujubes for more than four thousand years. As late as the middle of the nineteenth century, China had more jujube trees than any other type of fruit tree. (Persimmons, incidentally, were the second most abundant fruit trees).

Beyond China, jujubes sometimes go under the sobriquet of "Chinese dates." Though botanically unrelated, dried jujube and fruits of the date palm resemble each other in appearance, texture, and flavor. Jujube fruits range in size from that of a cherry to that of a plum, have a high concentration of sugar (about thirty percent fresh, about seventy-five percent dried), and one elongated pit. When just ripe, the surface of the fruit is the color of mahogany and as shiny and smooth as if buffed with a cloth. At this stage, the flesh is crisp and sweet, reminiscent of apple. If the fruit is left to ripen a bit longer, the skin begins to wrinkle as the fruit loses water, and the flesh changes from light green to beige and becomes spongy, i.e., more datelike.

Jujube plants traveled beyond Asia centuries ago. The Roman scholar Pliny recorded that jujubes were brought from Syria to Rome sometime near the end of Augustus's reign. Plantings subsequently spread throughout southern Europe and northern Africa. The olive-sized fruits from seedling trees still find their way onto dessert trays in southern Europe today.

The first jujube plants to reach America crossed the Atlantic in 1837 and were planted in Beaufort, North Carolina. The plants evidently aroused some interest as ornamentals, for in 1854 the United States Patent Office distributed jujube throughout the middle Atlantic and southern states.

Interest in the gustatory value of jujube was spurred when U.S. Department of Agriculture plant explorer Frank Meyer began sending propagating wood of types with superior fruits from China to America in 1908. Because jujubes also tolerate drought, Meyer's chief in Washington, David Fairchild, saw great promise in this plant for developing agriculturally barren regions of the Southwest. In his enthusiasm, Fairchild would show up at social events in Washington—a get-together hosted by Alexander Graham Bell (Fairchild's father-in-law) or a banquet for the National Geographic Society (Society founder Gilbert Grosvenor was father-in-law to another of Bell's daughters), for example—with jujubes for everyone to sample.

In part because of the tree's handsome appearance and its adaptability to many soils, jujubes today are not uncommon dooryard trees across America's southern tier. Jujube breeding continued through the 1950s at the United States Department of Agriculture's research station in Chico, California, and jujubes were used for one of the Tennessee Valley Authority's reforestation projects. The International Tree Crops Institute even studied the possibility of converting the fruit's abundant sugar to alcohol fuel.

But the fruit itself never has caught on. Say "jujube" and most Americans think of a fruit-flavored gumdrop.

Description of the Plant

Jujube is a small tree—rarely more than thirty feet high—with small, glossy leaves and a naturally drooping habit, accentuated when the branches are weighed down with fruits. Plants send up suckers from their roots, and these suckers can appear many feet from the mother plant. Branches on some clones are armed with intimidating spines over an inch long. Fortunately, other clones and older trees have few or no spines.

Jujube has a complicated growth and branching habit that is unique among fruit plants. Each leaf axil contains two types of buds: a larger main bud, which is just like a shoot bud on any other plant; and a smaller lateral bud, which can grow into a shoot the same season it forms. Depending on the location, type, and vigor of a bud, it might remain dormant or grow into a permanent or a deciduous shoot, possibly a fruit-bearing shoot.

Jujube

As the growing season commences, each node of a woody branch has the possibility of producing one to ten branchlets, with older branches producing the most branchlets. Most of these branchlets are deciduous, dying in winter and falling from the plant in spring. Here and there a robust shoot might appear instead of a branchlet and this shoot becomes part of the permanent structure of the tree. Shoots of intermediate vigor are half-deciduous, losing only their distal portions at the end of the season.

Small, inconspicuous, yellow flowers grow in clusters of one to half a dozen or more in leaf axils of the growing branchlets. Flower buds are initiated the same year the flowers open. The plants have an extended blossoming period that continues sporadically throughout the growing season, with the first blossoms to mature being those closest to the base of a branchlet. Artificial lighting, such as a streetlight, can further prolong the flowering period. Individual flowers, however, are receptive to pollen for only a day or less.

Pollination needs of the jujube are not clearly defined. Some cultivars need cross-pollination and others are either self-fertile or set parthenocarpic fruits, but these needs might change with climate. Allegedly self-fertile clones commonly set more and larger fruit with cross-pollination. That said, there are some cultivars, such as 'Silverhill', 'Swoboda', and 'Leon Burk', that set prodigious crops in isolation, yielding stones with aborted kernels.

Three hundred years ago, the Chinese writer Li Shi Chen described forty-three varieties of jujube; today, China has over eight hundred varieties. Most jujube plants in Europe and America are seedling trees with fruits of variable quality. My first introduction to the fruit was not favorable: I joined a Chinese couple in gathering fruit from beneath a tree growing in the shadow of the Capitol in Washington, D.C. This tree (now called 'Admiral Wilkes') evidently was not one of the better clones, for I found the fruits insipid. Years later, the fruits of a tree at the Brooklyn Botanical Garden in New York, though small, were tasty enough to renew my interest in the plant.

Frank Meyer sent to America eighty-three varieties that he collected in China. Many of the descriptions of cultivars listed at the end of this chapter are from his *Agricultural Explorations in the Fruit and Nut Orchards of China*, issued in 1911. The most commonly planted cultivars in America are 'Li' and 'Lang'. In addition to those cultivars listed, Meyer also reported a rare, ornamental cultivar in China that was called 'Dragon's Claw' ('Lung Tsao Tsao Shu') for its gnarled and twisted branches and a white-fruited jujube, of which I have heard no more.

Cultivation

Though the jujube is native to hot climates where temperatures range from twenty to one hundred and twenty degrees Fahrenheit, the tree will survive winter cold to at least minus twenty-two degrees Fahrenheit. The plant revels in summer sun and heat, with the lack of either limiting fruit production more than winter cold as one progresses north planting these trees. For best production in northern areas, site the plant in the sunniest and warmest microclimate, such as near a south-facing wall. Looking to the other extreme of jujube cultivation, the need for a mere 150 hours of winter chilling before buds will awaken in spring makes jujube right at home in subtropical climates.

Jujubes tolerate many types of soils. Meyer reported seeing trees in China that were productive even when growing "in an inner courtyard where the ground has been tramped until it is hard as stone." Jujubes also tolerate a wide range of soil moisture conditions, as evidenced by their native habitats, where rainfall might be as little as five or as much as eighty inches each year. Cultivated trees grow well between rice paddies in China and in the dry soils of the American Southwest. Sometimes, rain during ripening splits the fruit.

Given adequate heat and sun, jujube trees will thrive without special care. The plants bloom late enough to escape spring frosts and virtually no pests attack the plant or the fruit. What little pruning the plants need is directed toward developing a spreading habit in the young tree. On a mature tree, pruning back some of the oldest permanent branches and side branches near the cuts encourages growth of young permanent branches to replace the old ones; best fruits are borne on permanent branches up to ten years old.

Meyer reported that the Chinese would cut out a ring of bark from the trees right after blossoming in order to increase yield, with some sacrifice of sweetness in the ripe fruit. The ring was made with a saw cut each year at a different level on the trunk, beginning when trees were six or seven years old.

The ground around jujube trees should never be cultivated. Any root damage induces the plants to send up suckers.

Propagation

Plants grown from seed usually do not bear high-quality fruit, but could be used as rootstocks or ornamentals. Germination is enhanced by opening the stone and extracting the two kernels contained within. (Depending on pollination, some stones will be hollow—and some large-fruited cultivars always have hollow stones.) An easy way to open a stone is to carefully cut it lengthwise along one edge with pruning shears.

Stratify the kernels under cool, moist conditions for two months unless you first nip off the pointed end of the seed, in which case no stratification is needed. It is important that the peat moss, perlite, or whatever medium in which the seeds are being stratified is just moist, not wet. Never expose the kernels to temperatures below freezing. Expect an average of about fifty percent of the seeds to germinate, less from large-fruited clones or from plants that have been self-pollinated, more from small-fruited ones or from plants that have been cross-pollinated. The kernels are slow to germinate and seedlings often require two years of growth before they are large enough to be grafted.

Suckers, root cuttings, and grafts are ways to propagate superior jujube clones. A clone to be propagated by suckers or root cuttings must be on its own roots, that is, it should not be a grafted tree. Success with root cuttings is variable, depending on the clone, and plants grown from root cuttings will not develop the taproot of trees grown from seed. Stem cuttings root with difficulty.

Grafted plants grow vigorously. Chip budding, T-budding, and whip-and-tongue grafting have all been successful—as long as scionwood is not chosen of stems destined to be deciduous. Jujube plants are precocious. Grafted trees have even been known to bear some fruit in the same season in which they were grafted!

Harvest and Use

The hundred pounds of fruit that a single jujube tree can produce do not all ripen at the same time, so the fruits must be picked every few days for a month or more. As a green fruit ripens, it first turns almost white and then, within a few days, becomes mottled reddish brown. For "fresh" eating, i.e. when the fruit is still crisp, harvest those fruits that are brown but still firm. Soon after the skin becomes completely brown, it begins to wrinkle, and the yellow flesh within becomes soft and spongy. While that skin color change is taking place, sugar concentration of the fruit rises. Jujube fruits also are extremely rich in vitamin C, containing 400 to 1,000 milligrams of this vitamin per hundred grams.

The fruits can be picked underripe—when they turn from green to almost white—to finish ripening off the tree. Such fruits will not be as sweet as those ripened on the tree, though.

Crispy ripe fruits will keep for one to two months at fifty degrees Fahrenheit; at room temperature, the fruits may be stored for a week to a month. The length of the storage period probably depends on the humidity, with longer storage possible in drier air. Never store the fresh fruit at temperatures below thirty-six degrees Fahrenheit or chilling injury, indicated by sunken areas in the fruits, will result.

Under dry conditions, on or off the tree, ripe fruits continue to lose moisture, shrivel, and become darker and spongy inside. Eventually they will drop from the tree. Dried fruits will keep for up to a year at cool temperatures and just over fifty percent relative humidity.

In China, jujubes are eaten fresh, dried, smoked, pickled, candied, and as a butter. The fruit can also be boiled with rice or baked with breads, much like raisin bread. Meyer reported in 1911 that the very spiny branches of wild jujube plants were used as fencing in China, and their small, sour, though pleasant-tasting, fruits were collected by "old women and children" for pastes and preserves.

Here is the recipe for real jujube candy (Chinese "honey jujubes"), quoted from Meyer's 1911 report.

The Chinese take large, sound, dried fruits and boil them thoroughly in sugared water, after which they are taken out and dried in the sun or wind for a couple of days. When sufficiently dry they are given a slight boiling again and are partly dried. When dry enough to be handled, the skin is slashed lengthwise with a few small knives tied together. Then the fruits are given a third boiling, now, however, in a stronger sugar water, and for the best grades of honey jujube honey is added. When this process is finished they are spread out to dry, and when no longer sticky are ready to be sold.

Cultivars

'Chin Sze Tsao': medium-sized tree; the fruits are light brown, small, and very sweet; used to make "honey jujube."

'GA866': from the fruit-breeding program at Chico, California; the crispy fruits are long, broad, firm, and very sweet.

'Hu Ping Tsao' ('Bottle Jujube'): tree is small and spineless, with few suckers; fruit is large and oblong; so named because in China the shiny red fruits are soaked for several months in weak spirits before being eaten.

'Lang': upright tree is almost thornless; fruits ripen right after 'Li' and are two inches long by one and a half inches wide, and pear-shaped with a thin, shiny skin; do not harvest until fully red; flavor is sweet with a hint of caramel; good fresh but at its best dried.

'Lang Tsao' ('Mellow Jujube'): tree is large and spreading; fruit is red, small, oblong, mellow-sweet, and a poor keeper.

'Li': many-branched tree; fruits are among the largest of any jujubes, round and two inches in diameter; often seedless or nearly so; excellent flavor.

'Ming Tsao': tree is small, erect, suckering, and not spiny; fruit is oblong, light brown, an inch and a half long, and sweet.

'Mu Shing Hong Tsao': tree grows large and old, eventually with few branches, spines, or suckers; the fruit is reddish brown and tapered, medium-sized, sometimes soft-kerneled ("seedless"), and a good keeper.

'Sherwood': seedling tree accidentally imported from China with some camellias; usually thornless; tree has a narrow weeping habit and is slow to begin bearing; the late-ripening fruits are large and have excellent flavor.

'Silverhill': a tree found in Silverhill, Alabama; large tree with relatively few suckers or thorns; late-ripening; prolific bearer of elongated fruits each about an inch across; fruit flesh is solid and sweet.

'So': tree is slow growing and ornamental with its downward-curving branches; moderate crops of crispy, round, good-quality fruits ripen early.

'Tsui Ling Tsao' ('Fragile Jujube'): tree has few suckers and no spines; fruit is oblong, a poor keeper, and breaks easily if dropped.

'Tun Ku Yu Tsao': fruit has a flat shape and is very sweet.

'Twen Ku Lu Tsao': tree has few suckers; fruit yields are low; fruit is dark brown, flat, and very sweet, but a poor keeper.

'Wuhu Tsao' ('Seedless Jujube'): this cultivar is functionally seedless; the fruits are dark reddish brown and can be eaten almost without noticing the soft stone; every year some of these small and very sweet fruits were sent to the Chinese emperor.

'Ya Tsao': tree is small, erect, very spiny, and suckering; fruits are dark brown and tapering, an inch and a half to two inches long and not very sweet.

'Yuen Ling Tsao' ('Su Hsin Tsao'): the spreading tree is especially cosmopolitan in its soil preferences; fruits are round, of variable size, with a purplish red skin, and eaten smoked.

'Yu Tsao' ('Tooth Jujube'): usually thornless; tooth-shaped fruits, good flavor.

Shipova

A Sweetie with a Blush

BOTANICAL NAME
×*Sorbopyrus auricularis*

PLANT TYPE
Deciduous tree

POLLINATION
Self-fruitful, but probably only partially so

RIPENING SEASON
Late summer

Shipova. Speak the name. It makes a pleasant sound, especially with the middle syllable emphasized and drawn out ever so slightly. Intoning the name is equally pleasant to the lips, the end of each syllable leaving the lips poised for the beginning of the next: Shi. . . po . . . va. Beyond such pleasantries, little is known about shipova, the most uncommon of the uncommon fruits between the covers of this book. Shipova is not now and has never been widely eaten, and even its origins are murky.

Poor flavor cannot be blamed for shipova's obscurity. A close flavor comparison would be with pear, which, as we will soon see, is also one of the "pear-rents" (pardon the pun) of this unusual hybrid. The buttery flesh—a bit more meaty than a pear—melts with each bite to fill the mouth with semisolid, sweet and fragrant ambrosia.

The name "shipova" sounds to me like something of beauty in a Nabokov story—and shipova, the fruit, similarly does not disappoint when it comes to appearance. Picture a small pear about two inches across and rounded so as to retain just a hint of pear-ness. The skin is golden yellow with a red blush on the side kissed by the sun.

Shipova's uncommonness also cannot be blamed on its being a "new kid on the block." The origin of the tree can be traced way back to sometime before

1610, in Europe, and it made its way to America in the early part of the twentieth century. Over the years, it picked up more than its share of both botanical and common names. The former have included *Pyrus malifolia*, denoting a pear with apple-like foliage, *Pyrus tomentosa*, denoting a pear with downy foliage, and *Bollwilleria auricularis*, *Azarolus pollvilleriana*, and *Sorbus bollwylleriana*, the latter names no longer having any botanical standing.

The name "shipova" tagged along on a plant brought to America from Yugoslavia in 1959, allegedly as a fall-ripening pear with apple-like leaves. Shipova proved not to be a pear at all, but identical to the plants introduced earlier in the twentieth century. The origin of its name is not clear, one suggestion being that it derives from the Slavic word *sipurak* or *sipac*, meaning "fruit of the rose," which shipova is, if "rose" is taken to mean the whole rose family.

Another plant, later proving identical to shipova, was introduced into America in 1986 from Macedonia under the name 'Smokvarka'. This name, though less euphonious and appetizing sounding than "shipova," is not cryptic at all. It means "little fig fruit," a description that is almost correct. The fruit does look a little like a fig even if it's not particularly little for a fig. As to flavor, it's a little like a fig only in that both are heavenly. I am, anyway, going to continue to call the fruit shipova.

Description of the Plant

Shipova is one of those rare hybrids that occur between two different genera. One parent is the common, or European, pear, *Pyrus communis*. The other parent is a species of *Sorbus*, probably *S. aria*, the common whitebeam. You may recognize that *Sorbus* is the genus that includes mountain ashes, those familiar ornamental trees having pinnate leaves and bearing flat-topped clusters of white flowers often followed by bunches of brightly colored fruits. Whitebeams lie within a different division of *Sorbus* from mountain ashes, the most obvious difference being that whitebeams' leaves are simple and covered with a downy felt that gives them a snowy appearance, especially on their undersides and early in the season.

With fat buds and downiness inherited from its whitebeam parent, shipova appears in spring almost like a magnolia in bud. The pear parent plays an equally minor role when it comes to shipova's growth habit. Rather than the predominance of upright shoots and the many narrow, angled crotches common to pears, shipova's growth habit is relatively open, with naturally spreading branches and wide-angled crotches.

Shipova's leaves unfold covered in a downy whiteness, much of which is lost on the uppersides as they mature. The tree is especially comely with the whiteness of its leaves highlighted against a backdrop of some dark-leaved plant, a Norway spruce, for example. The leaves also look pretty fluttering in a breeze, alternately showing off their white undersides and then their green topsides. The leaves stay healthy throughout the growing season, then turn, in autumn, a mix of pale salmon-pink and yellow.

Shipova bears its flowers on spurs, which are stubby branches elongating just a fraction of an inch each year, and also on short branches about six inches long. The flower buds open to yield clusters of blossoms, each of which spreads its white petals three-quarters of an inch to an inch across. I've counted over twenty blossoms in a single cluster! Rose-colored stamens (the male flower parts) emerge near the center of each blossom. Woolliness from the whitebeam parent manifests itself even in the flower, on the sepals, which are the petal-like appendages situated just beneath the actual petals.

The various introductions of *Sorbopyrus* into America have not all been identical. Two so-called 'Baciu' clones, from Romania, are smaller in all respects than shipova, with fruit that also differs from shipova in shape but not in taste or texture. (These two clones also were first brought in as pears.) Shipova is probably the clone that has been described as ×*Sorbopyrus auricularis* var. *bulbiformis*, or ×*Sorbopyrus bulbiformis*, which besides being larger in all respects, also bears rounder fruits.

'Bulbiformis' or shipova or whatever else you call this plant is a *Sorbopyrus* seedling that evidently originated before 1834. The first American introductions, which, as previously mentioned, subsequently proved to be the same as the later introduction named shipova, can be traced back to a tree growing on the grounds of the Paris Museum of Natural History. Cytological analysis, as well as shipova's robust nature, and, possibly, its frequent lack of viable seeds indicate that this clone is a triploid. With two sets of pear chromosomes and one set of whitebeam chromosomes, shipova probably originated as a seedling from the pollination of ×*Sorbopyrus* with pear. (The 'Baciu' clones have only one set of chromosomes from each parent.)

Although shipova fruit is very pearlike in flavor and appearance, its whitebeam parent has not necessarily been an idle onlooker in developing that flavor. Whitebeam is a plant that also has been enjoyed for the taste of its fruits. Many *Sorbus* species, in fact, have been enjoyed as such, justifying a short detour to see what they offer as "uncommon fruits for every garden."

Although their flavors can be very good, gustatory limitations of edible *Sorbus* are mostly small size and mealy texture. Whitebeam fruits, for instance, are scarlet and sweet, a good start for any fruit, but a mere half-inch across, dry, and mealy. Still, a good nibble. *S. yuana* yields olive-sized fruits sweeter than pears, but with their own unique flavor.

Before being eaten, some *Sorbus* fruits must be bletted, or allowed to soften after harvest (just like medlar, another uncommon fruit). The wild service tree or chequerberry, *S. torminalis*, is one such fruit and among the more popular *Sorbus* for eating. The cherry-sized fruit has a russet skin and, once bletted, develops a sweet and interesting taste that was once valued as a sweet treat and for making chequerberry beer. The berries were also reputed to make an effective love potion. The sorb-apple (*S. devoniensis*, also commonly called French hales or Fontainebleu service) reputedly develops the flavor, sweetness, and texture of dates upon bletting.

The service tree (*S. domestica*) yields a cute fruit that I chanced upon years ago, on the grounds—and on the ground—of the Arnold Arboretum. They look like miniature 'Bartlett' pears, so I picked one up and tasted it. The first one was sweet, soft, and aromatic. The next puckered me up; it evidently had not thoroughly bletted. I was not the first to enjoy these fruits, also called sorb-apples, for they were grown in Tudor orchards, and Theophrastus mentioned their cultivation in the fourth century B.C. This service tree and the just-mentioned wild service tree, incidentally, are not to be confused with *Amelanchier* species, also sometimes called service trees, and another uncommon fruit of this book.

As unusual as intergeneric hybrids are among plants generally, *Sorbus* has not confined its distant marriages only to pear. Among the more interesting ones as far as uncommon fruits is ×*Amelosorbus* because the other parent in the marriage is that other "service tree" of this book, *Amelanchier*. This hybrid was raised at the Arnold Arboretum around the middle of the twentieth century and was described as having leaves intergrade between both parents. It produced almost no normal pollen and few fruits. No mention was made of the flavor of the fruit.

Cultivation

Specifics of shipova cultivation are hard to pin down because relatively few trees have been grown throughout the world, despite the plant having been around for four hundred years. Still, we can make some educated guesses from conditions enjoyed by those few plants and from the likes and dislikes of shipova's parents.

Downy leaves would suggest that the plant enjoys a site in full sunlight and that it might tolerate some amount of drought. My experience bears this out, but drought tolerance is probably also due to the tree's robust top growth being matched below ground with roots that can reach far to find water. Like most cultivated fruits, shipova probably also enjoys a well-drained, moderately rich soil. Cold-hardiness is at least to Zone 4.

Shipova sets fruit without cross-pollination. And even if pollination does take place, the few or no viable seeds that result suggest that fertilization is rarely the case. Still, yields are not high and it is possible that some sort of pollinator might provide a further boost to productivity. But with what do you pollinate a triploid tree whose parents come from two different genera? Possibilities include a pear, a common whitebeam, or one of the other ×*Sorbopyrus* clones, such as 'Baciu'. It would be interesting to note if shipova would yield more fertile seeds, perhaps even larger fruit, with one of these other trees as a neighbor.

Perhaps the main shortcoming of this plant is the way it takes its time to yield its first fruits. Seven to ten years after planting is a typical waiting period. In my experience, neither bending down branches nor summer pruning—both of which are often effective in hastening fruiting of pears—has any effect on shipova. Rootstocks that induce precocity in pear, such as 'Quince A' and 'Old Home × Farmingdale 51', may prove effective in bringing shipova into earlier bearing, assuming they were also graft compatible with shipova.

Be careful pruning this plant because excessive pruning can induce vigorous, yet unfruitful, regrowth. In its youth, the plant needs nothing more than removal of misplaced branches, mostly with thinning cuts. Branching seems adequate without the need for heading cuts. Mature trees should need only light pruning because fruits are borne on short branches and on spurs that can bear year after year. Eventually, branches with old spurs may need invigoration by being cut back or by having their spurs thinned out a bit.

Shipova is a carefree fruit tree. Late frosts should cause no worry because shipova blooms late, about two weeks after pears. Insects and diseases should likewise cause little concern, and freedom from pests is one more thing keeping this tree looking pretty all season long.

One disease that could threaten shipova is fire blight, common to almost all members of the rose family. Fire blight most readily infects excessively vigorous shoots, so avoid severe pruning, heavy fertilization, or other practices that coax such growth. Planting lawn almost right up to the trunk provides a means of regulating growth: Let the grass grow longer and absorb more nutrients and water if shipova's growth seems excessive; mow lower if the tree needs to make more growth.

Put some care into siting shipova not only for best growth and because of its ornamental qualities, but also because the tree will be there for many, many years. A tree grafted in 1901 at the Arnold Arboretum was still alive as of this writing, in 2002 (even if only barely so).

Propagation

Not to be redundant about a lack of information, but little is also known about propagating shipova. Like the apple and the pear, shipova is propagated most readily and easily by grafting. Unlike the apple and the pear, for which a range of rootstocks exist that affect tree size, precocity, and adaptation to specific site conditions, little is known about possible rootstocks for shipova.

Generally, shipova is propagated on one of the clonal pear rootstocks. Testing needs to be done as to what species (*Sorbus*, pear, even quince, which is compatible with many pears) and clones are compatible and which ones might be used for adaptability, early bearing, and, if desired, size control.

It might be interesting to see how the tree grows even on its own roots. An own-rooted shipova would be hard to come by because shipova, like other mature pear and apple clones, is hard to root. The etiolated shoot method, described in the "Propagation" appendix, might be successful in producing such a tree. Otherwise, the only own-rooted shipova would be the original tree.

Harvest

Harvest shipova fruits when fully ripe, at which point their skins will be yellow. Cup the fruit in your palm, then roll the fruit upward with a slight twist. If truly ripe, it will part cleanly where the fruit stalk is attached to the tree. Picked slightly underripe, the fruit will store for months under refrigeration.

Medlar

Lost in the Middle Ages

BOTANICAL NAME
Mespilus germanica

PLANT TYPE
Small, flat-topped, deciduous tree

POLLINATION
Self-fertile

RIPENING SEASON
Fall

I t is time for dessert two hundred, perhaps even two thousand, years ago. We have a platter of medlars brought to the table. The fruits resemble small, russeted apples, tinged dull yellow or red, with their calyx ends (across from the stems) flared open. Better yet, let's take the suggestion of a past enthusiast and "send [medlars] to the table with vine leaves or other such garnishings . . . so dressed, medlars contrast well with bright, rosy apples."

Open a medlar; inside, the flesh is as soft as a baked apple. The flavor has a refreshing briskness with winy overtones, like old-fashioned applesauce laced with cinnamon. Embedded in the pulp are five, large, stonelike seeds.

The medlar may have been cultivated as far back as thirty centuries ago. It is hard to know for sure, because "medlar" was a name once applied to the cornelian cherry, stone fruits (*Prunus* spp.), and especially the medlar's close relatives, hawthorn and cotoneaster. Even today, medlar can mean some fruit other than *Mespilus germanica*. I once planted seeds of *nispero* (Spanish for medlar) brought back from Spain. The resulting plants turned out to be loquats (*Eriobotrya japonica*), sometimes called Japanese medlars.

The true medlar perhaps reached its peak of popularity during the Middle Ages. In the ninth century, the medlar was included in the catalogue of mandatory plants for the royal estates in Charlemagne's *Capitulare de villis* ("decree concerning towns"). Medlar trees were familiar denizens of walled monastery gardens of the Middle Ages, and fittingly, a tree is growing in the re-created monastery garden of the Cloisters, the medieval branch of the Metropolitan Museum of Art in New York. One of the Unicorn Tapestries (c. 1500) hanging at the Cloisters depicts medlars. The medlar was a market fruit in Europe as late as the nineteenth century.

Today, the medlar is rarely cultivated in Europe or anywhere else. The fruit admittedly could be, and has been, described in less than laudatory tones. "A crabby-looking, brownish-green, truncated, little spheroid of unsympathetic appearance," wrote one author. "Open-arse" and its variations "openars" and "open-ers" were English names for the fruit a thousand years ago, and allude to the large open disc between the persistent calyx lobes. Shakespeare's Mercutio was more delicate with his choice of words, calling the fruit "open et cetera" in *Romeo and Juliet*. The French bestow upon the medlar the unflattering nickname *cul de chien*.

Perhaps the mushy, brown interior is to some moderns more akin visually to a rotten, than a baked, apple. No matter, few people today have had the opportunity to sample this fruit so highly esteemed in past centuries. The only way to become familiar with the medlar today is to plant one.

Description of the Plant

There is some question as to the original home of the medlar, for dense thickets of scraggly and thorny wild medlars now are naturalized over much of Europe. The greatest diversity amongst wild medlars, suggesting a possible point of origin for this plant, is along the west coast of the Caspian Sea. But leaf impressions of the medlar have been reported in interglacial deposits in the former East Germany, lending support to Linnaeus's choice of *germanica* for the specific epithet.

In comparison with its wild siblings, the cultivated medlar has taken on an air of elegance, lacking thorns and becoming a flat-topped, small tree, usually no more than twenty feet high. Not too elegant, though, for the elbowed contortions of the branches, so evident in winter, lend an air of rusticity that never allows even cultivated plants to be pressed into formal attire. Under cultivation, a medlar can be long lived. A tree planted in Hertfordshire when James I was king of England (he reigned from 1603 to 1625) was reportedly still alive in 1988. Occasional dieback of branches is something I've noticed on many medlars, including my own, which adds to the rusticity of the tree

Medlar

and the worry of us gardeners, although pruning easily gets the tree back in shape and new growth is soon bearing fruit.

In summer, medlar's elbowed branches are hidden beneath lush, green, lance-shaped leaves. Variegated forms also exist: var. *argenteo-variegata*, whose leaves are flecked with white, and var. *aureo-variegata*, whose leaves are flecked with yellow. In autumn, medlar leaves turn warm, rich shades of yellow, orange, and russet.

A medlar in bloom, festooned as it is with large white or slightly pink blossoms, each one to two inches across, is every bit as showy as a wild rose. Some European cities, among them Lochem and Goor in Holland, have medlar flowers in their city emblems. In contrast to those of most other fruit trees, medlar flowers open up after the plant has pushed out a few inches of growth. The blossoms are born singly on the ends of short shoots that grow in spring from lateral buds on year-old wood and from spurs on older wood. A whorl of dark green leaves behind each flower contrasts and frames the blossom.

Almost every medlar flower will set fruit. The blooms open late enough so that spring frost is rarely a hazard, and the flowers do not need cross-pollination. Some pollination occurs in the absence of insects because as the flowers open, the outward-facing stigmas readily touch the inward-facing stamens. And if pollination should not occur, the medlar has a strong tendency to set fruit parthenocarpically, that is, without any pollination whatsoever.

For all the centuries that medlars have been cultivated, remarkably few clones have been selected for superior fruit. There are a few thousand cultivars of apple, yet only a handful of medlar cultivars.

Medlars have been hybridized with related genera. Medlar's closest of kin is the hawthorn, and hybrids between the two genera, designated ×*Crataegomespilus*, have been produced by crossing the medlar with either *Crataegus laevigata* or *C. monogyna*. The Russian plant breeder I. V. Michurin used medlar in breeding with the goal of improving the gustatory quality of mountain ash (*Sorbus* spp.).

Chimeras, or graft hybrids, also have been noted between medlar and hawthorn (these particular chimeras are called hawmedlars, or, botanically, +*Crataegomespilus*). Chimeras occur when adventitious buds at the graft union grow so that the resulting shoot combines the characters of the rootstock and the scion. The first medlar-hawthorn chimera was reported in 1898.

As might be expected, if you hybridize two ornamental plants, the resulting offspring very likely also will be ornamental. Such is the case for some of the sexual and graft hybrids between medlar and hawthorn. I would not expect incorporating "blood" of the somewhat austere hawthorn or mountain ash fruits into medlar to improve the flavor of medlar fruits, though.

Cultivation

Medlar trees are hardy at least to USDA Hardiness Zone 5, though individuals within a population of seedling trees planted near Chicago have survived where the mercury has dipped to almost minus thirty degrees Fahrenheit. The site for the tree should be sunny, and the soil should be well drained and reasonably fertile. Soil requirements vary somewhat with choice of rootstock (see the following section on propagation).

Because of possible delayed incompatibilities between scion and rootstock, a medlar tree should be planted with its graft union a couple of inches below soil level. Soil covering the medlar scion eventually will induce the scion to form its own roots. This rule cannot be followed with a medlar trained as a standard by being grafted high on some ramrod-straight rootstock.

The medlar is an attractive specimen tree standing alone in a lawn. Because the medlar is a small tree, it is equally at home mingling with other shrubs in a shrub border. Just make sure the plant is not shaded.

A medlar tree needs training in its early years to build up an attractive and sturdy framework. Beyond that, what little pruning is needed is confined to the removal of dead and crossing branches and the thinning out of spindly wood to admit light and air into the tree canopy. Be careful not to prune off the extremities of too many branches, for this is where most of the flowering shoots arise.

Though the medlar shares some pest problems common to its kin in the rose family, these pests rarely become serious enough to warrant concern or mention. No pests have called attention to themselves on my tree after almost two decades.

Propagation

Medlar is most commonly and most easily propagated by grafting. When I created my present medlar tree, I used a friend's medlar for scion wood, but did not have a medlar rootstock. No matter.

> He does the savage Hawthorn teach
> To bear the Medlar and the Pear.
>
> (Abraham Cowley, 1678)

Or, quoting eighteenth-century poet Ambrose Philips,

> Men have gathered from the hawthorn's branch
> Large medlars imitating regal crowns.

Medlar can be grafted upon rootstocks of pear, quince, hawthorn, amelanchier, and, of course, medlar. The quince is the recommended rootstock for moist soils, the hawthorn for dry soils (*Crataegus monogyna* or *C. laevigata* are probably most suitable), and the pear for heavier soils. Quince roots have a dwarfing effect on the resultant tree, but this effect is lost as scion rooting takes place on grafted trees whose graft union is below ground level. The pear is generally considered the best of the three rootstocks. (Fortunately, pear was the rootstock that I had available.)

The crooked stem of the medlar is unsuitable where a very straight trunk is needed for a tree trained as a very formal "standard." To create such a tree, graft the medlar high on a straight trunk of pear.

Medlar seedlings are likely to be inferior to their parents, but not to the same extent as, for example, apple seedlings. This is no great consolation, though, because only about one out of ten thousand apple seedlings bears fruit that matches either of its parents in flavor. Medlar seeds need cool, moist stratification, but may not germinate until their second spring, especially if seed is not fresh when sown.

Cuttings root with difficulty. Some success has been reported with early summer softwood cuttings treated with 5000 ppm IBA in 50% isopropanol solution and grown under mist. Alternatively, try the etiolated shoot method described in Appendix 5 ("Propagation").

Harvest and Use

Medlars are rock-hard and puckery when ready for harvest and must be allowed to soften before becoming edible. This softening is called "bletting," a word coined in 1839 from the French word *blessi*, which denotes a particular type of bruised appearance found in fruits such as the medlar and the persimmon. Chemically speaking, bletting brings about an increase in sugars and a decrease in acids and tannins (tannins cause the unripe fruits to be puckery).

Though the fruit is picked rock-hard, it must be thoroughly matured on the tree before harvest. Fruit picked too early shrivels in storage and never attains good flavor. The entire growing season is needed for the fruits to mature, even beyond the first few frosts of autumn. This has fueled the myth that a frost is needed to ripen the fruits (the same myth is promulgated for the persimmon, whose fruits also need a long season, but not frost, before they are ready for picking). The fruit will not be harmed by a few degrees of frost.

Medlars are ready for harvest when the leaves are just beginning to fall, at which stage the fruits part readily from the branch. Leaving fruits on the tree late in the season adds to the medlar's show of beauty, for the nude branches become quite ornamental with their scores of little medlar pompoms. To ensure that the fruits do not rot in storage, pick them on a dry sunny day. Be gentle; the fruits' hardness belies their need for careful handling.

Set each harvested fruit in a cool room calyx end down and not touching its neighbor. Some gardeners just set medlars on a clean shelf or on a bed of straw; others "plant" the fruits in clean sand, sawdust, or bran. In Chaucer's day, gardeners evidently were not overly fastidious about where they bletted their medlars:

> But if I fare as dooth an open-ers [medlar];
> That ilke fruyt is ever lenger the wers,
> Til it be roten in mullok or in stree [in rubbish or in straw].
>
> (*Canterbury Tales*, 1387)

Less fastidious gardeners also might let ripe fruits just drop from the trees and blet on the ground.

Bletting requires from two weeks to a month, at which time the hard, cream-colored interior turns brown and mushy. Do not touch the fruits except to remove them for eating; they will show you they are fit to eat when their skins darken. Once bletted, medlars keep for several weeks.

The easiest way to eat a medlar is to suck the fruit empty, leaving skin and seeds behind. The fresh fruit is (was?) the classic accompaniment to port at the end of a meal. The pulp can be scooped out and folded into cream for a dessert dish. Medlars also have been eaten cooked in a number of ways, such as baked whole, stewed with butter, or roasted over a fire. The fruit is well suited to the usual array of jams, jellies, tarts, and syrups. You can make a refreshing drink by pouring boiling water over the fruit, then drinking the cooled liquid.

In the past, medlar wood was prized for its durability, and the fruits for their medicinal virtues. The wood was prescribed for spear points, cudgels, fighting clubs, walking sticks, and canes. In herbal remedies, the fruits were considered effective, according to the herbalist Culpeper, writing in the seventeenth century, to "strengthen the retentive faculty, therefore it stays Womens Longings: the good old Man cannot endure Womens Minds should run a gadding . . . very powerful to stay any Fluxes of Blood or Humours in Man or Woman . . . The Fruit eaten by Woman with Child, stayeth their Longing after unusual Meats."

Cultivars

In addition to those cultivars listed here, a number of other cultivars—'Puciolot', 'Pucia Supermol', 'Nèfle Précoce', 'Nèfle Tardive', 'Monstreux d'Evreinoff', 'Breda Giant', 'Nèfle d'Octobre', 'Sultan', 'Westerveld', 'Macrocarpa', and 'Marron'—have recently come to my attention, although I have little information about them beyond their names. Some of these cultivars could even be the same as each other or as one of those that follow, although "casual comparison" by Joseph Postman at the USDA germplasm facility in Oregon indicates that 'Puciolot', at least, bears particularly large fruit with good flavor. In the future, DNA "fingerprinting" could point the finger at aliases.

'Dutch' (also called 'Giant', 'Monstrous', and 'Dutch Giant'): this cultivar was listed in an English nursery catalogue of 1783, so has been around at least that long; tree is very vigorous and the branches spread to make the plant flat-headed almost to the point of weeping; fruit is large, often two and a half inches across, and has good flavor.

'Nottingham' (also called 'Common' and probably the same as 'Neapolitan' of older texts): perhaps the oldest extant cultivar of medlar; tree is somewhat straggly with an upright growth habit; fruit is yellowish brown with russet, and has long sepals; though the fruit is small, usually an inch-and-a half or less across, the rich, subacid flavor of 'Nottingham' is considered among the best of all medlars.

'Royal': this cultivar has characteristics intermediate between 'Dutch' and 'Nottingham'; tree is moderately upright with a rounded form; fruit is of moderate size, with good flavor.

'Stoneless' (sometimes called by non-English names 'San Noyan', 'Sans Noyau', or 'Sans Pépins'): the saving grace of this cultivar is that it is seedless and a good keeper; the fruit is only a half to three-quarters of an inch in diameter and most, but not all, gardeners agree that it has poor flavor.

Epilogue

The grower of uncommon fruits is almost alone in the wilderness, at least for the present. You might chat over the fence with your neighbor, comparing sizes of tomatoes or yields of apples, but you probably will not find common ground talking about the likes of maypops, medlars, or mulberries.

Fortunately, there are a few organizations devoted to uncommon fruits of temperate zones. These include: California Rare Fruit Growers (www.crfg.org); North American Fruit Explorers (www.nafex.org); and Northern Nut Growers (www.northernnutgrowers.org). Within the membership ranks of these organizations are people with whom you can share experiences, enthusiasm, even plants. In addition, my website (leereich.com) offers up-to-date information about uncommon fruits. So go . . .

> forward [and] graffe, set, plant and nourish up trees in every corner of your ground, the labor is small, the cost is nothing, the commodity is great, your selves shall have plentie, the poor shall have somwhat in time of want to relieve their necessitie.
>
> (John Gerard, *The Herball*, 1597)

Also, the activity is pleasant and the flavors are exquisite.

Appendix 1

Nomenclature

E very plant has a scientific name that is a Latin or latinized binomial, the first word of which refers to the plant's *genus* and the second word of which refers to a subdivision of genus, the *species*. Thus, the musk strawberry, *Fragaria moschata*, and the alpine strawberry, *Fragaria vesca*, are two different species within the genus *Fragaria*. Note that the genus and species names are always italicized or underlined. And if the genus referred to is obvious, it may be abbreviated, so, for example, *Fragaria vesca* could be written *F. vesca*.

Sometimes there exist within a species large enough subpopulations of similar plants to warrant further subdivision—those plants are a "botanical variety." An example of this is found in medlar, *Mespilus germanica*. Within this species, there occur plants with white-flecked leaves, and these are designated *M. germanica* var. *argenteo-variegata*.

Scientific names avoid the confusion that sometimes results with common names. "Gooseberry" is a common name for *Pereskia aculeata*, *Physalis peruviana*, *Davyalis hebecarpa*, and other plants not at all related to the true gooseberry (*Ribes uva-crispa* and *R. hirtellum*). If you are put off by scientific names for plants, take heart: nomenclature could be worse. Before the days of Carl von Linne, the eighteenth-century originator of the present system, catnip was known as *Nepeta floribus interrupte spicatis pedunculatis*. Isn't *Nepeta cataria* less cumbersome?

A "seedling" is what grows when you take a seed out of a ripe fruit and plant it. Except where viable hybrids are produced between different species (or, more rarely, between different genera), seedlings are the same genus and species as their parents. Sow seeds of medlar, *Mespilus germanica*, and the resultant seedlings also will be *Mespilus germanica*. But just as all siblings in a human family are similar, though not exactly alike, plant seedlings also differ from each other. How much they differ depends on the particular species.

The word "seedling" does not refer to the size of a plant, but to the fact that the plant was propagated by seed (rather than by a cutting or by grafting, for example). A seedling plant is a seedling its whole life—even a fifty-foot apple tree could be a seedling.

If a particular seedling proves its worth in horticulture—perhaps with better-tasting fruit, increased tolerance for cold, or prettier flowers—then that seedling becomes worthy of a name and dissemination. Such plants are elevated to the status of "cultivated variety" or, joining these two words, "cultivar." (Older texts just use the term "variety" or "horticultural variety," the word "horticultural" here differentiating such a plant from a "botanical variety.") Cultivar status was conferred on the seedlings that produced 'McIntosh' apple and 'Bartlett' pear—they received the cultivar names 'McIntosh' and 'Bartlett'. Using the 'Nottingham' cultivar (note the single quotes and non-Latin name used for cultivars) of medlar as an example, the complete name for a cultivar could be written *Mespilus germanica* cv. Nottingham or *Mespilus germanica* 'Nottingham'.

Except for plants whose seedlings all are very much like the parent plant, cultivars must be propagated by some method of cloning, such as stem cuttings, root cuttings, layering, and grafting. If seeds of these plants are grown, more seedlings, not cultivars, will result, unless one of those seedlings proves worthy of its own cultivar name.

Appendix 2

Pollination

"Pollination," the transfer of pollen from male parts of a flower (the stamens) to female parts of a flower (the pistils), is a necessity in order for most plants to form fruits. Effective pollination can occur only between flowers of the same type of fruit (usually within a species, sometimes between species). Therefore, strawberry flowers can pollinate strawberry flowers, but cannot pollinate pear flowers. Pollen is transferred by wind or insects (especially bees), or when the mere opening of a flower causes stamens to rub against pistils. Just how pollen is transferred varies with the type of fruit.

To the botanist, a "perfect" flower is one with both stamens and pistils. But not all plants have perfect flowers. Some plants have flowers that are either staminate (male) or pistillate (female). If both sexes are on separate flowers of the same plant, the plant is "monoecious" (derived from Latin, meaning "one house"). On the other hand, if individual plants have either male or female flowers, the species is "dioecious" (meaning "two houses"). The kiwifruit plant is an example of a dioecious plant, and one male plant (nonfruiting) can provide enough pollen to sire a good crop of fruits on up to about eight female plants.

Even a plant with perfect flowers may need special accommodation, in the form of "cross-pollination," to set fruit. The female floral parts of "self-sterile" plants are finicky, and refuse to set fruit unless dusted with pollen from stamens of a different clone of that fruit. A different clone is represented by a cultivar with a different name, or by a seedling. Pawpaw, although perfect-flowered, needs cross-pollination to set fruit, so a cultivar such as 'Taytwo' will not set fruit unless it receives pollen from either a seedling pawpaw, or from a different cultivar, such as 'Overleese'. In this example, 'Overleese' or the seedling also will fruit, because of the 'Taytwo' pollen either receives.

For effective cross-pollination, flowers of two different clones must be within a hundred feet of each other and their bloom seasons must overlap. There are ways to get around having to put two different plants in the ground when growing fruits that need cross-pollination. Perhaps your neighbor is growing a suitable pollinator plant, though this is unlikely with uncommon fruits. If you know of a suitable pollinator plant that is not nearby, cut off some branches while the plant is in bloom, put the branches in a bucket of water, and set the bucket on the ground under your plant. The bouquet's pollen will stay viable long enough to pollinate your plant. Perhaps the most practical alternative is to graft a branch of a suitable pollinator right onto your plant. Your plant, then, will have two different clones growing on a common root system.

Plants whose flowers can set fruit with their own pollen are said to be "self-fertile" or "self-pollinating." Such plants need no special accommodation for pollination and will set fruit in isolation.

Self-sterile and self-fertile are two ends of a spectrum, and many types of fruit plants lie somewhere in between. These intermediate types set some fruits without cross-pollination, but their fruits are larger and more plentiful if their flowers are cross-pollinated.

This whole matter of pollination is greatly simplified in the case of a plant such as persimmon, some cultivars of which can set "parthenocarpic" fruits. Such fruits form without any pollination at all. Not only is a pollinator branch or plant unnecessary, but parthenocarpic fruits also are seedless.

Appendix 3

Siting and Planting

A congenial home, above and below ground, is necessary to keep a plant healthy and productive. Climate is perhaps the most limiting factor that determines what can be grown, but even climate can be modulated right at the planting site. And though it is the rare site that has perfect soil, soil is easily altered to suit the needs of a plant.

Climate

To gardeners, "hardiness" usually refers to the lowest temperature a plant can tolerate in the dead of winter. Spring frosts may nip flowers and tender, new growth, but it is the cold that comes in the dead of winter that kills a plant or cuts it down to the ground. Before setting any woody plant in the ground, it is important to know both the minimum temperature expected at the site and the minimum temperature a plant can tolerate.

Decades of weather data have been used to prepare the accompanying U.S. Department of Agriculture Plant Hardiness Zone Map. Squiggly lines overrunning the map bracket each zone, from 1 through 10, delineating the average annual minimum temperature within each zone—not the length of the winter, not the chance of late spring frosts, only the probable minimum temperature.

Cold in winter is not the only aspect of climate worth considering when planting fruits. Summer temperature, humidity, and rainfall have more influence on how well a plant grows rather than on whether or not the plant will survive. Summer weather also might influence fruit flavor and, for certain heat-loving plants, whether or not fruit ripens.

Rainfall need not be a consideration if plants are watered. Once established, plants may thrive on only rainfall, but all plants require watering

Figure E. USDA Plant Hardiness Zone Map (Courtesy Agricultural Research Service, U.S. Department of Agriculture).

throughout their first growing season. To figure out how much water to apply, first estimate the ground area encompassed by a plant's roots by assuming that the roots spread to about the same breadth as the tops. Each week, then, apply a half-gallon of water per square foot of root area covered. This amount of water is equivalent to one inch of rainfall, so if a rain gauge indicates that an inch of water has fallen, forgo watering for a week hence.

Any parcel of land, from a forty-acre farm field to a quarter-acre lot, has "microclimates," where pockets of air and soil are colder, warmer, even more or less humid, than the general climate due to the influence of slopes, walls, and pavement. These microclimates may represent the equivalent of moving to the next colder or warmer hardiness zone, in the latter case allowing you to grow a fruit not adapted to your general climate. (When growing a plant that is just barely cold-hardy in your area, eke out maximum cold-hardiness from the plant by avoiding anything that stimulates late-season, sappy growth, such as late summer pruning, fertilization, and watering.)

Microclimates are important when growing plants that blossom early in the season, for frozen blossoms will not form fruits. Early season bloomers need microclimates that either do not warm up early in spring, so blossoming is delayed, or sites that are not apt to receive frost after plant growth is under way.

South-facing slopes stare directly at the sun, so these slopes warm up early in spring and are hot in summer. Therefore, a south-facing slope can be used to hasten fruit ripening on a plant like persimmon, which blooms late but needs a long season when grown near its northern limit. The sun glances off north slopes, delaying their warming in spring and keeping them cool in summer—ideal for early blooming, cool-loving plants like gooseberries and currants.

If a slope actually has some elevation to it, the air is going to cool by one degree Fahrenheit every three hundred feet up. Avoid planting at the very top of a slope, though, because the top is most windy. For early-blooming fruit plants, also avoid the very bottom of a slope. Cold air is heavier than warm air, and flows downhill, collecting in low areas as would water. This effect even is noticeable in small depressions on relatively flat land. Avoid such sites especially for low-growing early bloomers like strawberries.

Like a south slope, a wall or pavement will raise the air temperature nearby by a few degrees in winter and summer.

Appendix 3

Soil

Though the uncommon fruits in this book hail from all corners of the world and include plants as diverse as ground-hugging shrubs and stately trees, they all have surprisingly similar soil requirements. Simply put, these plants, along with most cultivated plants, need a soil well supplied with air (yes, roots must breathe!), water, and nutrients.

Aeration must be the first consideration, since plants are unable to utilize nutrients in even fertile soils if the roots have no air. Waterlogged soil results when water displaces air out of the soil pores. There are two causes for this condition: either the water table is high, so water is rising up into the soil from below; or the soil has pores so small that they cling to excessive amounts of water by capillary action.

Test for high water table by digging a hole a couple of feet deep and noting when and how long water remains in the hole. If water is present for much of the year, especially during the growing season, the options are to choose another site, raise roots above the water, or lower the water. Raise roots by building up a mound of soil, then planting on top of the mound. Not only must the mound be sufficiently high to take the roots up out of the water, but the mound also must be sufficiently wide so as not to dry out too quickly. To lower the water instead, drain it in either open trenches or buried, perforated, plastic pipe to lower ground. This, of course, assumes there is lower ground somewhere nearby. (The Natural Resources Conservation Service, listed in the telephone directory as a subheading under U.S. Department of Agriculture, provides technical assistance for drainage.)

The small particles that comprise clay soils can result in small soil pores becoming clogged with water. Soils high in clay are sticky and smooth when wet, and mold well. The way to aerate a clay is to aggregate—glue together— the small particles into larger units. Large pores form between the large aggregates, and these large pores cannot hold capillary water; they fill with air. At the same time, though, the small pores within each large aggregate hold water for plants.

"Glue" for such soils is humus, which is derived from the decomposition of anything that once was living. Materials such as compost, peat moss, manure, rotted leaves, and sawdust are sources of humus. Thoroughly mix these materials into the soil for quick results, then just lay them on the surface to maintain high levels and reap other benefits of mulches.

Sandy soils are composed of large particles, and represent the opposite extreme from clay soils. Sandy soils feel gritty when wet and are not sticky when they are wet or dry. Such soils have plenty of air, but dry out too readily. Trudging water all season long to the plants is one cure, but a more practical approach is to modify the soil so it holds more water. Once again, an abundance of humus remedies the problem. In this case, the spongelike nature of humus holds moisture in the soil. Laying humus materials on top of the soil as mulch is sufficient.

Loam soils are those containing a spectrum of particle sizes, and hence, a spectrum of pore sizes. These soils are well aerated and hold water, but can be made even more so with the addition of humus.

With aeration and water taken care of, now consider the soil's fertility. Soil must supply a plant with a baker's dozen of essential nutrients, and in order for the plant to utilize those nutrients, the soil's acidity (pH level) also must be in the correct range for the plant.

Most cultivated plants thrive best in a soil that is slightly acidic (pH between 6 and 7). Determine a soil's acidity either with a purchased kit, or by sending a sample to a testing laboratory (for location of a local laboratory, call the Cooperative Extension Service, listed in the telephone directory under the name of your county). If the soil is not sufficiently acidic, mix in sulfur. If the soil is too acidic, mix in ground limestone. The quantity of materials needed to change the acidity depends on how much of a change is needed and how much clay is in the soil. To change a soil one pH unit requires, per ten square feet, two-tenths to one pound of limestone or one-tenth to one pound of sulfur. The lower values apply to sandy soils and the higher values apply to clay soils.

Periodic fertilization is needed to replace nutrients removed from the soil by plant uptake, leaching, and volatilization. The three nutrients needed in greatest amounts by plants are nitrogen, phosphorus, and potassium, and these might be the only nutrients you need to add deliberately (the others come along for the ride).

Fertilizers are produced synthetically ("chemical fertilizers") or are derived from natural sources ("natural fertilizers"). Any fertilizer you buy will have three numbers on the bag or box, and from the three numbers you can determine the actual concentrations of, respectively, nitrogen, phosphorous, and potassium in the bag. Commonly available ratios for chemical fertilizers are 20–20–20, 10–20–10, and 5–10–5. Examples of natural fertilizers include compost (3–1–2), manure (0.5–0.05–0.5), wood ashes (0–1–7), greensand (0–0–2), rock phosphate (0–2–0), soybean meal (7–2–1), bone meal (4–12–0), and blood meal (13–0–0).

Chemical fertilizers usually are more concentrated sources of nutrients than are natural fertilizers, but chemical fertilizers also are more apt to wash out of the soil or burn plant roots. Note that except for compost, natural fertilizers are high in one nutrient—nitrogen, phosphorus, or potassium—rather than all three; therefore, use natural fertilizers in combination for balanced nutrition. Also, do not eschew natural fertilizers for their low concentration of nutrients—it is this non-nutritive bulk that helps make soils porous and hold water.

Whether using synthetic or natural fertilizers, find out what concentration of nutrients the fertilizer contains, and adjust your application accordingly. Nitrogen commonly is the most needed nutrient—often the only nutrient needed, if any, when high humus levels are maintained—and a general recommendation is to add the equivalent of two-tenths of a pound of actual nitrogen per hundred square feet each year. This could be supplied, for example, by two pounds (about four cups) of 10–10–10 or three pounds of soybean meal. The compost or leaf mold (but not the peat moss) mentioned earlier to improve aeration and water-holding capacity of soils also provides sufficient nourishment if a one-inch layer is spread on top of the soil annually.

Planting

> Plant trees on Michaelmas and command them to grow,
> Plant trees at Candlemas and entreat them to grow.

This English adage is not applicable without caveats in climates with rigorous winters. Fall planting (Michaelmas is September 29) does permit plants to settle in place, perhaps even some roots to grow, well before tops begin growth the following spring. In fall, the ground also has good tilth for digging. In contrast, digging in spring (Candlemas is February 2) must be delayed until the soil thaws and dries some. Pending this delay, there is danger of the tops of plants growing before their roots establish or, perhaps, before you even get their roots in the ground.

What about the caveats? First, some plants, such as persimmon and pawpaw, just do not take well to fall planting. When transplanted, such plants like to be removed from the soil, then be put right back in, just before growth begins. This is not a consideration if plants are transplanted, with their roots intact, from containers. The second caveat arises from the fact that all plants are in danger of being heaved out of the soil as it freezes and thaws through the cold months. Prevent heaving with a thick layer of mulch to insulate the soil.

When digging out soil from the planting hole, dig only deeply enough to get the plant set as deep in the ground as it was at the nursery. Make the hole about twice the width of the root ball, tapering the depth from ground level at the edges to full depth at the center. Rough up the inside of the hole to provide a surface for easy root penetration.

If lime or sulfur is needed to change the acidity of the soil, this is a good time to thoroughly mix it into the soil of the planting hole. Both these materials move only slowly through soil so otherwise would take too long to work their way down to the roots. Beyond the planting hole, just spread these materials on top of the ground; by the time roots extend beyond the hole, the effects of the lime or sulfur will have leached down into the soil. Do not, however, mix fertilizer into the planting hole or it could burn new roots. Do not mix in peat moss or other organic materials either, or roots will not venture beyond the resulting fluffy soil. And as the organic materials decomposed, the soil in the planting hole would settle.

Set the plant in the planting hole so that the old soil line on the stem is at the same level as the ground. If the plant is bare root, soak the roots in water for half a day before planting. Then trim off dead and broken roots, and fan the remaining roots out in the planting hole, working quickly so the roots are not exposed to excessive drying. If the plant is in a container, remove it, then tease the outer layer of roots away from the soil ball before setting the plant in the hole. Backfill soil into the hole, tamping it with your fingers to make sure there are no large pockets of air amongst the roots. When the hole is filled, form a low basin around the plant to contain water and mulch the bare soil with woodchips, straw, or some other organic material.

Thoroughly water the soil, then water weekly once growth begins in earnest. Preparing the soil, watering, and keeping weeds at least two feet back from the stem will give plants a rousing start in their critical first season.

Appendix 4

Pruning

The uncommon fruits of this book run the spectrum when it comes to need for pruning. Not requiring any pruning are plants like raisin tree and mulberry, yet plants like Asian pear and black currant must be pruned every year. A number of the uncommon fruits—pawpaw, American persimmon, and Nanking cherry, for example—are in a category "betwixt and between": pruning is beneficial, but not absolutely necessary.

When pruning is necessary, make all cuts with a clear objective in mind and in such a way as to facilitate healing. Except where noted in the chapters for each fruit, prune plants when they are dormant, sometime from when the leaves have fallen in autumn until before growth commences again. Pruning wounds heal most quickly if cuts are made just before growth begins, though. Delay pruning until the latter part of the dormant period where winters are severely cold, so that cold-injured limbs can be noted and removed. No wound dressings are necessary on pruning cuts.

Tools of the Trade

First-century A.D. Roman writer Columella described six specialized parts to the *vinitoria falx*, the pruning hook for grapes; the modern fruit grower likely will use a couple or so different pruning tools. No matter what the tool, it must be sharp. A crisp, clean cut heals best.

Use a tool appropriate to the thickness of the branch to be cut. For small branches up to a half-inch across, a hand pruning shear suffices. Lop off branches up to an inch and a half in diameter with a long-handled, appropriately named, lopper. Larger limbs call for some type of pruning saw. A pole pruner reaches high into a tree to make pruning cuts. Some pole pruners have both a lopper and a saw at their end—very useful but not quite the six-in-one *vinitoria falx* of Columella.

How to Cut

Cut in such a manner as to facilitate healing. When large limbs of a tree need removal, prevent the falling limb from stripping bark off the trunk by first making a slight undercut into the limb a few inches out from the trunk. Then saw through the limb from above, slightly farther out on the trunk than the undercut. With the bulk of the limb removed, cut off the remaining stump close to, but not flush with, the trunk. A slight collar is needed for the wound to heal over.

Cuts on small branches heal best if made just above and sloping away from a bud. Too much wood left above the bud results in a dead stub, which might provide entrance for disease. If the cut is too close to the bud, that bud dries out and dies.

On young branches, there are two basic types of pruning cuts; which one you choose depends on the response you want to elicit from the plant. First is the "heading cut," a cut that shortens a branch by some amount. The heading cut awakens buds beneath the cut, inducing branches to form. Severe shortening of a branch results in a vigorous response from just a few buds; slight heading results in less response from a greater number of buds. Heading cuts, then, are useful where branching is desired or where a weak limb needs stimulation.

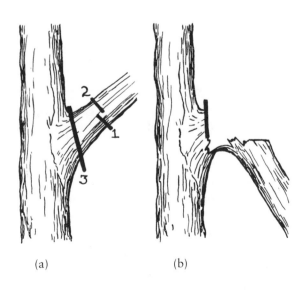

(a)   (b)

Figure F. Pruning large limbs: (a) correct; (b) incorrect.

247

(a)   (b)   (c)   (d)

Figure G. Pruning small branches: (a) correct—bud just below cut will grow; (b) long, slanting cut will dry out bud; (c) stub left above bud will rot; (d) cut is too close to bud, so bud will die.

The other type of cut is the "thinning cut," which is what you do when you remove a branch completely right at its origin. There is no local response to this cut, so thinning cuts are the obvious choice where growth is too dense within a plant.

Objectives in Pruning

The objective in pruning a young fruit tree is to plan for the future. With age, limbs will need to be strong enough to support both their own weight and that of their luscious bounty. Proper training also will shape the nascent tree to a form that allows all the branches to be bathed in air and sufficient light, even when the tree grows old. (This training does not apply to bushes because bushes, by definition, do not grow large enough to have heavy limbs or shade themselves, and because bushes commonly renew themselves with new branches from ground level.) Keep pruning to a minimum on young plants, for excessive pruning is a sure way to delay fruiting.

Train a young tree either to a "central leader" or "open center" form. The central leader tree has the shape of a Christmas tree. Scaffold branches grow out around a single trunk and as you look up the trunk, the scaffolds become successively shorter. Create such a tree by allowing only one, vigorous, upright branch to grow as the trunk (the central leader). Head the central leader (cut off about a third of the previous season's growth) each winter to induce branching, but always maintain growth from the uppermost bud as a continuation of the central leader. If any branches try to overgrow the central leader, ruthlessly cut them out or bend them to the horizontal. Head back a weakly, but well-positioned, scaffold branch to one or two buds, one of which should send out a shoot with renewed vigor.

As each winter's heading cuts induces branching around the central leader, select scaffold branches that are well positioned and will remain sturdy as the tree ages. Since the height of a scaffold branch never changes, remove any branches less than two feet above the ground, or whatever other height you desire for the lowest branch. Scaffolds that come out at wide angles from the trunk are stronger than those at narrow angles, so either selectively retain wide-angled scaffolds, or carefully widen the angles and prop the branches open with notched sticks or weights. Scaffolds directly across from each other on the trunk will weaken with age, so also choose scaffolds that are arranged in a spiral fashion moving up the trunk. And finally, allow ample room for each scaffold to develop—a half-foot vertically from one to the next.

An open center tree has the form of a goblet, with three or four main limbs radiating outward and upward. Develop an open center tree essentially the same way as the central leader, except that after three or four scaffold branches of about equal vigor have been selected, lop off the central stem above where the top branch comes off. The following winter head back scaffold branches so they branch and fill the volume of the tree.

Fruit trees can be trained to a form that combines the central leader and the open center forms, the "modified central leader." A modified central leader tree begins life as a central leader tree, then the central leader is lopped off high within the tree so the tree is open center from there on up.

ONCE any tree or bush reaches its allotted size and begins to bear fruits, the objectives in pruning are to maintain fruit quality, production, and plant health.

When you prune off a branch, you also are removing flower buds and, hence, potential fruits. Thus, pruning increases fruit quality by allowing a plant to divert more energy into fewer remaining fruits.

Figure H. Two ways of training a tree. (a) central leader: (i) at planting,
(ii) end of first season, (iii) end of second season, (iv) end of third season;
(b) open center: (i) at planting, (ii) end of first season, (iii) end of second season.

Continued productivity of a fruit plant depends, in part, on using pruning to stimulate a certain amount of new growth each year. How much pruning is needed depends on the bearing habit of the fruit. A plant like black currant, which bears mostly on one-year-old wood, needs more severe pruning than a plant like Asian pear, which bears much of its fruit on short growths (spurs) on old wood. Know the fruit-bearing habit of the particular plant!

An unpruned tree or shrub can become a tangled mass of branches, shade creating weak, unproductive wood and disease festering in the dank air. In trees, the upper branches tend to grow more vigorously than the bottom branches, so the bottom branches get too shaded, then weak and unfruitful. Counteract this tendency using thinning cuts to open spaces in the tops of trees, and heading cuts to invigorate the lower branches. Renew overgrown shrubs by cutting away at ground level some of the oldest shoots. Also maintain plant health by pruning diseased branches off any tree or shrub.

Pruning

Trees, young or old, periodically send up watersprouts from their limbs. Watersprouts are vigorous branches, shooting vertically skyward, that sap a tree's energy, are not fruitful, and cast shade within the plant. Remove watersprouts at their bases as soon as you notice them.

A final reason for pruning is aesthetic. If you have allotted a certain space for a plant and with age it begins to outgrow that space, pruning is in order to bring the plant back within bounds.

Appendix 5

Propagation

E nthusiasm for growing and eating uncommon fruits likely will create a need for skills in plant propagation. The road that leads to that first bite into a particularly choice fruit might begin with planting a seed or with making a piece of twig become a whole plant. Where space is limited, a tree can be created with each branch of a different cultivar. The following are basic, yet serviceable, directions for common methods of propagating fruit plants.

Plants are propagated either by sowing seeds or by cloning. *Seed propagation* usually results in plants that are different from each other and from their parents, though some plants come "true" from seed, which means seedlings are uniform and like the parent. *Cloning* always produces plants identical to each other and to the plant from which they came.

Most cultivated fruits, including the uncommon ones of this book, do not come true from seed, but seed propagation can be used to develop new cultivars of these plants. Whereas fruits of most seedlings are almost always inferior to their parents' fruits (only an estimated one out of ten thousand apple seedlings will produce fruit even as good as that of its parent!), seedlings of many of the uncommon fruits of this book often produce fruit as tasty as that of their parents. This is not an inherent trait of "uncommon" fruits, but speaks well of their intrinsic quality and, perhaps, their potential to become even better through deliberate breeding.

Nonetheless, with plants that do not come true from seed, you are playing the odds with seed propagation. Your one seedling may not match the quality of its parent, especially if the parent is a truly superior cultivar. In the case of dioecious plants, about half the seedlings will be males, which, of course, do not bear fruit. And males and females usually cannot be distinguished until they are old enough to flower.

One other drawback to seed propagation is that, in some cases, you must wait many years before a seedling bears its first fruit. This time period can be shortened by grafting a branch from the seedling onto a mature tree of that fruit.

Cloning is the only way to propagate cultivars of most fruit plants. Cloned plants also bear at a relatively young age, since the plant part used for propagation already is of bearing age.

THE OBVIOUS first step in propagating with seed is to procure seed. In some cases, seed can be bought. Otherwise, take seeds from a thoroughly ripe fruit. Extract small seeds by dropping whole fruits into a food blender with ample water, then giving the mixture a few short bursts with the appliance. Decant water and fruit pulp, and collect the heavier, viable seeds at the bottom.

After extraction, soak seeds in water for twelve to twenty-four hours. This leaches out possible germination inhibitors from the seed coat or bits of pulp adhering to the seed, and ensures that seeds are plump with water. Many seeds germinate best if not allowed to dry out from this point on.

Scarification, whereby you deliberately damage the seed coat, might be needed to allow seeds with hard coatings to imbibe water. The most convenient ways to scarify such seeds are either by nicking the seedcoats with a file, or by pouring near-boiling water over the seeds and letting them soak in the cooling water for twenty-four hours. Concentrated sulfuric acid also softens seed coats, but the timing is critical (and different for each type of seed) and the acid will burn your skin if not used with caution. Rinse seeds thoroughly with water after a sulfuric acid soak. A slow but easy way to soften seed coats is to keep seeds warm and moist for a couple of months. Put the seeds into a plastic bag filled with a mix of equal parts peat and perlite, previously wetted and then thoroughly squeezed free of excess moisture, and keep the bag at room temperature.

There also are biochemical roadblocks to germination—hormones within seeds that prevent germination until seeds are exposed to cool, moist conditions for a period of time. In nature, seedlings germinating in autumn would be threatened by winter's bitter cold, so these hormones serve the purpose of delaying germination until spring. You can simulate nature by putting seeds in the refrigerator (not the freezer, it is too cold to cause the hormonal changes needed) in a plastic bag of moist peat and perlite. The process is called *stratification* because the traditional method of stratifying seeds in the nursery business was to alternate layers (strata) of seeds and damp sand in boxes put outdoors in autumn.

Keep an eye on seeds stratifying in the refrigerator. Once the requisite hours of chilling are fulfilled, the seeds may sprout as suddenly as if a switch had been turned on. If you are not ready to plant the seeds, hold them at a lower temperature to slow growth.

Some seeds need either scarification or stratification before they will germinate, others need scarification followed by stratification, and still others require neither treatment.

When it comes to actually planting the seeds, sow them *au naturel*—outdoors in summer or fall at plants' permanent locations—or sow them in containers for future transplanting. The advantage of *au naturel* growing is that there is no transplant shock. But since such seeds are subject to the vagaries of nature (animals, microorganisms, insects, and weather), play the odds and plant a few seeds at each station, later thinning to the single healthiest seedling. Outdoors, cool weather on either side of winter's deep freeze fulfills stratification needs. Scarification needs are fulfilled as seed coats are weakened by freezing and thawing, soil microorganisms (especially if seed is planted while the soil is still warm in late summer or early fall), and/or the digestive tracts of animals (not desirable for *your* seeds, though, which you want to stay in place).

Whether sowing in a container or open ground, plant seed at a depth about four times the seed's thickness. The soil for direct-seeding outdoors should be just like that which would be suitable for planting beans or any other garden crop: weed free, crumbly, and enriched with organic matter.

For sowing in containers, use potting soil, not garden soil. Sprinkle small seeds over the surface of seed flats, then gently move the seedlings into individual pots once seedlings are large enough to handle. Sow large seeds individually in pots.

Indoors or outdoors, firm the soil over the seed after sowing to ensure good contact between seed and soil. Water thoroughly, and keep the seedbed or containers moist, but never sodden.

Once seedlings are up and growing, give them light (full sun or part shade, depending on the needs of the particular plant), and when required, water and fertilizer. Avoid damping-off disease of seedlings by not overwatering and making sure plants are not crowded. If seeds are started indoors in late winter, do not move them outdoors until warm weather has arrived, about the time you set out tomato transplants. Seedlings of even cold-hardy plants are tender to cold.

You now are on your way to fruit!

CLONING makes use of the fact that any piece of a plant, except certain parts of the flower, has the genetic potential to become a whole new plant. A new plant might begin life as a piece of shoot (stem cuttings and grafts), a piece of root (root cuttings), or as a small shoot still attached to a mother plant (suckers and layers). Though the original plant of any clone eventually dies, there is no theoretical limit to the longevity of a clone. The grape cultivar 'Sultana' originated at least 2000 years ago and lives on today from cuttings repeatedly taken over the centuries.

Softwood stem cuttings are cuttings made from new, actively growing shoots. They root quickly but require close attention since water lost through the leaves cannot be replaced until roots form.

Before taking softwood cuttings from a plant, have ready a "propagating frame." The humid atmosphere within the frame keeps leaves turgid until roots form. Fill flowerpots or other containers having drainage holes with a pre-moistened mixture of equal parts peat moss and either perlite or vermiculite. Then build a removable tent of clear plastic or glass to cover the pot or pots; an inverted jar suffices for just a few, small cuttings. Locate the propagating frame in bright light, but never direct sunlight or the cuttings will cook. (Professional plant propagators keep plants turgid with electronically activated nozzles that periodically blow a fine mist over the leaves, and stimulate rooting by applying gentle heat to the bases of the cuttings with special cables.)

Take softwood cuttings in early morning when plants are plump with moisture. The best time during the growing season varies from plant to plant, but the wood should never be overly succulent. Lateral shoots have a good degree of vigor for cuttings. Make cuttings two to five inches long, and whisk them quickly over to the propagating frame, or keep them wrapped in plastic, out of direct light, and cool until you are ready to plant them. Strip off all but the top two or three leaves and, in the case of plants with large leaves, cut the remaining leaves in half. Then slide the stems into the prepared pots or containers, water, and close up the frame.

Softwood cuttings form roots within a few weeks. Test for rooting by feeling for resistance when you give stems a slight upward tug. Once cuttings have rooted, acclimate them to the real world by increasing ventilation within the frame over the course of a couple weeks. Then repot the rooted cuttings into potting soil.

The etiolated shoot method is a variation on softwood cuttings. This method has been successful in rooting stems of many plants otherwise difficult, previously impossible, to root (such as stems or shoots from mature apple trees.) In late winter, put an opaque tube—of roofing paper or aluminum foil, for example—around and extending a few inches beyond the terminal bud of a plant stem. This tube will exclude light from the shoot that grows from the terminal bud until that shoot appears at the end of the tube, at which time the shoot's exposed leaves and stem will develop normally. A variation on this method is to completely shade a plant or stem before growth begins. When new, etiolated shoots are a few inches long, wrap each of their bases in some opaque material and gradually admit light to the plant or shoot. With either method, in late summer cut off the leafy shoots with their etiolated (bleached) basal portions and root them as you would any other softwood cutting. The etiolated shoot method is so successful because etiolated stems root so readily and because these etiolated stems, fed by their deep green parts developing later in light, are not starved for energy reserves.

Hardwood cuttings are cuttings made from dormant wood, usually stems that grew the previous season. Autumn, after the leaves have fallen, is the best time to take hardwood cuttings. Cut wood into foot-long lengths (or pieces with at least two buds) with each top cut just above a bud and each bottom cut just below another bud. Cuttings taken from the lower portions of shoots generally root better than do those from the upper portions.

With cuttings in hand, you now have a number of options on how to handle them. You could plant immediately, making a slit in the ground with a shovel, inserting each cutting up to its top bud and six inches from the next cutting, then firming the soil back in place with your heel. If the soil freezes and thaws through the winter, a mulch, removed in the spring, will be needed to keep cuttings from heaving out of the soil.

Alternatively, refrigerate cuttings until it is time to plant them in spring. Bundle the wood into a plastic bag, wrap this bag in a wet rag, then put the bag and rag into another plastic bag, well sealed to prevent drying.

The main danger with setting hardwood cuttings in spring is that the tops might grow too much before roots form. Therefore, plant as early in spring as possible. One way to abate the danger of tops growing before roots form is to give the cuttings a jump on spring by inducing them to form at least root initials in the fall. Do this by keeping the bundle of cuttings, wrapped in plastic and rags, at room temperature for about a month before it goes into the refrigerator.

Before the days of refrigerators and plastic bags, the same result was achieved by burying a bundle of cuttings, upside down, outdoors in well-drained soil. Since soil cools more slowly than the air in fall, the cuttings kept warm for a while. And even better, the bases of the cuttings began to feel the warmth of spring while the tops, deeper in the soil, were still cold. Cuttings with pre-formed root initials still should be planted as early in spring as possible.

Rooting of hardwood or softwood cuttings sometimes is facilitated by dipping the bottom ends of the cuttings in a rooting hormone before setting the cutting in the propagating medium. Old-time plant propagators would embed a grain seed in the split, bottom end of each cutting, and as the seed germinated, it released natural hormones. Today, rooting hormones such as IBA (indolebutyric acid) and NAA (naphthaleneacetic acid) are available as powders.

Root cuttings are made from pieces of root. Dig under a plant near its crown and cut off some of the thicker roots when the plant is dormant and the soil is not frozen. The thinner the root, the longer the cutting should be, with a pencil-thick root about four inches long.

Plant root cuttings either outdoors in good garden soil, or indoors in a pot filled with the same mix of peat moss and perlite or vermiculite recommended for softwood cuttings. Lay the cuttings either horizontally, with a half-inch covering of soil, or set them upright, with their tips just barely above the soil surface. In the latter case, make sure the end that is up is the same end that was closest to the plant's crown. Note that not all plants have roots that readily regenerate into whole new plants.

To propagate a plant by any *grafting* method, you take a scion, which is a short stem or even just a single bud of the plant you want to propagate, and join it to a rootstock (sometimes just called "stock"). The rootstock provides only roots, and all new growth above the graft will be from the scion. Often a rootstock will try to grow shoots of its own, and these should be promptly removed.

The closer the botanical relationship between stock and scion, the better the chance for a successful graft. For example, all pawpaw scions are compatible with all pawpaw rootstock, because all pawpaws are in the same genus and species. Often, interspecific grafts are successful, as in the case of an Oriental persimmon (*Diospyros kaki*) scion on an American persimmon (*D. virginiana*) rootstock. There are fewer examples of successful unions between genera, but oriental pear (*Pyrus pyrifolia*) can be grafted upon quince (*Cydonia oblongata*) rootstock. Rarely are grafts between botanical families possible.

Grafting is not difficult and was practiced as long ago as 1000 B.C. in China. I nonetheless do get a little nervous every time I graft because I hear in my mind the words "any fool can graft," spoken by one of my old horticulture professors to emphasize just how easy it is to graft.

Given a compatible stock and scion, there are three important prerequisites to a successful graft:

1) The cambium (the layer just below the bark) of the stock and the cambium of the scion must be held near each other. Where the cambiums of the cut portions of the stock and scion cannot be entirely contiguous, such as when stock and scion are different sizes, set the scion at one edge of the cut on the stock so that at least portions of their cambiums will be near to each other. Once stock and scion are in place, hold them there by wrapping with a rubber band (cut open), string, or tape. No matter what is used to hold stock and scion together, slit it after graft has knit together but before the plant is strangled at the graft union.
2) The graft union must not dry out. The sixteenth-century mix of wet clay and dung used to seal in moisture is replaced today by the more conveniently applied commercial grafting waxes, tree wound sealants, or plastic wrap.
3) The temperature must be warm, but not hot, while healing occurs.

If all three of these conditions are fulfilled, there are many ways by which a stock and scion can be joined. Three common methods are whip-and-tongue grafting, T-bud grafting, and chip-bud grafting.

Whip-and-tongue grafting is performed indoors in winter on potted or bare-root plants, or outdoors in spring just before or as growth commences. Stocks and scions one-quarter to one-half inch in diameter are best suited for this method. In autumn or winter, when temperatures are above freezing, collect leafless scions of wood that grew the previous season. Store the scions just like hardwood cuttings, wrapped and in the refrigerator, until the time of grafting.

To graft, make a smooth, sloping cut one to two inches long on both the top of the stock and the bottom of the scion. Then cut a tongue in each slope beginning a third of the way from the end of the wood, parallel to the sloping cut, and in a direction away from the cut end. The tongue should be half the length of the sloping cut. Fit the stock and scion together, wrap with a rubber band, and seal to prevent desiccation. Grafts made indoors should be kept warm for a couple of weeks, then moved to cold storage until you are ready for the plants to begin growth.

T-bud grafting uses only a single bud as a scion and is performed when the bark is slipping (easily peeled back from the wood), usually in late summer. Cut a T a little over an inch high into a smooth portion of bark on the rootstock. The cut should just penetrate the bark to solid wood.

On the scion plant, find a plump, well-formed, vegetative (not flower) bud on current season's growth. Cut off the leaf subtending the bud, leaving only a short piece of the petiole (leafstalk), which will serve as a handle. Next, make a shallow cut to remove the bud, beginning about a half-inch above it and ending a similar distance below it.

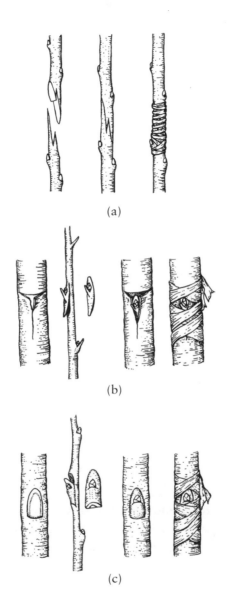

(a)

(b)

(c)

Figure I. Three grafting methods: (a) whip-and-tongue graft; (b) T-bud graft; (c) chip-bud graft.

Open the flaps of the T in the rootstock and insert the scion bud. (If the flaps do not open easily because the bark does not slip, try again in a couple of weeks, watering the plant thoroughly a few times during that period.) Wrap the flaps closed with a rubber band, covering all cut surfaces, but do not cover the bud itself. If the graft is a success, the petiole will drop cleanly from the bud in about two weeks. The following spring, cut the branch back to just above the grafted bud and allow new growth only from this bud.

Chip-bud grafting also utilizes a single bud, but can be done anytime during the growing season. On a smooth area of stem on the rootstock, make a downward-sloping cut about an eighth of an inch deep. An inch and a half higher on the stem, cut in, then down, to the other cut. Remove the chip. A similar chip, cut from the plant you wish to propagate, is the scion. Bind the scion chip to the waiting cut in the rootstock, then thoroughly seal the whole graft to prevent drying. Chip-bud grafts made in spring can be cut back to the graft after about two weeks to force growth that season; wait until the following spring with late-season chip buds.

Propagation by layers or suckers is relatively easy, since a new plant has both roots and stems when it is finally removed from the mother plant.

To *layer*, bend a one-year-old, dormant stem down to the ground in early spring. Bury a short segment of this stem under the soil, holding it down with a clip made of a piece of bent coat hanger, or with a brick. Slightly wounding the buried portion of stem sometimes helps stimulate rooting. Stake upright the portion of the stem beyond the buried segment. When roots have formed on the buried portion of stem, which usually occurs by the end of the season, cut off the rooted portion and transplant it.

A *sucker* is a shoot that rises at the base of a plant from below ground. Some plants have a more pronounced tendency to throw up suckers than do others. During the dormant season, dig—do not pull—suckers with roots attached from around the base of the mother plant. Then plant them. That's all there is to it.

Appendix 6

Mail-Order Sources for Plants or Seeds

ASIAN PEAR (*Pyrus pyrifolia*; *P. usuriensis*; *P.* ×*bretschneideri*)

Bay Laurel Nursery, 2500 El Camino Real, Atascadero, CA 93422, 805-466-3406; www.baylaurelnursery.com

Burnt Ridge Nursery, 432 Burnt Ridge Road, Onalaska, WA 98570, 360-985-2873; www.landru.myhome.net/burntridge/

Edible Landscaping Nursery, Route 2, Box 77, Afton, VA 22920, 800-524-4156; www.eat-it.com

Hidden Springs Nursery, 170 Hidden Springs Lane, Cookeville, TN 38501, 931-268-2592

Just Fruit & Exotics, 30 St. Francis Street, Crawfordville, FL 32327, 850-926-5644

One Green World, 28696 South Cramer Road, Molalla, OR 97038, 877-353-4028; www.onegreenworld.com

Pacific Tree Farms, 4301 Lynwood Drive, Chula Vista, CA 92010, 619-422-2400; www.kyburg.com

Raintree Nursery, 391 Butts Road, Morton, WA 98356, 360-496-6400; www.RaintreeNursery.com

Trees of Antiquity, 4395 Westside Road, Healdsburg, CA 95448, 707-433-6420; www.treesofantiquity.com

AUTUMN OLIVE (*Elaeagnus umbellata*)

Burnt Ridge Nursery, 432 Burnt Ridge Road, Onalaska, WA 98570, 360-985-2873; www.landru.myhome.net/burntridge/

Forestfarm, 990 Tetherow, Williams, OR 97544-9599, 541-846-7269; www.forestfarm.com

Hidden Springs Nursery, 170 Hidden Springs Lane, Cookeville, TN 38501, 931-268-2592

Musser Forests, P.O. Box 340, Route 119, North Indiana, PA 15701, 800-643-8319; www.musserforests.com

One Green World, 28696 South Cramer Road, Molalla, OR 97038, 877-353-4028; www.onegreenworld.com

BEACH PLUM (*Prunus maritima*)

All Seasons Nursery, 27 Derby Lane, Cranston, RI 02921, 401-828-1123; www.allseasonsnurseryonline.com
Fedco Seeds, P.O. Box 520-A, Waterville, Maine, 04903; www.fedcoseeds.com
Oikos Tree Crops, P.O. Box 19425, Kalamazoo, MI 49019-0425; 616-624-6233
Reeseville Ridge Nursery, 512 South Main Street, Reeseville WI 53579; 920-927-3291; www.wegrowit.com/Reeseville/ReesevilleRidgeCatalog.htm

BLACK CURRANT—AMERICAN (*Ribes americanum*)

Oikos Tree Crops, P.O. Box 19425, Kalamazoo, MI 49019-0425; 616-624-6233

BLACK CURRANT—CLOVE CURRANT (*Ribes odoratum*; *R. aureum*)

Burnt Ridge Nursery, 432 Burnt Ridge Road, Onalaska, WA 98570, 360-985-2873; www.landru.myhome.net/burntridge/
Edible Landscaping Nursery, Route 2, Box 77, Afton, VA 22920, 800-524-4156; www.eat-it.com
Forestfarm, 990 Tetherow, Williams, OR 97544-9599, 541-846-7269; www.forestfarm.com
Indiana Berry & Plant, 5218 W. 500 South, Huntingburg, IN 47542, 800-295-2226; www.inberry.com
Oikos Tree Crops, P.O. Box 19425, Kalamazoo, MI 49019-0425; 616-624-6233; 616-624-6233
One Green World, 28696 South Cramer Road, Molalla, OR 97038, 877-353-4028; www.onegreenworld.com
Raintree Nursery, 391 Butts Road, Morton, WA 98356, 360-496-6400; www.RaintreeNursery.com
Rare Fruit Nursery, 1065 Messenger Road, Grant's Pass, OR 97527, 541-846-7578; www.exoticfruit.com
Saint Lawrence Nurseries, RFD 2, State Route 345, Potsdam, NY 13676, 315-265-6739; www.sln.potsdam.ny.us
Whitman Farms Nursery, 1420 Beaumont NW, Salem, OR 97304, 503-585-8728; www.whitmanfarms.com

BLACK CURRANT—EUROPEAN (*Ribes nigrum*)

Burnt Ridge Nursery, 432 Burnt Ridge Road, Onalaska, WA 98570, 360-985-2873; www.landru.myhome.net/burntridge/
Edible Landscaping Nursery, Route 2, Box 77, Afton, VA 22920, 800-524-4156; www.eat-it.com
Indiana Berry & Plant, 5218 W. 500 South, Huntingburg, IN 47542, 800-295-2226; www.inberry.com

McGinnis Berry Crops Limited, 3583 Dove Creek Road, Courtenay, B.C. Canada
V9N 1P3; (250) 338-8200; www.berrycrops.net
Nourse Farms, 41 River Rd., South Deerfield, MA 01373, 413-665-2658; www
.noursefarms.com
One Green World, 28696 South Cramer Road, Molalla, OR 97038, 877-353-
4028; www.onegreenworld.com
Raintree Nursery, 391 Butts Road, Morton, WA 98356, 360-496-6400; www
.RaintreeNursery.com
Saint Lawrence Nurseries, RFD 2, State Route 345, Potsdam, NY13676; 315-
265-6739; www.sln.potsdam.ny.us
Whitman Farms Nursery, 1420 Beaumont NW, Salem, OR 97304, 503-585-
8728; www.whitmanfarms.com

BLUEBERRY, LOWBUSH (*Vaccinium angustifolium*)

Burnt Ridge Nursery, 432 Burnt Ridge Road, Onalaska, WA 98570, 360-985-
2873; www.landru.myhome.net/burntridge/
Forestfarm, 990 Tetherow, Williams, OR 97544-9599, 541-846-7269; www
.forestfarm.com
Hartmann's Plant Company, Inc., 310 60th Street, Grand Junction, MI 49056,
616-253-4281; www.hartmannsplantcompany.com
Raintree Nursery, 391 Butts Road, Morton, WA 98356, 360-496-6400; www
.RaintreeNursery.com
Saint Lawrence Nurseries, RFD 2, State Route 345, Potsdam, NY 13676, 315-
265-6739; www.sln.potsdam.ny.us
Tripple Brook Farm, 37 Middle Road, Southampton, MA 01703, 413-527-4626;
www.tripplebrookfarm.com

CHE (*Cudrania tricuspidata*)

Edible Landscaping Nursery, Route 2, Box 77, Afton, VA 22920, 800-524-4156;
www.eat-it.com
Hidden Springs Nursery, 170 Hidden Springs Lane, Cookeville, TN 38501, 931-
268-2592
Pacific Tree Farms, 4301 Lynwood Drive, Chula Vista, CA 92010, 619-422-
2400; www.kyburg.com

CORNELIAN CHERRY (*Cornus mas*)

(Ornamental varieties are available from many nurseries.)

Edible Landscaping Nursery, Route 2, Box 77, Afton, VA 22920, 800-524-4156;
www.eat-it.com
Forestfarm, 990 Tetherow, Williams, OR 97544-9599, 541-846-7269; www
.forestfarm.com
Hidden Springs Nursery, 170 Hidden Springs Lane, Cookeville, TN 38501, 931-
268-2592

John Gordon, Jr., 1385 Campbell Boulevard, North Amherst, NY 14120, 716-691-9371; www.geocities.com/nuttreegordon

One Green World, 28696 South Cramer Road, Molalla, OR 97038, 877-353-4028; www.onegreenworld.com

Raintree Nursery, 391 Butts Road, Morton, WA 98356, 360-496-6400; www.RaintreeNursery.com

Sherwood's Greenhouses, P, O. Box 6, Sibley, LA 71073, 318-377-3653

Whitman Farms Nursery, 1420 Beaumont NW, Salem, OR 97304, 503-585-8728; www.whitmanfarms.com

GOOSEBERRY (*Ribes hirtellum*; *R. uva-crispa*)

Burnt Ridge Nursery, 432 Burnt Ridge Road, Onalaska, WA 98570, 360-985-2873; www.landru.myhome.net/burntridge/

Edible Landscaping Nursery, Route 2, Box 77, Afton, VA 22920, 800-524-4156; www.eat-it.com

Hartmann's Plant Company, Inc., 310 60th Street, Grand Junction, MI 49056, 616-253-4281; www.hartmannsplantcompany.com

Hidden Springs Nursery, 170 Hidden Springs Lane, Cookeville, TN 38501, 931-268-2592

Indiana Berry & Plant, 5218 W. 500 South, Huntingburg, IN 47542, 800-295-2226; www.inberry.com

McGinnis Berry Crops Limited, 3583 Dove Creek Road, Courtenay, B.C. Canada V9N 1P3; (250) 338-8200; www.berrycrops.net

Nourse Farms, 41 River Road, South Deerfield, MA 01373, 413-665-2658; www.noursefarms.com

One Green World, 28696 South Cramer Road, Molalla, OR 97038, 877-353-4028; www.onegreenworld.com

Raintree Nursery, 391 Butts Road, Morton, WA 98356, 360-496-6400; www.RaintreeNursery.com

Stark Brothers Nurseries, Hwy. 54 West, Louisiana, MO 63353, 800-325-4180; www.starkbros.com

Trees of Antiquity, 4395 Westside Road, Healdsburg, CA 95448, 707-433-6420; www.treesofantiquity.com

Whitman Farms Nursery, 1420 Beaumont NW, Salem, OR 97304, 503-585-8728; www.whitmanfarms.com

GUMI (*Elaeagnus multiflora*)

Burnt Ridge Nursery, 432 Burnt Ridge Road, Onalaska, WA 98570, 360-985-2873; www.landru.myhome.net/burntridge/

Hidden Springs Nursery, 170 Hidden Springs Lane, Cookeville, TN 38501, 931-268-2592

One Green World, 28696 South Cramer Road, Molalla, OR 97038, 877-353-4028; www.onegreenworld.com

Mail-Order Sources for Plants and Seeds

Pacific Tree Farms, 4301 Lynwood Drive, Chula Vista, CA 92010, 619-422-2400; www.kyburg.com

Raintree Nursery, 391 Butts Road, Morton, WA 98356, 360-496-6400; www.RaintreeNursery.com

Sherwood's Greenhouses, P.O. Box 6, Sibley, LA 71073, 318-377-3653

JOSTABERRY (*Ribes nidigrolaria*)

Edible Landscaping Nursery, Route 2, Box 77, Afton, VA 22920, 800-524-4156; www.eat-it.com

Hidden Springs Nursery, 170 Hidden Springs Lane, Cookeville, TN 38501, 931-268-2592

Indiana Berry & Plant, 5218 W. 500 South, Huntingburg, IN 47542, 800-295-2226; www.inberry.com

One Green World, 28696 South Cramer Road, Molalla, OR 97038, 877-353-4028; www.onegreenworld.com

Raintree Nursery, 391 Butts Road, Morton, WA 98356, 360-496-6400; www.RaintreeNursery.com

Saint Lawrence Nurseries, RFD 2, State Route 345, Potsdam, NY13676, 315-265-6739; www.sln.potsdam.ny.us

JUJUBE (*Ziziphus jujuba*)

Burnt Ridge Nursery, 432 Burnt Ridge Road, Onalaska, WA 98570, 360-985-2873; www.landru.myhome.net/burntridge/

Edible Landscaping Nursery, Route 2, Box 77, Afton, VA 22920, 800-524-4156; www.eat-it.com

England's Orchard & Nursery, 316 State Route 2004, McKee, KY 40447-9616, 877-965-2228; www.nuttrees.net

Fork & Spade, c/o Scenic Nursery, 1313 Scenic Drive, Modesto, CA 95355, 800-829-5919: www.forkandspade.com

Hidden Springs Nursery, 170 Hidden Springs Lane, Cookeville, TN 38501, 931-268-2592

Just Fruit & Exotics, 30 St. Francis Street, Crawfordville, FL 32327, 850-926-5644

One Green World, 28696 South Cramer Road, Molalla, OR 97038, 877-353-4028; www.onegreenworld.com

Raintree Nursery, 391 Butts Road, Morton, WA 98356, 360-496-6400; www.RaintreeNursery.com

Roger and Shirley Meyer, 16531 Mt. Shelly Circle, Fountain Valley, CA 92708, 714-839-0796

JUNEBERRY (*Amelanchier* spp.)

(Ornamental varieties are available from many nurseries.)

Burnt Ridge Nursery, 432 Burnt Ridge Road, Onalaska, WA 98570, 360-985-2873; www.landru.myhome.net/burntridge/

Edible Landscaping Nursery, Route 2, Box 77, Afton, VA 22920, 800-524-4156; www.eat-it.com

Forestfarm, 990 Tetherow, Williams, OR 97544-9599, 541-846-7269; www.forestfarm.com

Hartmann's Plant Company, Inc., 310 60th Street, Grand Junction, MI 49056, 616-253-4281; www.hartmannsplantcompany.com

Hidden Springs Nursery, 170 Hidden Springs Lane, Cookeville, TN 38501, 931-268-2592

Oikos Tree Crops, P.O. Box 19425, Kalamazoo, MI 49019-0425; 616-624-6233

One Green World, 28696 South Cramer Road, Molalla, OR 97038, 877-353-4028; www.onegreenworld.com

Raintree Nursery, 391 Butts Road, Morton, WA 98356, 360-496-6400; www.RaintreeNursery.com

Roger and Shirley Meyer, 16531 Mt Shelly Circle, Fountain Valley, CA 92708, 714-839-0796

Saint Lawrence Nurseries, RFD 2, State Route 345, Potsdam, NY 13676, 315-265-6739; www.sln.potsdam.ny.us

Sherwood's Greenhouses, P.O. Box 6, Sibley, LA 71073, 318-377-3653

KIWIFRUIT, HARDY KIWIFRUIT, SUPER-HARDY KIWIFRUIT (*Actinidia* spp.)

Burnt Ridge Nursery, 432 Burnt Ridge Road, Onalaska, WA 98570, 360-985-2873; www.landru.myhome.net/burntridge/

Edible Landscaping Nursery, Route 2, Box 77, Afton, VA 22920, 800-524-4156; www.eat-it.com

Hartmann's Plant Company, Inc., 310 60th Street, Grand Junction, MI 49056, 616-253-4281; www.hartmannsplantcompany.com

Just Fruit & Exotics, 30 St. Francis Street, Crawfordville, FL 32327, 850-926-5644

One Green World, 28696 South Cramer Road, Molalla, OR 97038, 877-353-4028; www.onegreenworld.com

Raintree Nursery, 391 Butts Road, Morton, WA 98356, 360-496-6400; www.RaintreeNursery.com

Rare Fruit Nursery, 1065 Messenger Road, Grant's Pass, OR 97527, 541-846-7578; www.exoticfruit.com

Roger and Shirley Meyer, 16531 Mt Shelly Circle, Fountain Valley, CA 92708, 714-839-0796

Sherwood's Greenhouses, P.O. Box 6, Sibley, LA 71073, 318-377-3653

Trees of Antiquity, 4395 Westside Rd., Healdsburg, CA 95448, 707-433-6420; www.treesofantiquity.com

Tripple Brook Farm, 37 Middle Road, Southampton, MA 01703, 413-527-4626; www.tripplebrookfarm.com

Whitman Farms Nursery, 1420 Beaumont NW, Salem, OR 97304, 503-585-8728, whitmanfarms.com

LINGONBERRY (*Vaccinium vitis-idaea* var. *vitis-idaea*; *V. vitis-idaea* var. *minus*)

Forestfarm, 990 Tetherow Road, Williams, OR 97544-9599, 541-846-7269; www.forestfarm.com

Hartmann's Plant Company, P.O. Box 100, Lacota, MI 49063-0100, 616-253-4281; www.hartmannsplantcompany.com

One Green World, 28696 South Cramer Road, Molalla, OR 97038, 877-353-4028, www.onegreenworld.com

Raintree Nursery, 391 Butts Road, Morton, WA 98356, 360-496-6400; www.RaintreeNursery.com

Saint Lawrence Nurseries, RFD 2, State Route 345, Potsdam, NY 13676, 315-265-6739; www.sln.potsdam.ny.us.

MAYPOP (*Passiflora incarnata*)

Edible Landscaping Nursery, Route 2, Box 77, Afton, VA 22920, 800-524-4156; www.eat-it.com

Hartmann's Plant Company, Inc., 310 60th Street, Grand Junction, MI 49056, 616-253-4281; www.hartmannsplantcompany.com

Logee's Greenhouses, 55 North Street, Danielson, CT 06239, 860-774-8038; www.logees.com

Niche Gardens, Route 1, Box 290, Chapel Hill, NC 27516, 919-967-0078; www.nichegdn.com

Oikos Tree Crops, P.O. Box 19425, Kalamazoo, MI 49019-0425; 616-624-6233

One Green World, 28696 South Cramer Road, Molalla, OR 97038, 877-353-4028; www.onegreenworld.com

Tripple Brook Farm, 37 Middle Road, Southampton, MA 01703, 413-527-4626; www.tripplebrookfarm.com

Raintree Nursery, 391 Butts Road, Morton, WA 98356, 360-496-6400; www.RaintreeNursery.com

Woodlanders, Inc., 1128 Colleton Avenue, Aiken, SC 29801, 803-648-7522

MEDLAR (*Mespilus germanica*)

Edible Landscaping Nursery, Route 2, Box 77, Afton, VA 22920, 800-524-4156; www.eat-it.com

Hidden Springs Nursery, 170 Hidden Springs Lane, Cookeville, TN 38501, 931-268-2592

One Green World, 28696 South Cramer Road, Molalla, OR 97038, 877-353-4028; www.onegreenworld.com

Raintree Nursery, 391 Butts Road, Morton, WA 98356, 360-496-6400; www.RaintreeNursery.com

MULBERRIES (*Morus* spp.)

Burnt Ridge Nursery, 432 Burnt Ridge Road, Onalaska, WA 98570, 360-985-2873; www.landru.myhome.net/burntridge/

Chestnut Hill Nursery, Route 1, Box 341, Alachua, FL 32615, 904-462-2820; www.chestnuthillnursery.com

Edible Landscaping Nursery, Route 2, Box 77, Afton, VA 22920, 800-524-4156; www.eat-it.com

Forestfarm, 990 Tetherow, Williams, OR 97544-9599, 541-846-7269; www .forestfarm.com

Hidden Springs Nursery, 170 Hidden Springs Lane, Cookeville, TN 38501, 931-268-2592

Just Fruit & Exotics, 30 St. Francis Street, Crawfordville, FL 32327-4257, 850-926-5644

One Green World, 28696 South Cramer Road, Molalla, OR 97038, 877-353-4028; www.onegreenworld.com

Raintree Nursery, 391 Butts Road, Morton, WA 98356, 360-496-6400; www .RaintreeNursery.com

Saint Lawrence Nurseries, RFD 2, State Route 345, Potsdam, NY 13676, 315-265-6739; www.sln.potsdam.ny.us

Tripple Brook Farm, 37 Middle Road, Southampton, MA 01703, 413-527-4626; www.tripplebrookfarm.com

Whitman Farms Nursery, 1420 Beaumont NW, Salem, OR 97304, 503-585-8728, whitmanfarms.com

NANKING CHERRY (*Prunus tomentosa*)

Cultivars unavailable; seedlings available from many nurseries, including:

Hidden Springs Nursery, 170 Hidden Springs Lane, Cookeville, TN 38501, 931-268-2592

Edible Landscaping Nursery, Route 2, Box 77, Afton, VA 22920, 800-524-4156; www.eat-it.com

Forestfarm, 990 Tetherow, Williams, OR 97544-9599, 541-846-7269; www .forestfarm.com

Oikos Tree Crops, P.O. Box 19425, Kalamazoo, MI 49019-0425; 616-624-6233

Raintree Nursery, 391 Butts Road, Morton, WA 98356, 360-496-6400; www .RaintreeNursery.com

Saint Lawrence Nurseries, RFD 2, State Route 345, Potsdam, NY 13676, 315-265-6739; www.sln.potsdam.ny.us

PAWPAW (*Asimina triloba*)

Burnt Ridge Nursery, 432 Burnt Ridge Road, Onalaska, WA 98570, 360-985-2873; www.landru.myhome.net/burntridge/

Dutch Mountain Nursery, 7984 North 48th Street, Route 1, Augusta, MI 49012

Edible Landscaping Nursery, Route 2, Box 77, Afton, VA 22920, 800-524-4156; www.eat-it.com

England's Orchard & Nursery, 316 State Route 2004, McKee, KY 40447-9616, 877-965-2228; www.nuttrees.net

Forestfarm, 990 Tetherow, Williams, OR 97544-9599, 541-846-7269; www
.forestfarm.com

Grimo Nut Nursery, R.R. 3 Lakeshore Road, Niagara-on-the-Lake, Ontario LOS
1JO Canada, 905-934-6887; www.grimonut.com

Hidden Springs Nursery, 170 Hidden Springs Lane, Cookeville, TN 38501, 931-
268-2592

John Gordon, Jr., 1385 Campbell Boulevard, North Amherst, NY 14120, 716-
691-9371; www.geocities.com/nuttreegordon

Nolin River Nut Tree Nursery, 797 Port Wooden Road, Upton, KY 42784, 270-
369-8551; www.nolinnursery.com

Oikos Tree Crops, P.O. Box 19425, Kalamazoo, MI 49019-0425; 616-624-6233

One Green World, 28696 South Cramer Road, Molalla, OR 97038, 877-353-
4028; www.onegreenworld.com

Peterson Pawpaws, LLC, P.O. Box 1011, Harpers Ferry, WV 25425; 304-535-
3125; www.petersonpawpaws.com

Raintree Nursery, 391 Butts Road, Morton, WA 98356, 360-496-6400; www
.RaintreeNursery.com

Sherwood's Greenhouses, P.O. Box 6, Sibley, LA 71073, 318-377-3653

Trees of Antiquity, 4395 Westside Rd., Healdsburg, CA 95448, 707-433-6420;
www.treesofantiquity.com

PERSIMMONS (*Diospyros* spp.)

Bay Laurel Nursery, 2500 El Camino Real, Atascadero, CA 93422, 805-466-
3406; www.baylaurelnursery.com

Burnt Ridge Nursery, 432 Burnt Ridge Road, Onalaska, WA 98570, 360-985-
2873; www.landru.myhome.net/burntridge/

Edible Landscaping Nursery, Route 2, Box 77, Afton, VA 22920, 800-524-4156;
www.eat-it.com

England's Orchard & Nursery, 316 State Route 2004, McKee, KY 40447-9616,
877-965-2228; www.nuttrees.net

Fork & Spade, c/o Scenic Nursery, 1313 Scenic Drive, Modesto, CA 95355, 800-
829-5919; www.forkandspade.com

Grimo Nut Nursery, R.R. 3 Lakeshore Rd., Niagara-on-the-Lake, Ontario LOS
1JO Canada, 905-934-6887; www.grimonut.com

Hidden Springs Nursery, 170 Hidden Springs Lane, Cookeville, TN 38501, 931-
268-2592

John Gordon, Jr., 1385 Campbell Boulevard, North Amherst, NY 14120, 716-
691-9371; www.geocities.com/nuttreegordon

Just Fruit & Exotics, 30 St. Francis Street, Crawfordville, FL 32327, 850-926-
5644

Nolin River Nut Tree Nursery, 797 Port Wooden Road, Upton, KY 42784, 270-
369-8551; www.nolinnursery.com

Oikos Tree Crops, P.O. Box 19425, Kalamazoo, MI 49019-0425; 616-624-6233

One Green World, 28696 South Cramer Road, Molalla, OR 97038, 877-353-4028; www.onegreenworld.com
Raintree Nursery, 391 Butts Road, Morton, WA 98356, 360-496-6400; www.RaintreeNursery.com
Sherwood's Greenhouses, P.O. Box 6, Sibley, LA 71073, 318-377-3653
Trees of Antiquity, 4395 Westside Rd., Healdsburg, CA 95448, 707-433-6420; www.treesofantiquity.com
Tripple Brook Farm, 37 Middle Road, Southampton, MA 01703, 413-527-4626; www.tripplebrookfarm.com

RAISIN TREE (*Hovenia dulcis*)

Forestfarm, 990 Tetherow, Williams, OR 97544-9599, 541-846-7269; www.forestfarm.com
Just Fruit & Exotics, 30 St. Francis Street, Crawfordville, FL 32327, 850-926-5644
One Green World, 28696 South Cramer Road, Molalla, OR 97038, 877-353-4028; www.onegreenworld.com
Pacific Tree Farms, 4301 Lynwood Drive, Chula Vista, CA 92010, 619-422-2400; www.kyburg.com
Sherwood's Greenhouses, P.O. Box 6, Sibley, LA 71073, 318-377-3653

RED AND WHITE CURRANTS (*Ribes petraeum*; *R. rubrum*; *R. sativum*)

Burnt Ridge Nursery, 432 Burnt Ridge Road, Onalaska, WA 98570, 360-985-2873; www.landru.myhome.net/burntridge/
Edible Landscaping Nursery, Route 2, Box 77, Afton, VA 22920, 800-524-4156; www.eat-it.com
Hartmann's Plant Company, Inc., 310 60th Street, Grand Junction, MI 49056, 616-253-4281; www.hartmannsplantcompany.com
Indiana Berry & Plant, 5218 W. 500 South, Huntingburg, IN 47542, 800-295-2226; www.inberry.com
McGinnis Berry Crops Limited, 3583 Dove Creek Road, Courtenay, B.C. Canada V9N 1P3; (250) 338-8200; www.berrycrops.net
Nourse Farms, 41 River Rd., South Deerfield, MA 01373, 413-665-2658; www.noursefarms.com
One Green World, 28696 South Cramer Road, Molalla, OR 97038, 877-353-4028; www.onegreenworld.com
Raintree Nursery, 391 Butts Road, Morton, WA 98356, 360-496-6400; www.RaintreeNursery.com
Saint Lawrence Nurseries, RFD 2, State Route 345, Potsdam, NY13676, 315-265-6739; www.sln.potsdam.ny.us
Trees of Antiquity, 4395 Westside Rd., Healdsburg, CA 95448, 707-433-6420; www.treesofantiquity.com
Whitman Farms Nursery, 1420 Beaumont NW, Salem, OR 97304, 503-585-8728, whitmanfarms.com

RUSSIAN OLIVE (*Elaeagnus angustifolia*)

Forestfarm, 990 Tetherow, Williams, OR 97544-9599, 541-846-7269; www .forestfarm.com

Hidden Springs Nursery, 170 Hidden Springs Lane, Cookeville, TN 38501, 931-268-2592

Musser Forests, P.O. Box 340, Route 119, North Indiana, PA 15701, 800-643-8319; www.musserforests.com

Saint Lawrence Nurseries, RFD 2, State Route 345, Potsdam, NY 13676, 315-265-6739; www.sln.potsdam.ny.us

SHIPOVA (×*Sorbopyrus auricularis*)

Burnt Ridge Nursery, 432 Burnt Ridge Road, Onalaska, WA 98570, 360-985-2873; www.landru.myhome.net/burntridge/

One Green World, 28696 South Cramer Road, Molalla, OR 97038, 877-353-4028; www.onegreenworld.com

Raintree Nursery, 391 Butts Road, Morton, WA 98356, 360-496-6400; www .RaintreeNursery.com

STRAWBERRY—ALPINE (*Fragaria vesca*)

Edible Landscaping Nursery, Route 2, Box 77, Afton, VA 22920, 800-524-4156; www.eat-it.com

Forestfarm, 990 Tetherow, Williams, OR 97544-9599, 541-846-7269; www .forestfarm.com

Hartmann's Plant Company, Inc., 310 60th Street, Grand Junction, MI 49056, 616-253-4281; www.hartmannsplantcompany.com

J. L. Hudson, Seedsman, P.O. Box 1058, Redwood City, CA 94064

Park Seed Co., Cokesbury Road, Greenwood, SC 29647-0001, 800-845-3369; www.parkseed.com

Pinetree Garden Seeds, New Gloucester, ME 04260, 207-926-3400; www. superseeds.com

Raintree Nursery, 391 Butts Road, Morton, WA 98356, 360-496-6400; www .RaintreeNursery.com

Siskiyou Rare Plant Nursery, 2825 Cummings Road, Medford, OR 97501, 541-772-6846; www.srpn.net

Tripple Brook Farm, 37 Middle Road, Southampton, MA 01703, 413-527-4626; www.tripplebrookfarm.com

STRAWBERRY—MUSK (*Fragaria moschata*)

Raintree Nursery, 391 Butts Road, Morton, WA 98356, 360-496-6400; www .RaintreeNursery.com

Index

Numbers in *italic* refer to color plates.

Index

Index

Index

Index

Index

Index

Riley, James Whitcomb, 41
rock cranberry. See *Vaccinium vitis-idaea*
Romulus, 174
root cuttings. See cuttings
rootstock, general discussion of, 257
Ruel, Jean, 178
Russian mulberry. See *Morus alba* 'Tatarica'
Russian olive. See *Elaeagnus angustifolia*
rust (*Gymnosporangium* spp.), 16

salad pear. See Asian pear
sand pear. See *Pyrus pyrifolia*
sandy soils, general discussion of, 242–243
Sargent, Charles Sprague, 42
sarvisberry. See *Amelanchier* spp.
saskatoon. See *Amelanchier* spp.
saskatoon bud moth (*Epinotia bicordana*), 16
saskatoon sawfly (*Hoplocampa* spp.), 16
scarification, general discussion of, 253
scientific name, general discussion of, 235
scion, general discussion of, 257
seedling, general discussion of, 235–236
seed propagation, general discussion of, 252–254
seeds, mail-order sources for, 261–271
self-fertile (self-pollinating) plants, general discussion of, 238
self-sterile plants, general discussion of, 237
Septoria leaf spot, 129
serviceberry. See *Amelanchier* spp.
service tree. See *Sorbus domestica*
shadbush. See *Amelanchier* spp.
shih. See *Cudrania tricuspidata*
shipova. See ×*Sorbopyrus auricularis*
silkworm industry, 88
silkworms, 88
silkworm thorn. See *Cudrania tricuspidata*
sipac, 220

sipurak, 220
siting, general discussion of, 239–244
Slate, George, 163, 166
The Small Fruits of New York, 121, 179
Smith, Captain John (of Jamestown settlement), 97–98, 138
Smith, J. Russell, 95
softwood cuttings. See cuttings
soil, general discussion of, 242–244
sorb-apple. See *Sorbus devoniensis*
×*Sorbopyrus auricularis* (shipova), 219–224, 48
   'Baciu', 221, 223
   'Smokvarka', 220
×*Sorbopyrus auricularis* var. *bulbiformis*, 221
×*Sorbopyrus bulbiformis*. See ×*Sorbopyrus auricularis* var. *bulbiformis*
Sorbus
   aria (common whitebeam), 220
   aucuparia, 17
   bollwylleriana. See ×*Sorbopyrus auricularis*
   devoniensis (sorb-apple), 222
   domestica (service tree), 222
   intermedia, 17
   torminalis (chequerberry), 222
   yuana, 222
soursop. See *Annona muricata*
sourtop. See *Vaccinium myrtilloides*
species, general discussion of, 235
Strachey, William, 106, 138, 142
stratification, general discussion of, 253
strawberry. See *Fragaria* spp.
suckers, general discussion of, 260
sugar apple. See *Annona squamosa*
super-hardy kiwifruit. See *Actinidia kolomikta*
sweetsop. See *Annona squamosa*

tcho sang. See *Cudrania tricuspidata*
Teas, John C., 91
Theophrastus, 222
thicket serviceberry. See *Amelanchier canadensis*
thinning cut, general discussion of, 248

286

Index